Introducing
Microsoft®
Exchange 2000
Server

JoAnne Woodcock

PUBLISHED BY
Microsoft Press
A Division of Microsoft Corporation
One Microsoft Way
Redmond, Washington 98052-6399

Library of Congress Cataloging-in-Publication Data
Woodcock, JoAnne.
    Introducing Microsoft Exchange 2000 Server / JoAnne Woodcock.
       p. cm.
    Includes index.
    ISBN 0-7356-0960-8
    1. Microsoft Exchange Server (Computer file)   2. Client/server computing. I. Title.

  QA76.9.C55 W66 2000
  005.7'13769--dc21   00-028170

Printed and bound in the United States of America.

1 2 3 4 5 6 7 8 9   QMQM   5 4 3 2 1 0

Distributed in Canada by Penguin Books Canada Limited.

A CIP catalogue record for this book is available from the British Library.

Microsoft Press books are available through booksellers and distributors worldwide. For further information about international editions, contact your local Microsoft Corporation office or contact Microsoft Press International directly at fax (425) 936-7329. Visit our Web site at mspress.microsoft.com. Send comments to *mspinput@microsoft.com*.

Acquisitions Editor: Juliana Aldous
Project Editor: Lynn Finnel

TABLE OF CONTENTS

Introduction ix

Acknowledgments xiii

PART I: OVERVIEW

CHAPTER ONE

Exchange, Then and Now 3

An Exchange Overview 4

Exchange from 1996 to the Present 5

    Exchange Version 4.0 5

    Exchange Version 5.0 12

    Exchange Version 5.5 14

    Comparing Exchange Versions 4.0 through 5.5 17

    Exchange 2000 19

    The Messaging 20

    The Messages 23

    The Messengers 25

CHAPTER TWO

The Network 27

Network Topology 27

    The Server and Its Clients 29

    Dedicated Servers 31

The Network and Active Directory Services 34

    Organization Structure 34

    Windows 2000 and Exchange 2000 34

    An Overview of Active Directory Services 35

Active Directory Services and Network Views 38

    The Physical View 39

    The Logical View 40

    Domain Controllers 47

    An Everyday Analogy 47

Active Directory Services and Exchange 2000 49
   Windows 2000 49
   Logical and Physical Hierarchies 49
   Active Directory Services Terminology 50
   Directory Replication 50
   Peaceful Coexistence 51

CHAPTER THREE

A Visual Tour of Exchange 2000 53

Windows 2000 Server 53
The Exchange Installation Wizard 55
A Good Place to Start 55
The Microsoft Management Console 58
   Running the MMC 58
   Creating a New Console 59
   Some Representative MMC Consoles 60

CHAPTER FOUR

Exchange 2000 Installations 77

Customer Concerns 77
Centralized vs. Decentralized Administration 78
   Administrative Groups and Routing Groups 79
   Using Administrative and Routing Groups 80
Sites, Domains, and Other Groups 83
   Sites 84
   Domains 84
   Organizational Units 85
   Active Directory Groups 86
Installation, Coexistence, and Migration 88
New Installations 89
   The Process 89
   What Happens 90
Coexistence 90
   Coexistence with Earlier Exchange Versions 91
   Coexistence with Other Systems 94
Upgrades and Migration 95
   Upgrades 95
   Migration 100

PART II: UNDER THE HOOD

CHAPTER FIVE

Windows 2000 and Active Directory Services   105

Soul of a New Directory 105
  Directories and Directory Services 105
  Domains, Trees, and Forests: A Recap 107
  How It Works 120
Windows 2000 and Exchange 126
  The Directory 126
  Transport 129
  Name Resolution 129
  Windows 2000, Exchange 2000, and Business 130

CHAPTER SIX

Information Storage and the Web Store   133

The Web Store Concept 133
  Evolving Communication Needs 134
  New Needs, New Approaches 134
  Features of the Web Store 136
  Benefits for the Enterprise 141
  The Web Store and Administrators 142
  Microsoft Windows 2000 Integration 144
  The Web Store and Knowledge Workers 144
Exchange Technology That Makes It Happen 147
  Exchange 5.5 vs. Exchange 2000 148
  Storage Groups and Multiple Databases 149
  Data Storage and Access 151
  Front-End/Back-End Servers 154
  The Installable File System 155
  Clustering 155

CHAPTER SEVEN

Scalability and Reliability   159

Multiple Databases 160
  Single-Instance Storage 160
  Transactions and Transaction Logs 161
  Log and Data Drives 162

Clustering 163
    The Cluster Itself 164
    Virtual Servers and Resource Groups 165
    Clustering and Exchange 166
    Nodes and Storage Groups 166
Load Balancing 167
    Network Load Balancing Service in a Nutshell 168
Distributed Configuration 169
    "Epoxy" 169
    Creating a Front-End Server 169
    Routing Requests to the Back-End Server 170
    Front-End/Back-End Servers and Outlook Web Access 171

CHAPTER EIGHT

Information Flow and Routing   173

A Myriad of Destinations 173
Message Flow and Message Routing 174
Message Flow 174
    Separation of Powers: IIS and the Information Store 175
SMTP 177
    Advantages of SMTP 177
    SMTP from the Administrator's View 177
    Inside SMTP 184
    Inbound Message Flow 185
    Outbound Message Flow 186
Message Routing 186
    Delivery on the Same Server 187
    Delivery in the Same Routing Group 187
    Delivery to a Different Routing Group 188
    Delivery Outside the Organization 189
    Single vs. Multiple Routing Groups 190
    Connectors Linking Routing Groups 191
    Communicating with Other Mail Systems 195
    Link State Information 195

CHAPTER NINE

Internet Integration   199

Internet Protocols 200

Networking Models: An Overview 200
Internet Protocols, Exchange, and IIS 204
WebDAV **214**
HTTP and WebDAV 215
WebDAV Features 216
Outlook Web Access **218**
Outlook Web Access Clients 219
The Logon Process 220
Accessing the Store 220
Outlook Web Access Installations 221

CHAPTER TEN

Real-Time Communication   225

Instant Messaging **226**
Instant Messaging from the Client Side 226
Instant Messaging from the Server Side 228
Authentication Methods 235
Messaging Architecture and the RVP Protocol 236
Chat **238**
Chat Servers 239
Chat Channels 240
Chat Security 241
Data Conferencing **243**
The Conferencing Platform 243
The Conference Management Service 245
The Conference Technology Providers 245
The Video Conferencing Service 247
A Final Word 250

PART III: APPENDIXES

Glossary   255

Index 287

INTRODUCTION

This is a book about Microsoft Exchange 2000 Server, code-named Platinum during its pre-beta and beta development period. As the title states, this is an "Introducing" book—a book designed to introduce Exchange 2000—and so its primary goal is to show you what new features the product includes, why they are important, and how Exchange itself differs from its predecessors.

Who Is This For?

Even though this book is an introduction to Exchange 2000, it isn't necessarily for the end users who might one day find themselves clicking and dragging through an Exchange 2000 mailbox. Although those individuals are more than welcome—indeed, might find it quite useful—to learn about what makes Exchange Server tick, this book is intended primarily for the IT administrators who are or will be called upon to implement and administer Exchange in their organizations. As such, the content assumes familiarity with networking and Internet technologies. Although an understanding of Microsoft Windows 2000 is also valuable, it isn't essential, as the book does cover Microsoft Active Directory services, Windows 2000 domains, and Windows services (such as IIS) as they relate to Exchange 2000.

Exchange 2000 Itself

As for the product itself, of all the changes in Exchange 2000 Server, one stands out far more than the others: its tight integration with Windows 2000. This integration is part and parcel of Exchange 2000 in a number of different ways, the most prominent of which is undoubtedly the Exchange 2000 reliance on Windows 2000 Active Directory services for directory administration and management. Unlike any other version of Exchange, Exchange 2000 Server does away with its own directory and, instead, uses Windows 2000 Active Directory services as the single source of information about objects throughout the organization, from users to printers.

Like its predecessors Exchange 4.0, 5.0, and 5.5, however, Exchange 2000 Server remains a messaging and collaboration product. And, as is the case with any significant new version of a software product, Exchange 2000 layers a substantial bit of "oomph" onto the foundation built by its ancestors. This added capability appears in a number of different areas, but some of the most important include

- **Increased integration of Internet protocols and technologies** for example, in using Windows 2000 DNS naming, in the use of the Internet-standard SMTP as a native messaging protocol, and in the use of URLs and browsers for accessing both mail and public folders

- **Improved reliability and scalability** as shown by support for clustering, a front-end/back-end separation of protocol and database servers, and use of multiple databases

- **Centralized, more efficient management** exemplified by use of the Microsoft Management Console for administration

- **Collaborative capability** in the form of instant messaging, chat, and server-based conferencing, including video conferencing

- **Enhanced information store technology** that acts as the foundation for the Web Store—a new concept that blends messaging, a file system, and collaboration to provide users with a multimedia repository for information ranging from e-mail and voicemail to Web pages, faxes, and documents

About This Book and Exchange 2000

As of the time this book was completed and readied for printing, Exchange 2000 Server wasn't a released product. The majority of the book was written and edited on the basis of Exchange beta releases and documentation, but was checked for a final time against the first Exchange 2000 Release Candidate. As a result, there might well be differences between the Exchange 2000 described and illustrated here and the Exchange 2000 that you eventually hold in your hands. Overall, however, the Exchange 2000 presented here shouldn't differ substantially from the final product.

Of course, any differences resulting from errors in substance or interpretation are inadvertent and are as much regretted as they are regrettable.

Exchange Versions

Although this book covers Exchange capabilities ranging from e-mail to instant messaging and conferencing, it's important to note that Exchange 2000 Server itself won't provide all of these capabilities in a single package. The released product will appear in three different versions:

- **Exchange 2000 Server,** for midsized organizations and branch offices
- **Exchange 2000 Enterprise Server,** which adds support for multiple databases and clustering
- **Exchange 2000 Conferencing Server,** which includes capability for voice, video, and data conferencing

Where needed, the following chapters provide reminders that this or that feature is included in a particular version of Exchange 2000.

That said, it's on to Chapter 1 and a look at Exchange Server, past and present...

ACKNOWLEDGMENTS

To a great extent, this book is a case of "déjà vu all over again" in that many of the people involved in its development, editing, and production are people who contributed greatly to another book of mine on networking, done about a year ago. They are Juliana Aldous (acquisitions editor), Lynn Finnel (project manager), and Sybil Ihrig of Helios Productions (project manager, illustrator, and compositor). This book also benefited from the skills of three new acquaintances, Tracy Thomsic (acquisitions), Fran Aitkens (copy editor) and Douglas Giles (technical editor). All deserve thanks for lending their abilities and considerable knowledge, not to mention good cheer and endless patience, to the project. None is, of course, in any way responsible for errors or omissions in the result.

In addition to these book-related folk, thanks also to two people associated with Exchange 2000 itself who made their own valuable contributions: Thomas Rizzo, Lead Product Manager, and John Speare, Technical Writing Manager.

And finally, on a personal note, special thanks as always to Kate, Mark, and the four-footed clan (especially Nia), all of whom give far more than they ever could receive. This is the last time they will see public thanks, but private gratitude will be theirs far into the future. Thanks, guys. Ten-four, over and out.

PART I

OVERVIEW

CHAPTER ONE

Exchange, Then and Now

Since its debut in 1996, Microsoft Exchange Server (from here on just called Exchange) has become widely known and used as a back-end messaging product. In the minds of many if not most customers, Exchange and its desktop clients, including Microsoft Outlook and Microsoft Outlook Express, have become synonymous with e-mail. However, Exchange is more than just an e-mail server. Even though mail almost certainly has ranked as its number one task, Exchange is called Exchange, not MailCarrier or, considering some of the transmissions it has had to deliver, JunkMail or SpamU2.

If you look up the word *exchange* in Miriam Webster's *Tenth Collegiate Dictionary,* you find it defined as "reciprocal giving and receiving" or as "a place where things or services are exchanged." Both these definitions make it clear that the concept of an exchange covers much more than sending and receiving messages, even if those messages can contain fancy formatting or attached documents, images, and other objects. An exchange in Webster's sense more closely resembles the goings-on at a marketplace or a town hall meeting than at a post office.

The point behind this introductory spiel is, of course, that Exchange, the product, has always lived up to the idea behind its name—not only through its support for the "reciprocal giving and receiving" of e-mail, but also through its support for the trading of information through mechanisms ranging from calendars and bulletin boards to public and private folders, custom applications, task management, document routing, and remote access. And nowhere is the concept of freely exchanged information more evident than in the upcoming new version of Exchange, code-named Platinum during its development phase. In this latest version, known formally as Microsoft Exchange 2000, Exchange supports delivery of not only e-mail, but also voice mail, streaming video, Microsoft Office 2000 documents, and World Wide Web content, and it can enable instant messaging, video teleconferencing, and chat sessions.

In short, Exchange in all versions has always supported collaboration by being the engine behind those all-important (though often vaguely defined) activities collectively lumped in the category known as groupware. Now, in

Exchange 2000, it expands its support for group activities to cover the tried-and-true as well as enhanced and newly developed technologies unknown to earlier versions.

An Exchange Overview

Of course, knowing that Exchange supports collaboration is all well and good, but life is usually about specifics. So exactly what does Exchange have to offer, how has it changed in its relatively short life span from 1996 to the present, and what new features will it incorporate in Exchange 2000? Take a look.

To begin with, although Exchange has its own job to do, it's valuable to place it in context, as an integral part of Microsoft's BackOffice suite of server-based products. As such, Exchange is designed to work behind the scenes and to play nice with other Microsoft servers, such as

- **Site Server,** which is used for publishing to and managing an intranet

- **Proxy Server,** which is used for firewalls and network security

- **SQL Server,** which is used for databases and industrial-strength data warehousing

- **Systems Management Server,** which is used for centralized network administration

And, of course, Exchange and all other BackOffice products are built to run primarily over a network based on a Microsoft Windows NT or Windows 2000 foundation. In fact, as you'll see throughout this book, Exchange 2000, more than earlier versions of Exchange, is both dependent on and integrated with the server version of the Windows 2000 operating system. Directory management in Exchange 2000, for example, is tightly coupled to Windows 2000 and Microsoft Active Directory services.

As a product, Exchange first appeared as version 4.0. Since then, it has grown through versions 5.0, 5.5, and now to Exchange 2000. In every version, Exchange has concentrated on providing customers with a solid, inherently scalable, client/server-based messaging foundation, and changes in the product have been driven not only by the need for improvements in speed and reliability, but also by the need to focus on responsiveness to more powerful hardware and to changes in networking technologies and business practices. The Internet, for example, had a profound effect on the protocols and standards supported by Exchange version 5.5, and Web integration is an even more significant part of Exchange 2000.

Exchange has also grown to support what you might consider the "behavioral" needs of its users, meaning its ability to support people's reliance on being able to transfer information when, where, and as they want, sometimes asynchronously (through e-mail and document routing) and other times synchronously (through real-time chats and virtual meetings). And, of course, now that the Internet and the Web are practically synonymous with the online way of life, Exchange is adapting to this brave new world as well—for example, through incorporation of native Simple Mail Transfer Protocol (SMTP) message routing in Exchange 2000, and through features such as improved clustering that extend scalability to millions of users.

Where networks were once a dream of the future, they are now a cornerstone of the present. And Exchange, like its partners in the BackOffice suite and Microsoft's Windows 2000 DNA initiative, aims to help supply what business demands: connectivity, reliability, scalability, and whatever other "-ilities" move the freight of information along the tracks of either an internal or a global network infrastructure.

Exchange from 1996 to the Present

Although the goal of this book is to provide you with an introduction to Exchange in its latest incarnation, it doesn't hurt to see Exchange 2000 in light of the features and capabilities built into its predecessors. To set the scene, so to speak, the following sections provide a brief (and non-Darwinian) overview of Exchange as an evolving product.

Exchange Version 4.0

As already mentioned, Exchange was introduced in 1996 as version 4.0. Billed in the Microsoft Press book, *Introducing Exchange,* as "e-mail finally done right," Exchange 4.0 replaced Microsoft Mail as a group messaging platform. Designed to run on Windows NT 3.51 or later, Exchange 4.0 was an e-mail server with built-in scheduling, electronic forms, and support for high-end development tools to accommodate groupware and collaborative needs. In addition, even this early version of Exchange provided Internet connectivity through SMTP and Multipurpose Internet Mail Extensions (MIME) support for Internet mail, through remote access over an Internet connection, and through USENET newsfeeds and discussions.

Topologically, Exchange 4.0, like its 5.0 and 5.5 successors, was based on the nested concepts of an organization, multiple sites within the organization consisting of one or more permanently connected servers, and, of course, the servers themselves.

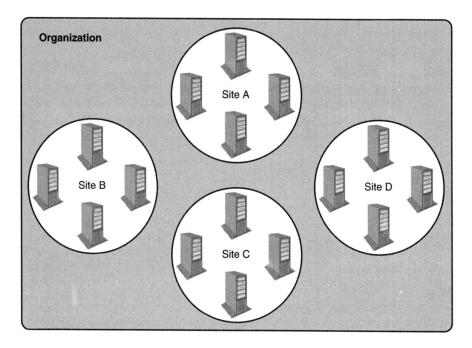

From an administrator's point of view, however, this broad topology—even though it could include many sites in many different geographic or functional locations—was visually unified into a single, centralized hierarchy known as the directory. This directory showed how the organization, its sites, and its servers were related. The graphical representation resembled the directory tree displayed by the Microsoft Windows 95 and 98 Explorer and the Outlook e-mail client.

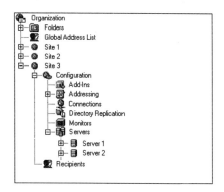

Internally, Exchange 4.0 was built on a foundation of four core components:

- **An information store** (also called the message store)
- **A directory**
- **A router** known as the message transfer agent, or MTA
- **The system attendant**

These components, working together, took on part of the messaging storage, routing, and delivery load for the organization. The components

- **Stored relevant messaging information** about the organization and its sites and servers
- **Controlled access to and use of this information**
- **Provided users with a single location,** known as the Universal Inbox, for message storage and retrieval
- **Routed and delivered messages,** within the organization and to and from other networks
- **Managed numerous housekeeping chores,** such as monitoring servers and connections and replicating directories and information across the organization

The Information Store

The information store was the Exchange database designed to hold all of the messages and documents shared and exchanged by users. To optimize performance and ensure that messages could be recovered, information about all transactions was recorded in a transaction log before being written to the database.

Although referred to as *the* information store, this database was actually made up of two databases, one public and one private. Depending on the installation, an Exchange server could be configured to hold both a public and a private information store, or it could be dedicated to one or the other for better performance.

The public part of the information store could be configured as one or many folders for use in housing documents, forms, bulletin board system (BBS) messages, and other information intended to be made publicly available, either to all or to a selected group of users. Because an Exchange organization might well include numerous servers spread across widely separated geographical sites, this public store was designed for automatic synchronization and replication to ensure that users throughout the organization could access up-to-date information.

The private store, as the name indicates, was private; it was the home of all user mailboxes. The public and private stores were the parts of Exchange visible to users as a graphical tree of folders and subfolders in the Exchange client window—a familiar and easily navigated representation of the time-honored directory/subdirectory structure known to people since the days of MS-DOS 2.0.

In Exchange 4.0, each public and private information store could reach a maximum size of 16 GB on any Exchange server. This physical limit, however, actually had a larger logical limit because the information store has always been implemented as a single-instance database— meaning that a message sent to multiple recipients, whether 10 or 10,000 individuals, is stored only once in the database. Recipients receive pointers to the message, rather than separate copies of the message itself.

The Directory

The Exchange directory was the equivalent of a centralized telephone book. Like the telephone white pages, it contained the information needed to identify mail recipients and public folders. Like the yellow pages, it also contained information about broader entities, including distribution lists—groups of users addressed by a single e-mail alias—and Exchange sites and servers. Although Exchange 2000, as noted earlier, shifts responsibility for directory services from the Exchange server to Windows 2000 and Active Directory services, the directory in many ways remains the same (or a similar) entity. Why is this? Because Active Directory services, though structured differently and controlled by a different "agent," didn't just come into being by itself; its origins lie in the directory implemented in Exchange.

At any rate, the Exchange directory services were structured so as to provide a unified view of the message recipients and resources available throughout the organization. And this view, the Global Address List, was in turn created from Directory objects, each listing the contents—mailboxes and so on—of an Exchange server. These Directory objects were, furthermore, endowed with customizable attributes, or properties, that could be used to define or limit their capabilities. So, in addition to basics such as user name, telephone number, and office location, the administrator could also use object properties for purposes such as setting limits on the size of user mailboxes, defining distribution lists, or even adding personal information about recipients.

From the recipients' perspective, the most important (visible) task performed by the Exchange directory was its creation of the Global Address List, in which they could find the name or e-mail address of someone to whom they needed to send a message.

Because the directory and the information in it needed to be maintained and synchronized both within and between sites, Exchange provided for directory replication in two ways:

- **Within a site,** whenever the directory on one server was updated, the changes were sent to all other servers in the site automatically. This ensured that all servers worked with the same information.

- **Between sites,** directory changes were routed to other sites at scheduled times. These updates were routed from a gateway type of server, designated as a bridgehead server, to another designated bridgehead server. The bridgehead server at the receiving site then communicated the changes to all other servers in its own site.

The Message Transfer Agent

The message transfer agent, or MTA, was the Exchange component that routed and delivered messages between servers within a site, to MTAs at other sites, and to and from other networks. Although the MTA was not needed for transferring messages between recipients on the same server, it was still the glue that held Exchange communications together. Only the MTA could direct and transfer messages between servers, and only the MTA was able to route messages to other Exchange sites or to "foreign" (non-Exchange) networks. The MTA performed this work by using several connectors. Each connector specialized in a particular type of delivery service.

- **Between Exchange sites with permanent high-bandwidth connections,** the MTA used the Exchange Server Site Connector, a fast and efficient means of delivery based on the use of remote procedure calls (RPCs) between the MTA on the sending server and the MTA on the receiving server. (RPCs are client/server or server/server Application Programming Interfaces [APIs] that enable a process on one computer to interact with a process on another system.)

- **For remote access,** as in the case of an offsite employee calling in for e-mail, the MTA used the Dynamic RAS Connector, which was essentially a site connector designed for an asynchronous rather than a permanent LAN connection. The Dynamic RAS Connector was dependent on Windows NT for dialup RAS support.

■ **For site-to-site transmissions over low-bandwidth connections,** over an X.400 backbone, or to a public X.400 network, the MTA used the X.400 Connector, which also allowed the administrator to control both when connections could occur and how large messages could be.

■ **For Internet transmissions,** the MTA used the Internet Mail Connector, which supported SMTP and messages based on plain text, MIME, Microsoft Mail, and UUENCODE and UUDECODE.

■ **For transmissions to PC-based, Microsoft Mail networks,** the MTA could deliver mail via the Microsoft Mail Connector.

The System Attendant

The System Attendant ran in the background, making sure that everything ran smoothly and that mail was routed correctly. In addition, it took care of certain vital tasks. This was the part of Exchange that

■ **Built the routing tables** used by the MTA in determining where and how messages were to be delivered

■ **Handled new e-mail addresses**

■ **Checked on directory replication**

■ **Oversaw the link monitor,** which kept a virtual eye on connections between sites and between Exchange servers and other system servers, and did the same for the server monitor, which was responsible for the status of Exchange

■ **Served as a security watchdog** by storing and managing digital signatures and encryption for mailboxes

The Four Together

Although the actual procedure followed depended on whether a message was being sent to a user on the same server, on a different server in the same site, on a different site, or on a different network, the four pieces worked together more or less as shown in the following illustration.

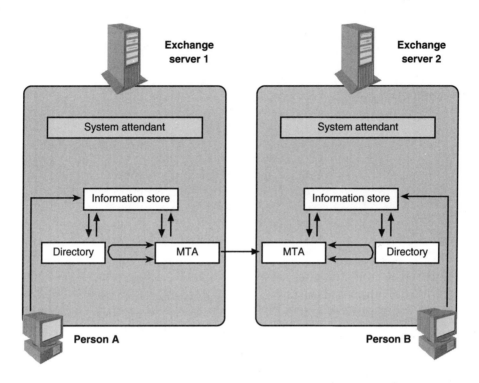

An illustration can't show the dynamics of message delivery because of the variables mentioned in the preceding paragraph. But in this example, a typical communications sequence between two servers, the following operations occurred:

1. Person A on server 1 sent a message to person B on server 2

2. The message was first delivered to the information store on server 1

3. The information store checked the directory to resolve the address

4. The directory provided the addressing information to the information store

5. Because the recipient was on a different server, the MTA on server 1 sent the message to the MTA on server 2

At this point, routing and delivery would vary. If the recipient were on the same server, the information store would not route the message to the MTA, but instead it would write the message to the user's inbox. Similarly, if the recipient were on a different network, the MTA on server 1 would route the message to the information store for delivery through a connector.

Though the methods might differ, in each case the information store, the directory, and the MTA would work in concert to find the recipient and to route and deliver the message reliably.

Exchange Version 5.0

Although version 5.0 of Exchange did not differ structurally (in terms of core components) or topologically (in terms of the organization/site/server hierarchy) from its version 4.0 predecessor, it did push into new territory in three main areas: the Internet, collaborative capabilities, and enhanced support for migration and coexistence with other messaging systems. Appearing in early 1997, this version also brought with it a new messaging client, Microsoft Outlook 97, and gave users the ability to transmit encrypted and signed messages through its support for security keys and digital certificates.

The Internet

Exchange 5.0 added support for the Internet (and intranets) in two primary ways: through its support for a number of additional standard Internet protocols and through its support of HTTP and the Microsoft Active Server platform.

Internet protocols   Although Exchange 4.0 included SMTP and X.400 support, version 5.0 added support for a number of Internet standards, all of which were implemented natively so as to inhibit negative effects on both performance and scalability. These Internet protocols included

- **POP3, the Post Office Protocol,**   which opened the door for any and all POP3-enabled Internet mail clients, including Netscape Navigator Mail and Eudora, to access Exchange servers to retrieve mail transmitted over the Internet

- **HTTP, the Hypertext Transfer Protocol, and HTML, the Hypertext Markup Language,**   about which no explanation should be needed other than to say that both made it possible to extend Exchange messaging and groupware to Web clients and intranets

- **NNTP, the Network News Transfer Protocol,**   which enabled Exchange to function as an Internet news server—to host discussion groups and to replicate newsgroups as public folders to other NNTP-based servers

- **LDAP, the Lightweight Directory Access Protocol,**   which enabled LDAP clients (including Microsoft Internet Explorer and

Netscape Navigator) and applications to perform directory searches over TCP/IP connections

■ **SSL, the Secure Sockets Layer,** which ensured secure communications over the Internet

NOTE: If these acronyms still have a tendency to clump together in your mind like the macaroni in alphabet soup, don't worry about it. They're all defined in the Glossary, if actual details are necessary here and now. The important thing to remember is that these are all Internet protocols and so contributed to the Exchange 5.0 support of that ever-growing global network.

The Active Server platform Another Internet-related aspect of Exchange 5.0 was its support of the Microsoft Active Server platform. Through the use of scripting languages, such as VBScript and JScript, and through Active Server Pages (ASP), developers gained the ability to add interactivity to Web and intranet pages. By blending the strengths of Exchange and other BackOffice components, such as the SQL Server relational database, with the Web, developers could create custom applications for such purposes as routing and tracking, contact lists, training, discussions, and so on.

In addition, Exchange 5.0 shipped with the Microsoft Active Messaging technology (renamed Collaboration Data Objects, or CDO, in Exchange 5.5). An interface, or link, between Exchange and the Microsoft Internet Information Server (IIS), Active Messaging enabled developers to tap into Exchange data, such as address books and messages, through IIS and render that information into HTML for viewing from—typically—an Active Server Page.

Although ASP and Active Messaging lie more in the developer's domain than the administrator's, their inclusion in Exchange clearly points up Exchange's increasing Internet focus. They are also, as described later in this chapter and in this book, significant developments in the product's continuing march toward the concept of a Web Store, as described in Chapter 6.

Microsoft Outlook 97

Outlook 97 was designed for 32-bit Windows systems, meaning Windows 95, Microsoft Windows NT 3.51 Workstation, and later systems. More broadly based than the earlier Microsoft Exchange Client and Schedule+ software, Outlook 97 shipped with Exchange, Microsoft Office 97, and as a separate application.

Though it built upon, extended, and interoperated with Microsoft Mail, Exchange Client, and Microsoft Schedule+, the goal of Outlook 97 was to provide users with a more comprehensive, one-stop environment capable of supporting a number of personal productivity functions, including

- E-mail (naturally)
- Both personal and group scheduling
- Contact and task management
- Journals and notes
- Document sharing through public folders and the Internet
- Custom groupware applications

Outlook 97 was essentially an outgrowth of the Microsoft "Information At Your Fingertips" mantra, a desktop information manager designed as the front-end partner to the back-end storage, routing, indexing, and directory management of Exchange.

Peaceful Coexistence

Finally, at least in terms of a broad overview, 5.0 extended Exchange in the areas of interoperability and migration from other mail systems. Along with migration tools for Novell GroupWise, Netscape Collabra, and IBM PROFS (Professional Office System), Exchange 5.0 enabled direct connections to cc:Mail through the Exchange Connector for Lotus cc:Mail. The latter feature, when installed, integrated the two systems to the point that Exchange and cc:Mail systems could synchronize directories, exchange messages, and provide cc:Mail users with the Exchange connectivity with the Internet and other supported systems.

Exchange Version 5.5

Exchange version 5.5, which appeared in late 1997, is the most current available version until Exchange 2000 is released. As you'd expect, version 5.5 continues the Exchange push toward more and better enterprise-level messaging, collaboration, and Internet support. Consequently, improvements are focused on these key areas.

Enterprise-Level Messaging

As noted earlier in this chapter, enterprise-level messaging emphasizes availability, scalability, and reliability, not to mention manageability and connectivity with non-Exchange installations. Exchange 5.5 aimed to please in all categories.

The "-ilities" Structurally, one of the most notable features in Exchange 5.5 was the elimination of size restrictions on the information store. No longer limited to a maximum of 16 GB, the message store in Exchange 5.5 can grow as big as it wants. The number of users that Exchange can handle per server is limited only by the capabilities of the hardware. By extension, since larger data stores mean larger, longer backups, Exchange 5.5 addressed this need as well by speeding backups to about 15 GB per hour and supporting advanced tape backup devices.

Although its unlimited message stores and enhanced backup capabilities addressed scalability and reliability issues, Exchange 5.5 support for the clustering services in Windows NT Server 4.0 Enterprise Edition was included to improve availability and fault tolerance. Clustering is the software-based union of two servers so that they can act as one. These services were embodied in the Microsoft Cluster Server (MSCS). MSCS must be installed before Exchange 5.5 can take advantage of clustering, but once installed, it ensures that mail delivery continues even if one of the clustered servers fails.

Manageability For users, especially those prone to action before thought, Exchange 5.5 introduced a failsafe of sorts. Rather than flushing deleted messages and folders when the client logged off or confirmed deletion, version 5.5 flagged and hid them for a period of time set by the administrator. Thanks to this feature, mistaken or unthinking deletions can be recovered by the user through the Recover Deleted Items command on the client Tools menu.

For broader administrative concerns, Exchange 5.5 introduced two new aids, address space scoping and SNMP support through MADMAN MIB. Address space scoping, although not a particularly intuitive term, refers to Exchange 5.5 support for traffic management through per-site, per-server, or per-organization restrictions that the administrator can apply to different connectors. MADMAN MIB, which sounds like the bad guy in an action movie, stands somewhat redundantly for Mail and Directory Management (MADMAN) Management Information Base (MIB), and is an Internet-standard means of managing network objects through SNMP. MADMAN MIB enables use of SNMP-based monitoring tools.

Connectivity On the connectivity front, Exchange 5.5 built up the interoperability stable with the inclusion of several new connectors, all of which, like earlier connectors, enabled use of Exchange in mixed messaging environments. The new connectors are:

- **The Lotus Notes Connector**
- **The PROFS Connector,** for the IBM mainframe-based Professional Office System
- **The SNADS Connector,** for IBM OfficeVision, based on the Systems Network Architecture (SNA) Distribution Services system

Internet Support

In terms of Internet support, perhaps the most significant change in Exchange 5.5 is its support of the Internet Message Access Protocol 4 (IMAP4), an Internet e-mail and bulletin-board access protocol that enables users of any IMAP4 client, such as Outlook Express and Netscape Communicator, to mail one another via Exchange. In addition, IMAP4 enables storage on the server as well as on the client machine and allows users to view message headers before downloading.

Version 5.5 of Exchange also supports the newer LDAP version 3, which allows for writable (as opposed to read-only) directory access so that users can, given administrative permission, change or update selected directory attributes, such as phone or fax numbers.

Exchange 5.5 added support for several other Internet-related standards:

- **MHTML, or MIME HTML,** which enables encapsulation of HTML documents in MIME messages
- **ETRN, or Extended TURN,** which allows a dial-up client to request delivery of queued messages from the server
- **SASL, or Simple Authentication and Security Layer,** which requires authentication from SMTP clients before a client/server connection is established

Collaboration

Finally, Exchange 5.5 included four significant improvements designed to provide users with more and better ways of working together.

- **Microsoft Exchange Scripting Agent,** a workflow-related tool that enables creation of "smart" event-driven or time-driven applications in VBScript or JavaScript. Running on the server, such applications can be used to initiate outcomes based on content submitted to a public folder—for example, routing an order form for processing or approval, depending on the monetary value of the order.

- **Collaboration Data Objects (CDO),** an object library known to Exchange 5.0 as Active Messaging, which enables developers to include collaborative features in Web-based Active Server Pages.

- **Microsoft Exchange Chat Service,** for real-time exchanges such as online meetings and conferences. An IRC (Internet Relay Chat) server, the Exchange Chat Service can host up to 10,000 simultaneous users participating from any IRC or IRCX (IRC Extensions) client.

- **Internet Locator Server (ILS),** a lookup tool designed to allow users to check the Exchange directory when they need (or want) to find out who else is online—for example, when they want to initiate a real-time activity such as group document editing or collaboration through a Microsoft NetMeeting session.

Comparing Exchange Versions 4.0 through 5.5

Before heading off into the world of Exchange 2000 and its features, you might find it useful at this point to see a summary of how Exchange has evolved up till now, the better to appreciate how and where Exchange 2000 extends existing capabilities or adds new functionality. Table 1-1 summarizes some of the features of Exchange versions 4.0, 5.0, and 5.5.

Exchange Features, Versions 4.0 through 5.5

Feature	Version 4.0	Version 5.0	Version 5.5
Information store	16 GB	16 GB	Unlimited
Connectors	X.400	X.400	X.400
	Site Connector	Site Connector	Site Connector
	Dynamic RAS	Dynamic RAS	Dynamic RAS
	Internet Mail	Internet Mail	Internet Mail
	Microsoft Mail	Microsoft Mail	Microsoft Mail
		Lotus cc:Mail	Lotus cc:Mail
			Lotus Notes

Table 1-1.   *(continued)*
Some significant features in Exchange versions 4.0 through 5.5.

17

Table 1-1. *continued*

Feature	Version 4.0	Version 5.0	Version 5.5
Connectors			PROFS
			SNADS
Internet	SMTP	SMTP	SMTP
		POP3	POP3
		HTTP	HTTP
		HTML	HTML
		NNTP	NNTP
		LDAP	LDAP
		SSL	SSL
		ASP	ASP
			LDAPv3
			IMAP4
			SASL
			MHTML
			ETRN
Collaboration	Public folders		
	Built-in scheduling		
	Forms		
		Outlook client	Outlook client
		ASP Pages	ASP Pages
		Active Messaging	Renamed CDO
			Exchange Scripting Agent
			Chat Service
			ILS

Exchange 2000

And now, at last, with past history duly acknowledged and surveyed, you come to Exchange 2000. In a sense it represents a brand-new paradigm, albeit one that maintains backward compatibility and continues the Exchange tradition of focusing on delivering messaging solutions that are scalable from the needs of small businesses to those of the enterprise.

> **N O T E :**   Although *enterprise* is not a particularly quantifiable term, it is used in this book to refer to very large organizations on the scale of Microsoft, Boeing, IBM, and the like. The term *organization* is used with less regard for size and so refers to businesses or groups ranging from small or medium-size to very large. Sometimes language and technology have trouble keeping up with one another.

But back to Exchange 2000. To begin with, according to a Microsoft white paper on product features and benefits published in July 1999, the changes and enhancements in Exchange 2000 are designed to address three primary areas:

- **Messaging**   the Exchange infrastructure
- **Messages**   Internet integration and single-location information management
- **Messengers**   accessibility reflecting the real-world needs of information anytime and from any device

Now for an overview of Exchange 2000; you'll find more detailed descriptions of the technologies later in the book. Here, although editors often tell writers to define terms when they first appear, the goal is to provide an overview of the product and point out the ways in which Exchange 2000 improves on earlier versions of Exchange. So, again, if you need to know exactly what a term means, right this very minute, refer to the Glossary.

The table at the top of the next page summarizes the changes described in the following sections.

New or Enhanced Features in Exchange 2000

Area	Feature
Messaging	Shift from Exchange directory to Active Directory services
	Distributed topology with components hosted on separate servers
	Multiple messaging databases
	Active/active clustering
	Administration through Microsoft Management Console
	SMTP implemented as a routing peer to X.400
Messages	Web Store for single-location message and document storage
	Enhanced development tools including CDO 3.0, OLE/DB and ADO integration, and server event model for synchronous processing
Messengers	Data conferencing server
	Instant messaging
	Chat service
	Unified messaging, including support for streaming media and wireless and handheld devices

Table 1-2
A summary of new or enhanced features in Exchange 2000.

The Messaging

Exchange 2000 incorporates a number of changes to the infrastructure, all of which (as usual) are intended to promote scalability, reliability, and performance.

Active Directory Services

One of the most significant changes in Exchange 2000 is its integration with Windows 2000. The most significant of these changes, in terms of implementation and migration, is the Exchange 2000 shift from using its own Exchange directory to using Windows 2000's Active Directory services for storage of all directory objects, including mailboxes, distribution lists, servers...everything. Whew! This is a big enough deal that it gets its own chapter later in the book (Chapter 5).

For now, note that this switch to Active Directory integration isn't based on whimsy. It's included to

- Improve speed and performance
- Provide administrators with a single directory for the entire enterprise—a single directory that can be managed from one place, with one set of tools
- Simplify directory management, for example, by basing distribution lists on Active Directory groups
- Extend Windows 2000 security to messaging and collaboration through use of the operating system's Access Control Lists (ACLs) in setting permissions for both Exchange data and Windows 2000 file shares
- Lower the cost of ownership

Although Active Directory services is the repository for user information, Microsoft doesn't expect every Exchange installation to jump onto the Exchange 2000 bandwagon immediately. For earlier versions of Exchange, Exchange 2000 therefore includes an Active Directory Connector that will, until the time is right for the enterprise, provide two-way replication between the Exchange directory and Active Directory services.

Topology

To improve scalability, Exchange 2000 implements a distributed configuration in which individual Exchange components, including directory services, can be hosted on separate servers. Although Exchange 2000 will still run on a single server for smaller organizations, this more flexible topology provides larger enterprises with the ability to host services that can accommodate large numbers of users, even into the millions.

Through this flexibility, administrators can divide and conquer, so to speak. For example, they can set up an Exchange system in which users connect to front-end servers and gain access to messages and other information stored on separate back-end systems. This same flexibility can also contribute to reliability. By segregating components on different servers, large enterprises can isolate system failures. In some instances, they can also reduce costs, for example, by using servers without RAID (Redundant Array of Independent [or Inexpensive] Disks) controllers for those components that don't require such care and feeding, such as protocol servers.

Multiple Databases

Throughout its history, Exchange has relied on a large message database whose integrity was secured through transaction logging. In Exchange 4.0 and 5.0, this message store could reach 16 GB in size; in version 5.5, the store size became unlimited, bounded only by hardware capabilities. Beginning with Exchange 2000, the message database becomes even more flexible and scalable, because it can now be split into multiple physical databases across several servers. The results are greater reliability, faster backup, and faster recovery, even though the whole can still be administered as a single data store.

Clustering

For reliability and scalability and Windows 2000 integration, Exchange 2000 supports two-way (with Windows 2000 Advanced Server) and four-way (with Windows 2000 Datacenter Server) active/active clustering.

This active/active clustering is new. Earlier releases of Exchange were based on an active/passive clustering model, meaning that Exchange ran on one clustered server but could be automati cally restarted on the other if an application or server failure occurred. In contrast, with active/active clustering, Exchange 2000 can run simultaneously on more than one server, and thus all of the servers in a cluster can process requests simultaneously. At the same time, the servers in the cluster can shift into recovery "mode" if one of the servers happens to fail. The upshot of this new clustering capability is increased reliability and lower cost by eliminating a dedicated fallback server.

Single-Console Management

Despite the numerous changes under the hood, Exchange 2000 facilitates administration through integration with the Microsoft Management Console in Windows 2000. Through the use of snap-ins (COM objects that represent single units of behavior and are used either individually or combined to create more complex tools), MMC and Exchange 2000 provide administrators with single-console management of Windows 2000 and both BackOffice (Exchange) and third-party applications through a learn-it-once interface and set of management tools.

SMTP

X.400, the messaging protocol supported by the ITU-T, is an internationally recognized e-mail standard and is widely used in Europe and Canada. It is, however, less common in the United States than SMTP, a host-to-host, TCP/IP mail transfer protocol. Although SMTP isn't exactly an official standard, it has been defined in IETF RFC 821 and so is well documented and does adhere to a defined code of behavior.

Although there are pro and con arguments for each of these standards, the fact is that both are widely used. Exchange has supported the X.400 standard since the beginning, and Exchange 2000 continues this support. In a more than casual nod to SMTP, however, Exchange 2000 also implements SMTP as a peer to X.400 for routing messages from one server to another, both within and between sites, to improve both reliability and throughput.

The Messages

Going beyond previous versions of Exchange, Exchange 2000 enhances the variety of messages and clients it supports. For example, Exchange now natively supports MIME content, so even audio and voice can be stored directly, without the need for conversion. In addition, Exchange 2000 supports XML and renders HTML and ASP pages scripts directly for more and better Web functionality. And, speaking of the Web...

The Web Store

Although Active Directory services represents the most significant change in Exchange 2000 infrastructure, to customers the new Web Store will undoubtedly represent the biggest visible change. As the embodiment of the Microsoft vision of unified document storage, the Web Store is the Exchange information store embodied in a Web-oriented concept that combines Exchange reliability and performance with Web accessibility and content presentation. Essentially, the Web Store is a one-stop facility for document storage and collaboration.

Through the Web Store, users can:

- **Store and directly access items** as diverse as e-mail messages and their attachments, voice mail, Microsoft Office 2000 documents, and (through FrontPage) Web sites and applications

- **Use the Web Store's built-in indexing and full-text search capabilities** to find what they need

- **Store document properties** to enable rapid, focused document retrieval, workflow, and collaboration

- **Manage documents through WebDAV** that enables remote file and document management over HTTP connections

And this richness of content is accessible through

- Outlook and any e-mail client that recognizes Internet standards
- URLs in a Web browser
- Office 2000 applications
- Wireless and handheld devices

Thus, users are now able to use the Exchange information store as a single location for collecting and managing documents, messages, tasks, and other project-related information, and they can use an e-mail client, a browser, an Office application, or (offsite) a wireless device to access any of that information.

Application Development

Exchange 2000 also offers developers their own set of goodies for creating collaborative and workflow applications. Some of these features, such as CDO, are Web-related. Others, such as OLE/DB and CDO Workflow Objects, are oriented more toward collaboration. The following list briefly describes these new or enhanced tools for application development:

- **Integration with Internet Information Server (IIS) and Active Server Pages** enables developers to use familiar tools for building Web-based applications

- **Integration of OLE/DB, a system-level programming interface, and ADO (ActiveX Data Objects),** an application-level programming interface, provides access to server-based BackOffice data and enables development of applications that make use of not only Exchange, but also SQL Server and other BackOffice products

- **An enhanced CDO 3.0 programming model** provides access to Exchange data, Internet protocol services, and MIME message parts and enables inclusion of workflow and collaboration features including calendaring, forwarding, and contact management in Web-enabled applications

- **CDO Workflow Objects** provides a library of tools based on transacted, synchronous events for applications designed to facilitate workflow and tracking

- **FrontPage 2000 integration** allows use of the Web Store for storage of Web sites and applications

■ **A server event model** supports development of applications that process objects based on events as they occur, including processing messages on arrival and performing tasks such as virus scanning or activating custom routing

NOTE: CDO, supported by integration with OLE/DB, ADO, and ADSI (Active Directory Services Interface), will replace MAPI, the previous Messaging API, in Exchange and Outlook. Microsoft will, however, continue to support MAPI for backward compatibility.

The Messengers

And finally, there are—broadly speaking—the "messengers," the means by which Exchange 2000 enables collaboration and delivers on one significant goal: unified messaging, anywhere and from any device.

Real-Time Collaboration

Exchange 2000 supports real-time collaboration in three ways: through data conferencing, instant messaging, and a Chat Server.

■ **The data conferencing server** is based on the ITU's T.120 standard—a suite of communication and application protocols for supporting real-time conferencing among numerous participants over different network types and connections. With this feature, which operates in situations ranging from one-to-one to many-to-many, users with T.120 clients, such as NetMeeting, can join virtual meetings and collaborate through a session that is started, managed, and closed down by the Exchange 2000 server rather than the initiator's workstation. In addition, using Exchange 2000 data conferencing means that users can rely on Outlook for scheduling meetings.

■ **Exchange 2000's instant messaging,** which is designed for immediate, unscheduled, one-to-one communications, enables individuals to check on others' online presence and send messages to them. The service is intended for quick, urgent sharing of information, as between members of a working group, though obviously it also opens the door to a potential landslide of "hey, how's it going" messages as well. The solution to the latter situation, alas, relies on the good sense and better manners of the participants.

■ **For open, many-to-many real-time communications, Exchange 2000, like Exchange 5.5, includes a Chat Server.** Now capable of hosting as many as 20,000 participants per server, the chat capability is designed for discussion-type forums that anyone can join. The service itself is automatically installed and easily set up by the administrator, who simply needs to define channels (chat rooms) and, if necessary, establish language restrictions or bans limiting access to certain users. Although generally thought of as a "fun" feature, real-time chat can also be useful in opening up a business discussion to participants in widely separated geographic locations.

Unified Messaging

Last, but not least for the future of communications, Exchange 2000 supports the concept of unified messaging. A step forward from the earlier support of a Universal Inbox by Exchange, unified messaging is designed to enable users to access not only e-mail messages, but also voice messages, streaming media, and Web Store content whenever they wish, and from both traditional (PC) and nontraditional clients, such as wireless and Windows CE-based handheld devices. In addition, Exchange 2000 supports telephone retrieval and forwarding of both voice and text to pagers.

So there you have it: Exchange history in a not-so-small nutshell. From the next chapter on, the focus turns to the future and to Exchange 2000.

CHAPTER TWO

The Network

Exchange in any version requires—of course—a network on which to run. The actual topology of the network—again, of course—varies tremendously with the business it serves. Such factors as size, logical organization of objects (people and other resources), geographic distribution of offices, physical LAN and WAN connections, and messaging needs all affect the size, scope, and layout of the network.

Exchange, especially Exchange 2000, is designed to provide the flexibility and scalability needed by networks of all shapes and sizes. It can be installed and run on a single network server, and it can also scale up to serve the demands of a million users. It can communicate with other messaging systems, such as Lotus Notes, and, as already mentioned, it supports the X.400 and SMTP protocols for Internet connectivity. But it needs a network, servers, and Microsoft Windows 2000 to run on, and one or more administrators (depending on the size and complexity of the organization) to help it do its job.

Network Topology

A small organization—defined in Microsoft's documentation as one with 500 or fewer users in one location—can manage nicely with a single, all-in-one Exchange server providing all messaging and collaboration services over LAN connections.

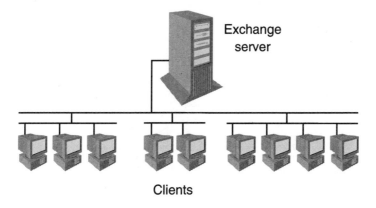

Exchange
server

Clients

In larger organizations, however, network topologies affect the way in which Windows 2000 and Exchange 2000 are deployed. In these organizations, LAN and WAN connections, the assignment of certain servers as domain controllers, and the grouping of the servers themselves are all factors to be considered.

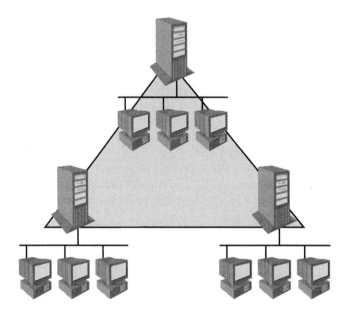

In addition, usage demands and network bandwidth can affect decisions on whether to parcel out services among different, dedicated servers—for example, by placing demanding services (such as conferencing) on high-performance hardware or isolating mailboxes on their own server to provide greater speed, serve a larger number of users, or avoid having other services interfere with mail transport and delivery.

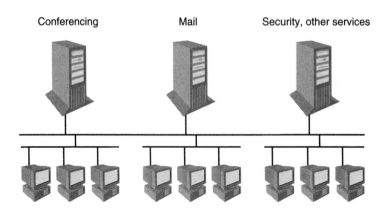

And, of course, there are also complex multi-server, multi-site organizations that can be spread out over a wide, even global, geographic area.

Site A

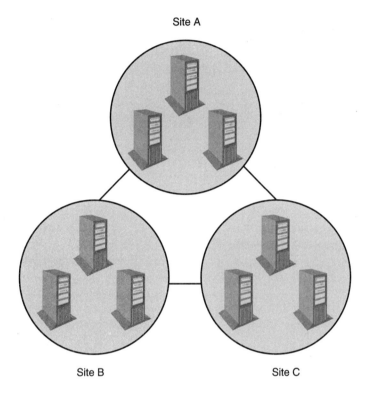

Site B   Site C

The structural and organizational permutations can appear to be endless, especially when the type of business is also brought into play. A manufacturing firm, for example, would center its operations around its products, whereas a wholesale distributor would more likely structure itself around its suppliers and its customers. And both the manufacturer and the distributor would differ from a service or information provider, which would be oriented around servers and associated hardware dedicated to handling high volumes of traffic.

The Server and Its Clients

Whether in a single server or multi-server environment, a single building or a multinational corporation—the heart of any client/server network is the server. For hardware, an Exchange 2000 server needs to be a machine with

- A Pentium 300 MHz or better microprocessor
- 128 MB of RAM (256 MB recommended)

- At least 2 GB of available storage space on the drive where it will be installed

- At least 500 MB of available storage space on the system drive

- A paging file (which is set through Control Panel | System | Advanced | Performance Options | Virtual Memory) equivalent to twice the amount of RAM in the system

- Windows 2000 Server installed

- A VGA or better monitor and CD-ROM drive

An Exchange client running Microsoft Outlook 2000 for messaging and collaboration should have

- At least 24 MB of RAM if it's running Windows 95 or Windows 98

- At least 72 MB of RAM if it's running Microsoft Windows NT Workstation 4.0 or later

NOTE: These are minimum requirements. As is usually the case with computers, it doesn't hurt to have more RAM and disk storage on the client or to have one or more powerful processors on the server, especially because, at the high end, Exchange 2000 runs comfortably on multiprocessor computers with multiple disk drives.

Where client software is concerned, the Exchange 2000 information store embodies the new Web Store concept for document, multimedia, and streaming media formats. This Internet-based, "one-stop shopping" storage is accessible not only with Outlook 2000, but also with other applications, including

- Outlook 97 and 98 and Outlook Express

- E-mail and newsgroup clients that support SMTP/POP3, IMAP, or NNTP

- World Wide Web browsers

- Microsoft FrontPage 2000 Web publishing application and Microsoft Office 2000 (through the File Open and File Save dialog boxes)

- The MS-DOS command line prompt

Dedicated Servers

Although small companies or divisions within a larger company can set up a reasonably no-muss, no-fuss Exchange organization on a single-processor, single-disk system, such a deployment is really only appropriate in a group with simple messaging requirements that can be handled by a relatively lightweight machine.

If the number of users or messaging traffic is too high, the demands place heavier loads on the server and can, if heavy enough, affect its performance. In such cases, the answer might be a multiprocessor system with multiple disk drives.

If the number of users and demand for services (especially high-bandwidth services such as conferencing) is very high, Exchange can be configured so that services run on different servers, with each server dedicated to a particular task. Depending on the load they must handle, these servers can range from single-processor computers to multiprocessor machines with vast amounts of disk storage. Through dedicated servers, Exchange can not only help distribute the messaging and collaboration load, it can also

- Direct heavy traffic or traffic with special demands (such as Internet connectivity) to machines specifically set up to handle the work

- Protect the network as a whole by restricting access to certain servers—an important consideration, especially when Internet access is involved

Exchange servers can be dedicated to particular tasks, such as those described in the following sections.

Mailboxes and Public Folders

Dedicating one or more servers to mail and public folders has the advantage of isolating these machines from demands and problems affecting other servers. If, in addition, public folders are maintained on a separate server, the company can allow public (external, or anonymous) access to the folders, while at the same time protecting the rest of the network by isolating it from potential security-related problems.

Outlook Web Access

Outlook Web Access, which was included in Exchange 5.5 and, earlier, in Exchange 5.0 Service Pack 1.0, provides remote users with just a limited amount of Outlook functionality, but it also does provide secure access to e-mail, calendars, and public folders through a Web browser. Outlook Web Access is designed for use by remote or roaming users and, because it doesn't require installation, it can also be used from multiple operating systems, in extranet applications, or by users who have systems with limited RAM or hard disk space.

Again, dedicating a separate server to Outlook Web Access protects the network by limiting access to a single server. In terms of network capacity, bandwidth and high-speed Internet access are additional factors to consider in dedicating a server, especially one expected to experience heavy usage.

Internet Mail

Internet mail servers, the delight of Internet e-mail and newsgroup users, must be reliable, workhorse machines ready to serve up messages 24 hours a day, 365 days a year—ideally without fail. These servers must also run IMAP4, POP3, and (for newsgroups) NNTP, but these protocols are routinely installed as part of Exchange messaging and collaboration. The main considerations, however, are (as is always the case with Internet access) bandwidth, high-speed access to high-volume servers, adequate modem connections to the network and hence to the server, and—because users maintain messages on the server—adequate disk space for individual mail stores.

Exchange Connectors

In deployments requiring high-traffic message routing to other systems or to earlier versions of Exchange, dedicated servers running some or all of the Exchange Connectors can help streamline operations and ease the burden on the mail server where the messages are actually stored.

Bear in mind that these connectors not only route messages to systems running products such as Microsoft Mail and Lotus Notes, but they also enable traffic flow over X.400 and SMTP and—through the Microsoft Active Directory Connector described in more detail later—to servers with Exchange-based (rather than Windows 2000-based) directories.

Conferencing

In terms of bandwidth demands and server processing and memory, conferencing, especially IP multicast videoconferencing, takes the prize in terms of being a demanding service. Of all the features supported by Exchange, conferencing may well be the one most deserving of

- The most powerful hardware
- Its very own server or servers
- High-bandwidth, high-speed, dedicated connections

Separating data conferencing, videoconferencing, or both, from the remainder of the messaging and collaboration setup can keep these services from slowing other services down. In addition, providing data conferencing through a separate server can—again—protect the network if individuals from within and outside the network frequently join together in conferences.

Chat

Chat services may or may not rank very high on an organization's list of needed features. However, the chat services provided by Exchange 2000 can actually perform a valuable service by providing users, both inside and outside the organization, with a real-time forum and a virtual room for specific discussions. One obvious use for such a feature would be to give employees the opportunity to routinely "meet" with one or more executives at scheduled times. Another use would be to provide an online environment, restricted to particular times and days, for interested parties to meet in a seminar-like atmosphere.

Although chat services don't place heavy demands on the server, it might be desirable to set aside a chat server in cases where

- There is heavy volume
- The chat is open to external visitors over the Internet and the server must be kept separate from the rest of the network

Instant Messaging

Instant messaging, a technology beloved by many Internet users and included with Exchange 2000, provides a way for individuals to maintain lists of contacts and to send real-time messages to those who are online. The Microsoft Instant Messaging client delivered by Exchange is a version of the instant messaging client provided by The Microsoft Network (MSN). On the screen, the client appears in a small window listing both the online and offline contacts.

In providing this service, Exchange relies on a home server, which is dedicated as an instant messaging server. A single home server can support up to 10,000 connections at the same time; organizations that need more connections will probably need several instant messaging servers.

When using instant messaging, users add new contacts to their list of contacts by sending a subscription to the contact's home server. Although little network overhead is involved in instant messaging and the messages themselves are ephemeral and not saved in the message store, administrators should consider the number of home servers that users will have to subscribe to.

The Network and Active Directory Services

Whether they are dedicated or not, Exchange servers run Exchange software, and as many documents, articles, and white papers will tell you, Exchange present is not the same as Exchange past. Even though Exchange 2000 can work seamlessly with earlier versions, the shift to Exchange 2000 involves a new way of looking at things that's based on the integration of Exchange 2000 with Windows 2000.

The most significant aspect of this integration is, of course, the switch from using an Exchange directory to relying on Windows 2000 Active Directory services. To a related but lesser extent, the shift also involves understanding Windows 2000 security. In terms of learning, the move to Exchange 2000 requires familiarity with a terminology in which some words are brand new and others, such as *site,* take on new, somewhat different meanings.

Organization Structure

Companies, like living things, grow and change. Sometimes structure just happens as the company adds to itself or diversifies. Other times, perhaps as the company matures, its leaders impose structure on it—a good example being the periodic reorganizations a company initiates to improve the work environment, address changing markets, or breathe new life into an organization grown accustomed to the old ways of doing things.

Whether structure just happens or is imposed, however, it's always people who determine how individuals fit together into groups. People determine which groups can or should combine to form larger departments. And, again, it's people who determine how those departments are related to other departments—which ones need to work together closely, which ones provide support throughout the company, and which ones (if any) are ancillary to or work independently of the main corporate body.

But, you think, so what? Usually, the person who administers the network is not the person who makes those decisions. Perhaps that's true. But an administrator who doesn't understand the structure of the organization can find it a tad difficult to figure out how best to map the organization—with its logical hierarchies and its physical network infrastructure—to the Active Directory domain or domains that will provide all users with the ability to find and communicate with one another.

Windows 2000 and Exchange 2000

Although all earlier versions of Exchange have run on top of Microsoft Windows NT, Exchange 2000 is the first to be so closely integrated with Windows

2000, the network operating system. This integration is designed to provide a solid, secure, and scalable roadbed over which Exchange 2000 can run its messaging and collaboration services. In terms of Exchange 2000, Windows integration is especially significant in two areas:

■ **Active Directory services,** which provides for unified administration of all network objects, including users, resources, messaging, configuration information, printers and other network devices, databases, and Web access

■ **Windows 2000 security,** which runs the gamut from authenticating users at logon to assigning network and messaging permissions to such tasks as creating distribution lists

As a side benefit, this same integration potentially leads to lower administrative and ownership costs because the same tools can be used from a single location to manage both the network and network messaging.

An Overview of Active Directory Services

Although Active Directory services is given its own chapter later in the book (see Chapter 5), its effect on Exchange 2000 and the way administrators view the enterprise is far-reaching enough for some of the basics to be covered here. In addition, because Active Directory terms permeate descriptions of Exchange 2000, people unfamiliar with the terms and what they mean can end up feeling like a dog chasing its tail: "I *would* understand X if only I knew Y, but to know Y, I should already understand X."

The Point of a Directory Service

At the risk of being overly simplistic, understanding Active Directory services and its importance to Exchange 2000 begins with the concept of a directory service. A directory service is an important, indeed an essential, tool in any enterprise of more than a few people; like a telephone book, it helps people find things. Traditionally, in messaging services, those "things" are other people and their attributes, such as first and last name, e-mail name, and so on. The larger the organization, the more important a directory service becomes in helping people to find and communicate with each other.

To be useful, a directory service must, among other things, provide a means of

■ **Storing user and other information** in a client-accessible database—the directory

■ **Ensuring that security is enforced,** that personal privacy is protected, and that resources cannot be accessed by unauthorized individuals

In replacing the Exchange directory, Active Directory services takes on those jobs.

Directory Access

Ultimately, all objects—from network resources up through users, groups, and the organization itself—must be uniquely named to be findable, accessible, or usable. To make the process of finding both painless to users and conceptually extensible to the entire Internet, Active Directory services relies on integration with the DNS (Domain Name Service) locator service, which is already widely used on both the Internet and in intranets to resolve "friendly" names into TCP/IP addresses. Like DNS, Active Directory services uses Internet-type names, such as *microsoft.com*. Such names can, in fact, be both Internet domain names and Windows 2000 domain names.

Although Active Directory services and DNS are tightly interwoven, it's important to remember that

■ **Active Directory services** is a repository of information

■ **DNS** is a tool for converting that information into a particular IP address, just as happens on the Internet

Active Directory services is, in a sense, a telephone book and DNS is the equivalent of a telephone operator able to resolve a person's name into a telephone number. The glue that binds the two is the LDAP protocol, which is used by the client to query DNS servers.

DNS

Anyone familiar with the Internet and even roughly aware of how it's structured is already familiar with DNS, the naming convention that enables computers anywhere in the world to find and communicate with one another. Although actual communication between these machines relies on IP addresses, it's the human-friendly DNS names that enable users to specify particular Internet sites and (although it might not always seem to be the case) to feel confident that there's order behind the apparent chaos of millions of interconnected computers.

In brief, DNS is the name service that organizes sites hierarchically, beginning with a single root domain and working downward through increasingly finer levels, through top-level domains (.com, .org, .gov, .edu, and so on), second-level domains (such as *microsoft.com, whitehouse.gov, washington.edu*), and subdomains (*law.washington.edu,* and so on), as shown in the following illustration.

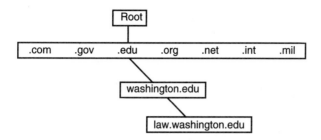

Namespaces

The term *namespace* appears over and over in references to both the Internet and to Active Directory services. (That's not unusual, because both are based on DNS conventions.) Although the term isn't particularly intuitive, it's not at all a difficult concept to master. A namespace is, simply, a bounded area within which a name can be resolved to the object it represents. Or, put another way, it's a name that encompasses a particular group of identifiable, locatable objects. A family's surname, for example, represents a namespace within which individual first names (and possibly middle initials) zero in on particular individuals.

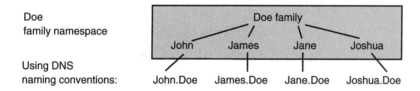

Given this definition and the preceding example, it's easy to see that the Doe family can, technically, be defined as a namespace, even though they can just as accurately be described as a family of potters, mechanics, farmers, or Internet wizards. Similarly, Active Directory services can be defined as a namespace, even though it, too, can be described in many ways—as a directory service, as a collection of named resources, or as an enterprise telephone book. The points to remember are that

- A namespace refers to a bounded area within which individual names can be resolved to particular objects

- Under DNS conventions, a namespace uses the familiar "dot" notation as it moves through increasingly specific levels of a domain hierarchy

- Namespaces and DNS names are important in the description of Windows 2000 domains, trees, and forests (groups of trees that don't share the same namespace), all of which are the building blocks not only of a Windows 2000 network, but also of the Exchange 2000 messaging infrastructure

Furthermore, because of this integration of DNS naming and its reliance on LDAP, Active Directory services is able to work across multiple operating systems, in the type of heterogeneous networking environment typical of many corporate networks. Because it's designed to function as a general-purpose directory, it's also able to incorporate other, more specific directories to reduce administrative loads and the need to maintain multiple namespaces.

Security

Because Exchange 2000 relies on Windows 2000 security, the messaging and collaboration functions are able to depend on the operating system's security APIs for privacy, network authentication, public keys for encryption and digital signatures, and development of secure enterprise and intranet applications.

Access Control Lists, or ACLs, provide protection for objects in Active Directory services. ACLs control

- **Who is allowed to see an object**
- **What properties of that object an individual can see,** for instance, first and last name and e-mail name, perhaps, but not other more sensitive information
- **What actions a given individual can perform on an object,** for instance, make changes to his or her own object

In addition, Active Directory services security allows an administrator to delegate administrative rights in certain circumstances and to certain individuals and groups. Such rights might, for example, grant administrative authority to add new users or set passwords, but only within a department or other clearly defined and circumscribed area.

Active Directory Services and Network Views

Whereas Exchange in earlier versions viewed the organization overall as a group of sites and servers, Exchange 2000, because of its integration with Active Directory services, takes a more extended view of the whole. There is, as always, the physical network on which Exchange runs. And there is, as before, the logical organization of regional offices, departments, users, resources, and other objects that need grouping for administrative purposes.

Where complexity—at least in concept—tends to enter the picture is in the blending of Active Directory services and Exchange. This happens because the two are interdependent and because Active Directory services brings with it

■ **Whole-network organization and administration,** including logon, permissions, and other security-related features, as well as Exchange-specific mailboxes, public folders, and group distributions

■ **New terminology** based on domains, forests, trees, and sites

Although understanding and appreciating the new features of the combined Active Directory services and Exchange 2000 organization might be somewhat difficult, at least initially, the key is to distinguish between viewing the organization and its network as a physical entity and as a logical collection of network resources.

The Physical View

On the physical side, Active Directory services—and, by extension, Exchange 2000—sees an organization in terms of sites. Although earlier versions of Exchange also referred to sites, the term has a somewhat different meaning in Exchange 2000. Formerly, a site was

■ A group of computers with permanent high-bandwidth connections. Under this definition, a site was not only a high-bandwidth subsection of a network, it was also an administrative unit.

Now, a site is

■ A group of computers belonging to one or more IP subnets—computers assigned the same subnet address as part of their longer, 32-bit IP address—characterized by permanent high-bandwidth (10 Mbps or faster) connections. Unlike earlier Exchange sites, these sites map the physical topology of the network.

Sites are no longer the administrative units they were under Exchange 5.5; they're determined primarily by topology and hardware in the sense of defining areas within a network that are linked by high-bandwidth connections, and they don't necessarily have to share the same namespace. Depending on network connections and how they are defined by the administrator, sites can span

■ A single IP subnet

■ A single domain (a collection of computers with its own security policy)

■ Multiple domains

As a rule, however, parts of a network separated by slower connections, such as WAN links or multiple routers, should be set up as different sites.

The Logical View

Superimposed upon this physical view of a network is a logical view through which administrators can view the organization as a hierarchy of objects arranged in manageable units known as domains, groups, trees, and one or possibly more forests. These units can parallel the structure of branches, offices, departments, and people in the actual organization.

Classes and Objects

To Active Directory services, all network users and resources are objects, and the objects are instances of object classes—categories or design blueprints, so to speak, for objects that represent something or someone real, in much the same way that a non-computer class named Bird might include in it a real-life instance of a canary.

Each object class defines the objects it can contain in terms of attributes, or characteristics. These attributes can be mandatory (also called *Must Contain*) attributes, meaning they must be present in every object in the class, or they can be optional (*May Contain*) attributes, meaning they can be present in some objects but not in others.

Here, for example, is a graphic showing an object—assume an Exchange user—and some typical attributes:

first name: Erwin
last name: Devguy
e-mail: bogusacct@msft.com
phone: 425-555-5555

Objects are like the atoms of the Active Directory universe; and like atoms, they are everywhere.

The Schema

Although objects represent instances of the classes to which they belong, they are actually defined in a special set of definitions known as the schema. This schema is stored in the directory and is composed of two kinds of objects:

■ **Class objects,** which define classes in terms of the mandatory and optional attributes mentioned earlier. Class objects also define object "lineage" in that they specify which higher-level classes can be parent classes of the objects they contain. In the real-life Exchange world, a class object is used to define a class such as Users.

■ **Attribute objects,** one per attribute, which specify the mandatory and optional characteristics of the objects in each class. In turn, the attributes are given a syntax, which specifies the type of data (for example text, true/false, integer) they can contain. To draw on real life again, the class Users might contain objects (instances of the class) named Tom, Dick, and Mary, and these objects might, in turn, be characterized by attribute objects defining such features as the person's given name and telephone number. The given name and telephone number would have to correspond to the syntax allowed for each attribute—say, text for one and numbers for the other.

The following illustration shows the relationships between classes and objects and their attributes.

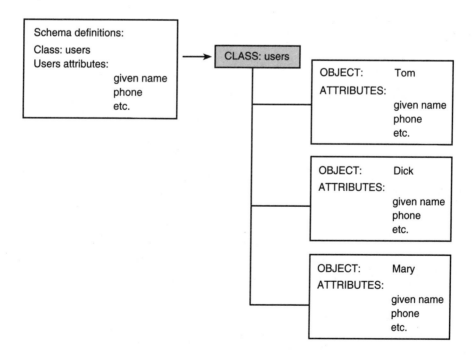

Domains

If objects—individual users, resources, and so on—are the atoms of an Active Directory structure, domains are the molecules. The parallel isn't exact, because domains can include related objects collected in containers called organizational units, but for purposes of a broader discussion, objects can still reasonably be considered "atomic" and domains "molecular."

To Windows 2000 and Active Directory services, a domain is a unit—a collection of network resources within a domain namespace. All objects and groups of objects in organizational units exist within domains, and each domain is characterized by a single security boundary—in other words, all objects within the domain share the same security permissions and restrictions.

However, although it's tempting to think of an Active Directory services domain as comparable to an Active Directory services site, the two actually have little to do with one another. A domain, unlike a site, isn't necessarily confined to a restricted area, such as a LAN. The computers can be located far from one another and connected in a number of ways—dial-up connections, ISDN, fiber optics, satellite, and so on. Even thinking of the possible combinations can be headache-inducing

- **A domain** can span a single site or multiple sites
- **A site** can span a single domain or multiple domains

For more on the differences and relationships between sites and domains, see the "An Everyday Analogy" section later in this chapter.

Aside from its DNS name, a domain is characterized by

- **One or more domain controllers:** computers designated as the domain "masters" in charge of handling user and domain security matters

- **A shared directory** and, by extension, centralized administration

- **Security policies** rights and permissions applied to a domain are limited to that domain and don't carry over into other domains (although trust relationships are automatically created when domains are joined to one another in the domain trees described in the next section)

- **Administrative authority** the ability to administer can be assigned on a domain-by-domain basis

- **Information storage** information about objects can be stored in a specific domain

Organizational Units

Hierarchically, organizational units sit between objects and domains. Unlike them, however, organizational units are containers for grouping other objects to make administration easier. In this respect, organizational units are much like Windows folders, which not only store files, but also can be assigned certain permissions, such as read-only or full-access sharing over the network. And just as folders can be set up to match the way a person thinks, works, and accesses files, organizational units can be set up to reflect the structure of an organization, especially because they can be arranged hierarchically, with one organizational unit containing others.

Unlike folders, however, organizational units can contain a multitude of object types, including user accounts, groups (collections of users, groups, and contacts), hardware such as computers and printers, and resources such as applications and file shares.

The smallest Active Directory services unit that can be given administrative authority, an organizational unit is, overall, an administrative tool for use in structuring and organizing resources at the domain level.

Trees

Trees, or domain trees, are one step above domains in the Active Directory services hierarchy. Trees contain domains arranged in a parent/child relationship—one in which all included domains represent a contiguous namespace. The following example uses real tree names to illustrate the relationship.

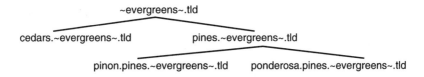

NOTE: In this example, .tld (rather than .com, .org, and so on) represents the top-level domain. The domain names themselves are surrounded by tilde symbols. These Internet no-nos make the names completely unusable, which is necessary to respect the ownership rights of potential real Internet sites. This convention will be followed in illustrations throughout the book.

As you can see, the tree structure is an old, familiar one. The only difference between this and, say, a directory tree lies in the DNS naming used. Note also that all branches of the tree exist within the namespace defined by the root domain, *~evergreens~.tld,* and that name resolution, as usual in DNS and on the Internet, moves to successively finer levels from right to left.

In terms of Windows 2000 and Exchange 2000, a domain tree such as this can represent an entire enterprise-wide Active Directory services implementation.

Forests

In some instances, if an enterprise finds it necessary to support multiple, non-contiguous domain trees—for example, *~evergreens~.tld* and a separate but closely related tree, *~spruces~.tld*—it can form a forest containing the separate trees, as shown below.

Forest

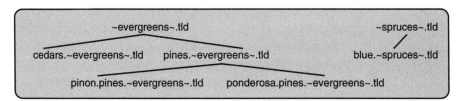

Although the forest itself doesn't need to be named, it does need to contain a root domain (assume *~evergreens~.tld* in the example), which can be the same as the organization's DNS name. Even though each tree within the forest represents a contiguous namespace, the namespaces of the domain trees are unrelated to one another. Importantly, however, the trees in a forest

- ■ **Share a common schema,** the definition of object attributes in each object class, and configuration information, including replication topology between servers.

- ■ **Include two-way, hierarchical trust relationships,** based on the Kerberos security protocol, that are known to all the trees in the forest. The trust relationships are established in such a way that the domains in a tree implicitly trust one another. Thus, for example, if the cedars domain establishes a trust relationship with the pines domain, and the pines domain establishes a trust relationship with the ponderosa domain, then cedars automatically trusts ponderosa.

- ■ **Can represent a single Exchange 2000 organization.**

On the other hand,

- ■ **A forest *does* represent the outermost boundary of the Active Directory domain structure,** which is another way of saying that the Active Directory domain structure can't become larger than the forest.

■ **Multiple forests can't be combined in a single Exchange 2000 organization.** Whereas Exchange 5.5 could span multiple Windows NT domains, under Exchange 2000, forest A and forest B can't be part of the same organization. This difference is significant because it means that forest A and forest B, if created

❑ Would require separate administration

❑ Would not benefit from automatic directory replication

❑ Would not be able to "see" the objects in the other forest's address list, which is an important consideration in terms of making the directory useful throughout the enterprise

Thus, all the domains and, therefore, all the users in the following forest could be in one Exchange organization.

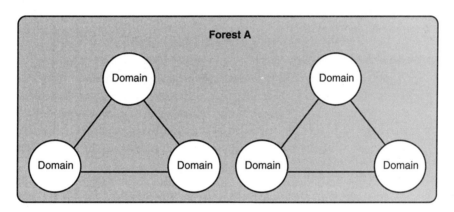

But the forests shown below could not.

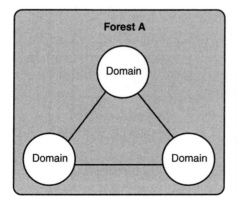 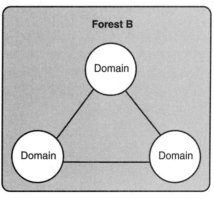

Naming Contexts

Within this structure of domains, trees, and possibly a forest, Active Directory services can consist of multiple naming contexts, which are contiguous subtrees of the directory and serve as boundaries for information within the structure. In a multiple domain environment, each server holds at least the following three naming contexts:

- The schema

- The configuration

- One or more user naming contexts—the actual directory objects

Within a given forest, the schema and configuration naming contexts are the same on all domain controllers; but the user naming context is unique to each server.

These naming contexts are fundamental to the enterprise-wide (forest-wide) Global Catalog maintained by Active Directory services for locating objects.

The Global Catalog

Although Active Directory services can be made up of numerous naming contexts, applications such as Exchange 2000 must be able to give their users the ability to locate objects throughout the forest, often without knowing much more than the object's name or another such common attribute, and certainly without knowing the tree, domain, or container hierarchy through which to travel to find the object.

To satisfy this need, as well as to support legacy protocols such as MAPI, Active Directory services maintains the Global Catalog, which is an efficient and effective solution in which any server acting as a domain controller can be designated a Global Catalog server holding the following:

- **A full replica of its own domain**

- **A partial replica for every other domain** in the Active Directory services tree or forest, which—by default—contains only a limited set of often-searched attributes, but includes enough to locate a full replica of the object being searched for

The Global Catalog is automatically generated during replication and includes any changes to information covered by global attributes (those included in the partial replicas).

Domain Controllers

An Active Directory domain, unlike domains under Windows NT, is multimastered, which means that all domain controllers, or DCs, have writable copies of directory information and so can function as equals rather than as primary and backup controllers. Domain controllers must, obviously, be running the server version of Windows 2000. Once they are, however, they can propagate replicas of directory information among themselves. Furthermore, should one domain controller fail, others in the same domain can take over directory access, because they all hold copies of the same directory information.

An Everyday Analogy

If the preceding descriptions of sites, domains, trees, and forests tend to blur, the following analogy might help. Be careful, however, not to push this analogy too far. It's included primarily to help distinguish the physical concept of a site from the logical concept of a domain.

Think of the physical network in terms of a dictionary. This dictionary (equivalent to the entire network) consists of many individual pages (the computers), each of which contains a unique word and its definitions (the computers' resources).

For efficiency, the "administrator" decides to group related pages alphabetically (sites), putting all the A words together in one site, all the B words in another, and so on. For those groups that are still too unwieldy, the administrator divides them into closely related subgroups—for example, by dividing the A words into those beginning AA through AD, those beginning AE through AG, and so on. Each of those smaller groups would be equivalent to a subnet. The same holds true for mapping network computers to sites, as shown in the following illustration.

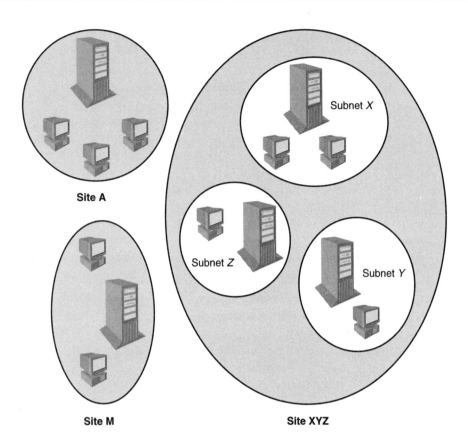

Site A

Subnet *X*

Subnet *Z*

Subnet *Y*

Site M

Site XYZ

This arrangement would work well in terms of randomly finding words in the dictionary, but it wouldn't work very well at all if the administrator needed to manage words that were related to one another—all words related to *transportation*, for example. In this case, the administrator could decide to create an "index" (comparable to the tree in the leftmost panes of Active Directory services and Exchange windows) that grouped words logically, by topic. So, for example, *transportation* might become one topic (domain) and *geology* might become another. Furthermore, within each topic, the administrator might designate subtopics (subdomains and smaller administrative units) so that *transportation* might be further divided into *airplanes, boats, cars,* and *oxcarts.*

Note that even though the dictionary would physically still be divided into alphabetic "sites," the topic-related "domains" could span anything from a single subnet (the word *alphabet*, perhaps) to multiple sites (*transportation*). Furthermore, the reverse also holds true—a single site (say, the letter A) could span multiple domains (*animals* to *airplanes*).

Active Directory Services and Exchange 2000

Obviously, Windows 2000, especially in its server versions, and Exchange 2000 are designed to meet different corporate needs. The one focuses on providing a reliable, scalable network operating system on which many applications can run. The other, taking advantage of Windows, focuses on providing a reliable, scalable messaging framework for the corporation and its users. Thanks to the integration of Exchange and Active Directory services, Windows 2000 and Exchange 2000 complement each other in many ways, among them

- Centralized, standardized administration
- Reliance on Windows 2000 Active Directory services for needs ranging from logon to security to managing mailboxes and users
- Use of forests, domains, trees, domain controllers, and sites as structural underpinnings

But it's also true that, given the basic difference in their responsibilities, there are certain factors to consider in installing Exchange 2000 in a Windows 2000 environment or migrating to Exchange 2000 in a mixed Windows environment. The following sections briefly define some of the issues involved.

Windows 2000

First of all, an obvious but nevertheless true observation: The primary domain controller must be running Windows 2000 before Exchange 2000 can be installed, either in a new installation or as an upgrade to an existing Exchange installation. In addition, the network must be running a DNS service.

Logical and Physical Hierarchies

In figuring out how to structure the Exchange organization, bear in mind that, as already mentioned and illustrated, Exchange 2000 can't span multiple forests. For users in the organization to be able to see and find one another through Active Directory services and the Global Catalog, they must be in the same forest. A forest, remember, represents the outermost boundary of the Active Directory domain structure. Even though the domain trees in the forest belong to noncontiguous (different) domain namespaces, they still share the same schema and configuration information.

Within this logical hierarchy of trees and domains, Exchange also divides and conquers in terms of the way it defines a site. While earlier versions of Exchange viewed a site as a collection of servers with permanent, dependable,

49

broadband connections, Exchange 2000 views the old concept of site in two different ways: administrative groups and routing groups.

An administrative group is, as the name indicates, an administrative tool, a means of grouping resources such as servers, public folder trees, and the like as a unit, typically for across-the-board access control. A routing group, in contrast, is a physical collection of servers linked by high-bandwidth connections. In this new view, a routing group more closely resembles the old concept of a site than does an administrative group.

Active Directory Services Terminology

Because Exchange 2000 is integrated with Active Directory services, the terminology for object classes in Exchange 2000 has changed

- What used to be a mailbox is now a Windows 2000 user, that is, someone who can log on to the network. A user account contains the individual's logon password, permissions for using network resources, and memberships in various groups.

- A custom recipient is now a contact, someone who can't log on but who is associated with an e-mail address and to whom, optionally, Exchange e-mail can be routed.

- A distribution list is now one of two types of groups, a security-based Windows 2000 group characterized by group permissions for network resources, or (more like the old distribution list) a group of users who receive bulk mailings.

   NOTE: Each of the preceding can also be either mailbox-enabled, meaning it's associated with an Exchange mailbox and can therefore send and receive e-mail, or it's mail-enabled, meaning it's associated with an e-mail address, but not with an Exchange mailbox and therefore relies on third-party messaging for sending and receiving mail.

Directory Replication

Another change based on Exchange 2000 integration with Active Directory services involves replication of attribute changes (such as a change in telephone extension number) to the Global Catalog. Whereas earlier versions of Exchange were required to replicate the entire object if one of the object's attributes was changed, under Exchange 2000 and Active Directory services, only the changed attribute is replicated to the domain controllers within a given domain. If the changed attribute happens to be one chosen for replication to the Global Catalog that serves the entire enterprise, it's also replicated to the Global Catalog servers for distribution to all other domains.

Peaceful Coexistence

Finally, though far from the least important of these considerations, Exchange 2000 server coexists and seamlessly communicates with earlier Exchange installations. For example, directory synchronization between Active Directory services and the Exchange directory is handled by the Exchange 2000 Active Directory Connector (ADC), an enhanced version of the ADC shipped with Windows 2000 that can be used to replicate site and configuration information upstream (from Exchange to Active Directory services), downstream (from Active Directory services to Exchange), or both.

In addition, an upgraded server is visible in both its Exchange site and its Active Directory services site, and the entire Exchange organization—old and new—can be administered centrally, from a single point. Furthermore, the Exchange server is capable of handling both MAPI-compliant applications—those built to exchange e-mail through the Microsoft Messaging API—and Internet clients.

CHAPTER THREE

A Visual Tour of Exchange 2000

The preceding two chapters have provided mostly conceptual overviews of Exchange 2000, some relating to earlier versions, others relating to Microsoft Windows 2000 and Microsoft Active Directory services. Those descriptions, however, haven't actually introduced the Exchange 2000 that appears on-screen in the numerous windows that enable administration and management of users, resources, and the servers themselves.

On-screen, Exchange is as familiar and yet as different as, say, London or Tokyo would be to a lifelong New Yorker. So, just as maps and guidebooks help a New Yorker learn about a new city, this chapter, operating on the assumption that a picture is indeed worth a thousand words, distills a portion of those thousands of "words" about Exchange into a visual tour. This tour, based on text and screen illustrations, should serve as an introduction to the Exchange 2000 environment.

Some of these illustrations may look familiar or be easily compared to existing Exchange features, especially because they show reliance on the Windows interface and their content (users, public folders, and so on). Others, such as the illustrations of the Microsoft Management Console (MMC), may represent new territory. Regardless, the illustrations as a whole represent a pictorial overview of Exchange 2000 and its on-screen environment.

Windows 2000 Server

Because Windows 2000 and Active Directory services are so intimately connected to Exchange and resource management, Windows provides a good starting point—like getting to know the international terminal and duty-free shop at the airport before departing for parts unknown.

At startup, unless told otherwise, Windows 2000 Server opens with a services- and network-management tool when the administrator logs on.

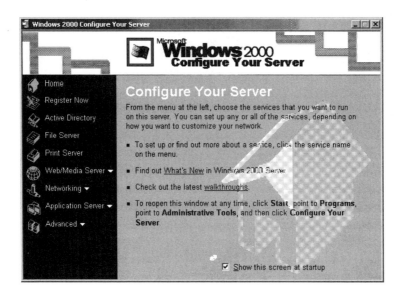

As the screen text indicates, this appears at startup if the check box, Show This Screen At Startup, remains selected. The screen is also accessible from Start | Programs | Administrative Tools | Configure Your Server. Once Windows 2000 Server has been installed, this program simplifies the tasks of adjusting the setup to meet the needs of a particular network. Briefly, the options listed on the left side of the window allow the types of customization listed in Table 3-1.

Windows 2000 Features and What They Do

Item	For customizing
Active Directory	User and security-related matters, including accounts, policies, permissions, and server roles in domains
File Server	Shared network files and folders
Print Server	Printers and related resources
Web/Media Server	Internet- and intranet-related resources, including World Wide Web, FTP, and multimedia sites
Networking	Network-related features, including protocols, DNS, DHCP, remote access, and routing
Application Server	Message queues and distributed applications
Advanced	Microsoft Terminal Server, certificates, remote installation, optional components

Table 3-1.
Features useful for customizing a Windows 2000/Exchange installation.

The Exchange Installation Wizard

Once Windows 2000 Server is up and running, the Microsoft Exchange 2000 Installation Wizard can be used to install, modify, or remove Exchange 2000 components. As the next illustration shows, the Component Selection screen—the first actual setup screen to appear after the wizard is started—includes an Action column to the left of a large, expandable Component Name column for selecting individual Exchange components. Selecting a component and then clicking in the Action column presents the installation choices None, Reinstall, Remove, and Change.

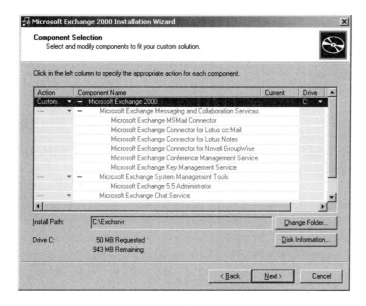

The rest of the Installation Wizard screens ask for account information (user name, domain, and password) and allow a review of choices before carrying out the specified actions.

A Good Place to Start

Both common sense and the documentation urge careful study and meticulous planning before installing Exchange, especially in light of such factors as

- The size of the organization
- Whether deployment represents a completely new installation or migration from or coexistence with earlier versions of Exchange

■ Network topology, site definitions, and administrative grouping of both servers and users

■ Number and types of administrators and roles to be played by each

These, of course, are issues that can only be handled, perhaps with consulting help, by those familiar with the organization.

For getting comfortable with Active Directory services and Exchange 2000, however, the familiar Help window is a fine starting point. Although Help itself needs no explanation, there *is* one possible point of confusion—the seeming changeability of the Help content because Windows 2000 and Exchange 2000 rely on the Microsoft Management Console (MMC).

MMC provides the environment within which administrators manage both Active Directory services and Exchange, but it doesn't always display the same Help content because it is just the frame within which tools, called snap-ins, perform the actual work. And because the work that goes on inside MMC can range from administering domains to managing Exchange, MMC Help both varies and yet stays the same.

That is, requesting Help from an MMC window brings up two distinct categories of Help, although they are combined and displayed in the same Help window. One category, the part that remains constant from one MMC window to the next, provides Help on MMC and how to use it. The other category, the part that changes from window to window, provides information on the snap-in running within the MMC.

For example, starting the MCC by choosing Start | Programs | Administrative Tools | Active Directory Users and Computers and then requesting Help calls up this window.

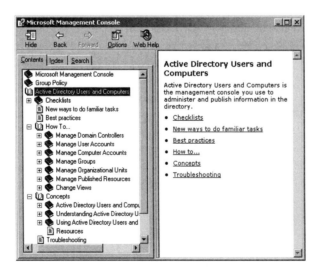

On the other hand, requesting Help after starting the MMC by choosing Start | Programs | Microsoft Exchange | System Manager produces this window.

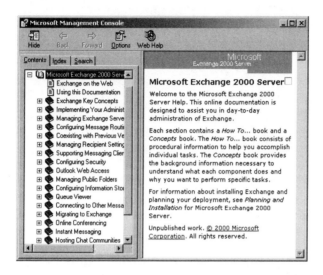

As you can see, Help can provide a considerable amount of both conceptual and "click here, drag there" assistance. For example, using the two Help windows illustrated above

- Searching on the word *checklist* in Users and Computers Help produces much useful information about Active Directory services, group policies, and terminal management, along with detailed lists that contain links to both background information and help on installation and administration

- Searching on the word *installation* in the Exchange Management Help window produces a long list of installation-related help topics, ranging from a FAQ on Exchange Conferencing (the Online Conferencing topic) to instructions on adding administrative groups, installing an X.400 Connector, migrating from Lotus Notes, and so on

And, as shown, to assist in sorting background information from step-by-step instructions, Help divides each Contents section into How To and Concepts sections.

As for the MMC itself...

The Microsoft Management Console

Visually and administratively, the MMC is one of the most significant features of Exchange 2000. The MMC provides the interface for viewing and managing an Exchange (and Active Directory services) implementation.

Although designed as a tool for unifying and simplifying system management, the MMC does not itself provide any functionality. It provides instead a common framework for tools—consoles—composed of one or more modules called snap-ins. Each of these snap-ins, in turn, is a COM object that represents, as Microsoft describes it, a single unit of management behavior—that is, a self-contained unit of "work" related to some aspect of system administration. "Building blocks" of code, these snap-ins come in two varieties, stand-alone and extension.

- **A stand-alone snap-in** is functional as-is and does not rely on any other snap-in to do its work

- **An extension snap-in** can provide functionality only when invoked by a parent snap-in

Like children's Lego blocks or TinkerToys, these snap-ins—both those shipped by Microsoft and those created by independent software vendors (ISVs)—can be assembled in different combinations to form tools for customized management. Within the MMC window, snap-ins are displayed on the left side (in the console tree) along with other items, including folders, other consoles, ActiveX controls, and even links to Web pages.

Running the MMC

Existing consoles, such as Exchange Management and Active Directory Users and Computers, are listed on the Programs menu. Those installed for Windows 2000 administration are on the Administrative Tools menu, and those for Exchange are on the Microsoft Exchange menu. They are also accessible through the Run command, which has the following syntax:

```
mmc path\filename.msc /a
```

where
`path\filename.msc` specifies the location of an existing console file, and
`/a` opens the file in author mode, to allow modification of the console.

Creating a New Console

The MMC can also be used to create new consoles. When started with the Run command with no parameters (click Start | Run, type **mmc** and then click OK), MMC displays the blank window shown below.

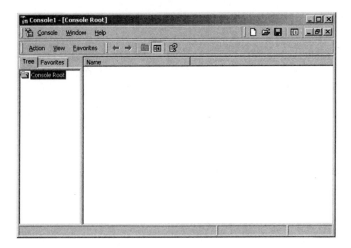

NOTE: The Console Root is the container for whatever tree the console author creates.

You can add (and remove) snap-ins through the Add | Remove Snap-in command on the Console menu, which produces the following window.

The next illustration shows a new console with the Exchange Folders snap-in added.

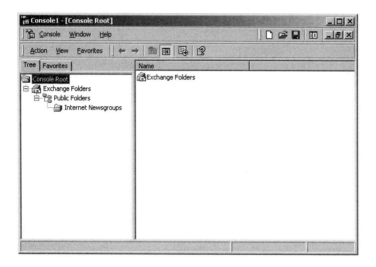

Some Representative MMC Consoles

Server configuration, Exchange installation, Help, and the MMC are all parts of understanding and administering Active Directory services and Exchange. There is also, of course, the question of what the Exchange installation itself looks like. To cover that, the following sections illustrate representative consoles for a computer in a domain with the DNS name *sample.local*.

Note that these illustrations show all Exchange components installed, and that the installation reflects Exchange "out of the box" rather than in any particular type of deployment, because real-world installations are bound to vary as much as the organizations that use them. Where needed, however, the illustrations do include example computers and users.

NOTE: These illustrations were based on a pre-release version of Exchange Server. Some details might differ in the released product.

Active Directory Services

For managing domains, sites, users, and other resources, Windows 2000 Server includes—among many other choices that depend on the installed components—three items on the Administrative Tools menu. These three are Active Directory Sites and Services, Active Directory Domains and Trusts, and Active Directory Users and Computers.

Sites and Services The Active Directory Sites and Services console is installed on every Windows 2000 domain controller. After installation of the Windows 2000 Administration Tools, it can also be used on other computers with access to a Windows 2000 domain.

The Sites and Services console is used for numerous site-related tasks, including

- Creating, renaming, and deleting sites

- Creating and deleting subnets

- Connecting to forests and domain controllers

- Delegating control

- Optimizing directory replication between sites through site links, which specify how sites are connected

By default, the Sites and Services window shows site information, as shown in the following illustration.

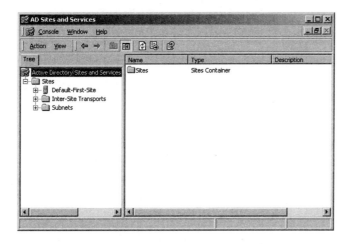

However, clicking the View menu and choosing Show Services Node changes the view to include service-centric information—that is, information that is stable, useful to many clients, and not reliant on the clients knowing the actual machine on which the service resides. Such information, when published by Active Directory services, can be accessed by clients, which can then access the service(s) themselves on network servers.

The following illustration shows the Services node, expanded to include Exchange information published in the directory.

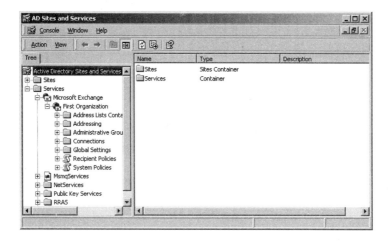

Domains and Trusts The Active Directory Domains and Trusts console is used for establishing and managing trust relationships between domains. These domains don't need to be in the same forest or to be Windows 2000-only. They can also include domains set up under earlier versions of Windows, and they can extend to non-Windows realms answerable to Kerberos V5 security.

The following illustration shows the Domains and Trusts console.

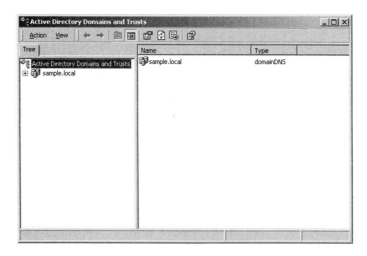

In addition to managing trust relationships, the Domains and Trusts tool is also used for

■ **Setting additional user principal name (UPN) suffixes** that can be used in place of the default DNS domain name at logon (For example, a user could log on as *jdoe@test* instead of as *jdoe@sample.local*.)

- **Identifying and changing the domain-naming operations master,** which is the one (and only) computer in a forest designated to control the addition and removal of domains in the forest

- **Switching operation** *irreversibly* from the default mixed mode (which enables Windows NT and Windows 2000 controllers to exist in the same domain) to native mode (Windows 2000 only) in an upgraded installation

Users and Computers The Active Directory Users and Computers console, arguably the one most needed on a day-to-day administrative basis, is the tool for managing

- Domain controllers

- Users and their accounts

- Computers

- Groups and organizational units

- Printers

- Shared folders

Users and Computers is accessible from the Programs menu, under both Administrative Tools and Microsoft Exchange, and appears in a window like the following.

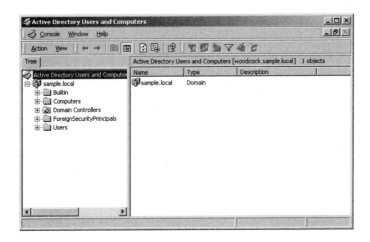

Adding new objects to reflect the organization's logical hierarchy is simply a matter of right-clicking the appropriate container, choosing New from the shortcut menu, and selecting the type of object (computer, contact, group, organizational unit, printer, user, or shared folder) to be added. For example, the following illustrations show the process of adding a new user.

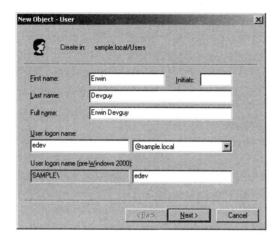

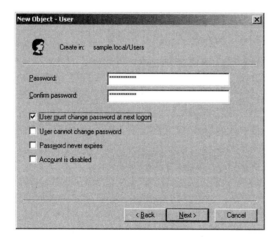

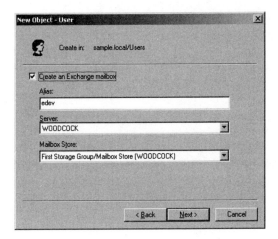

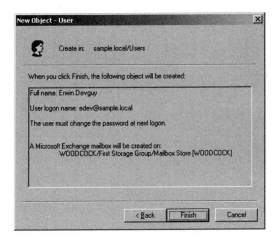

Later management involves either opening the object's property sheet or right-clicking and choosing an option from a shortcut menu. The next illustration shows the property sheet for a user.

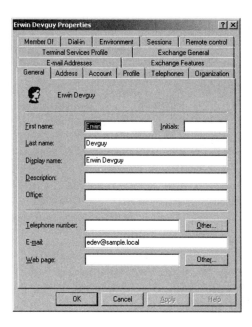

And this illustration shows the shortcut menu.

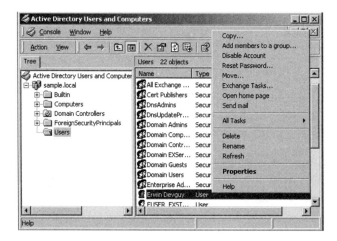

That, in essence, is a quick tour of Active Directory services and its administrative tools. (Chapter 5 deals with Active Directory services in more detail.) Exchange, as described in the next sections, offers tools of its own.

Exchange System Manager

The core of Exchange administration is the Exchange System Manager, an MMC console that (for benefit of those familiar with earlier versions of Exchange) replaces the Exchange 5.5 Administrator Program. The System Manager, which is shown in the following illustration, is essentially the tool to be used in managing all Exchange objects ranging from recipients and address lists to servers, chat, and policies affecting servers, public stores, and mailboxes.

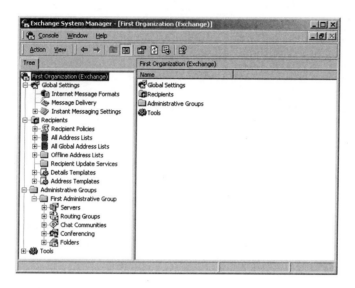

This partial list of the Help topics for this console illustrates the extent of activities that fall under the System Manager umbrella.

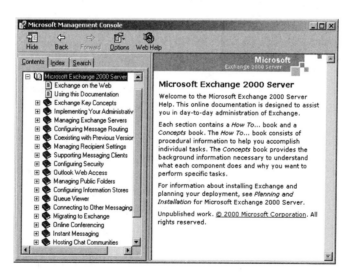

The next sections briefly describe the System Manager's approach to four primary tasks in Exchange 2000: managing administrative groups, managing routing groups, working with Active Directory Connector (for coexistence with earlier versions of Exchange), and migrating from earlier versions to Exchange 2000.

Managing administrative groups   Administrative groups are Active Directory objects that are collected together to simplify management of permissions. In Exchange 2000, administrative groups represent the administrative half of earlier Exchange sites. (The other half, described later, is routing groups.)

Creating an administrative group is simply a matter of right-clicking Administrative Groups in the System Manager tree, choosing New, choosing Administrative Group, and then typing a name and any desired administrative note in the dialog box that appears. Once created, an administrative group can be assigned its own policies.

Policies represent a new concept in Exchange 2000. In essence, a policy is a set of configuration settings that an administrator can apply across the board to multiple objects in the same class. Like a word processing template or a rule book, a policy simplifies management by providing a one-stop means of addressing the configuration of large numbers of similar objects.

Through the System Manager, an administrator can create, edit, and apply two types of policies.

- **Server-side system policies**   are applied to servers, public stores, and mailbox stores

- **Client-side recipient policies**   are applied to mail-enabled objects (objects with at least one e-mail address) in order to generate e-mail addresses. These objects include users, groups, contacts, and public folders.

The following illustrations show the nodes for both system policies and recipient policies (under the administrative group node) and an example of the limits that can be set for mailbox stores in a new policy.

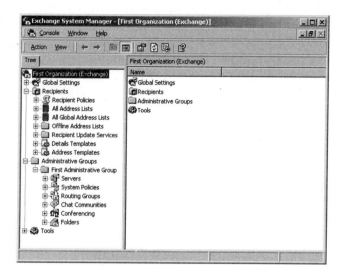

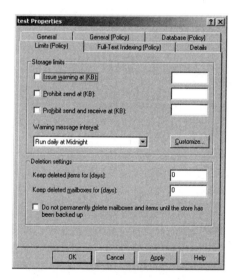

As mentioned earlier, administrative groups are designed to simplify permissions management. Exchange permissions are based on Windows 2000 security. However, to address the needs specific to messaging and collaboration, Exchange builds on the Windows security model by adding its own set of permissions known as extended permissions. These extended permissions affect the information store and public folders and cover such actions as

- Creating public folders
- Adding, mail-enabling, and managing public folders (modifying such features as access control lists, expiration dates, deleted item retention, and replica lists)
- Administering the information store

By default, child objects in Exchange 2000 inherit the permissions applied to their parent objects, so applying a set of permissions once to a parent object provides a quick and easy way to affect all child objects beneath the parent. This default behavior is also customizable and can be changed so that it affects, among other things

- The object itself and none other
- The object and its child objects
- Child objects only
- The object and its subcontainers
- Subcontainers only
- And so on, as shown in the following illustration

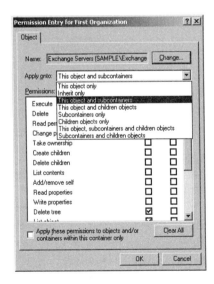

NOTE: During installation on the first server, Exchange sets up two default group accounts, Exchange Admins and Exchange Servers, both of which are viewable in the Users container of the domain tree in the Active Directory Users and Computers console. Because Exchange propagates permissions from parent to child objects, these accounts—and the permissions set for them—can serve as the basis for quickly implementing security throughout an Exchange organization.

Managing routing groups   Where administrative groups are designed to mirror the logical hierarchy of an organization, routing groups are designed to serve the physical connections between servers and groups of servers.

In an organization consisting of a single group of "well-connected" servers—those with permanent, high bandwidth connections—routing groups aren't necessary. However, a larger or more dispersed organization might easily include both well-connected servers and servers connected by slower or non-permanent links. In this type of environment, routing groups provide "single-hop" message routing to connect groups that must rely on slower connections. In essence, routing groups are the Exchange 2000 implementation of the physical sites linked by various connectors in earlier versions.

In connecting routing groups, Exchange 2000 relies on an SMTP or X.400 connector and bridgehead servers in each group that actually funnel all incoming and outgoing traffic between groups.

To create routing groups, however:

- **The Administrative Groups container**   must include a Routing Group container

- **This Routing Group container**   (displayed by selecting Display Routing Groups on the Administrative Views tab of the organization's Property sheet) is enabled only if the servers are running in native mode (Windows 2000 only)

Once routing groups are ready for connection, Exchange provides several options for actually linking the groups: a Routing Group Connector, an SMTP Connector, and an X.400 Connector. Of these, the Routing Group Connector is preferred, but

- **An SMTP Connector**   can be used if the routing groups belong to different forests, if scheduling is required, or if the connection requires custom authentication or encryption

■ **An X.400 Connector** can be used if the connection involves a non-Exchange system, X.400 connectivity already exists, or bandwidth is in short supply

To create a Routing Group Connector, right-click the Connectors folder under the routing group name, and choose New | Routing Group Connector from the shortcut menu, which produces the following screen.

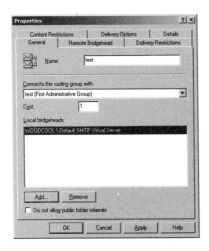

NOTE: A Routing Group Connector creates a one-way link between the originating group and the group to which it joins, so a second connector is needed to provide message transfer in the opposite direction.

Working with Active Directory Connector Active Directory Connector, which enables administrators to synchronize Active Directory services and the Exchange 5.5 directory, ships with both Windows 2000 Server and Exchange 2000. Although both are developed from the same code base

■ **The version shipped with Windows 2000** replicates information about directory objects to and from Active Directory services and the Exchange directory

■ **The version shipped with Exchange 2000** is enhanced to also replicate information from the configuration-naming context (information related to domain controllers and replication topology) and supports mixed Exchange sites

NOTE: Although much of the following information relates to both Windows and Exchange Active Directory Connectors, the remainder of this section focuses on the Exchange version.

Replication—whether from Windows to Exchange or from Exchange to Windows—relies on a connection agreement that must be established between an existing Exchange site and Active Directory services. This agreement defines the servers to be connected, as well as such information as

- **Exchange objects to be replicated**
- **Windows objects to be replicated**
- **Direction of replication**   one-way (Windows to Exchange or Exchange to Windows) or two-way (Note that adding a mailbox for a new user requires either a two-way connection or a one-way connection from Windows to Exchange.)
- **Replication schedule**   for example, continuous or at a specified time of day

Active Directory Connector runs as a service and needs to be installed only once on a server (with the help of the Active Directory Connector Installation Wizard). Once installed, the connector works through the MMC and its own snap-ins to enable the administrator to configure as many different connection agreements as are needed between the server and different Exchange sites. Each of these connection agreements can, of course, be configured differently.

When run from Exchange 2000, Active Directory Connector looks like this.

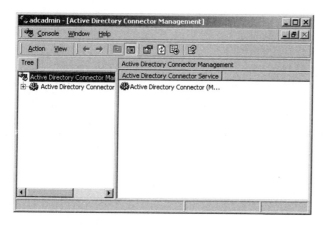

And new connection agreements are created on a property sheet like this.

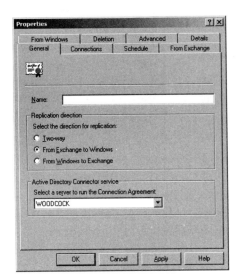

Active Directory Connector is especially valuable in the following situations:

- Replicating user information from the Exchange directory to Active Directory services
- Replicating data from Active Directory services to the old Exchange directory
- Centralizing directory management
- Enabling an Exchange 2000 deployment to coexist with an Exchange 5.5 installation

Migration   In addition to the numerous connectors that enable it to communicate with other message systems, Exchange 2000 also includes a Migration Wizard and a number of other tools that help in moving from another message system to Exchange. The Migration Wizard supports migration from the systems shown in the following illustration.

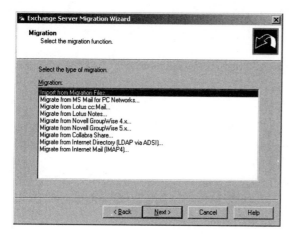

Through the wizard, administrators not only can specify the mail system to migrate from, but also can control which user accounts and mail the wizard migrates. In addition, depending on the system being migrated from, the wizard maps data and user information to Exchange and Active Directory services items and objects.

The wizard does *not* perform these tasks during migration:

- Move personal archives
- Convert custom applications
- Migrate distribution lists

It *does*, however, perform the following:

- Adds new users and converts contacts to users in Active Directory services
- Updates groups in Exchange
- Adds mail, calendar, and public folder information to the Exchange information store

The Migration Wizard performs its work in two steps, which can be carried out either separately or all at once.

- **In the first step** the source extractor component copies and saves data—directory and calendar information and messages—in migration-ready format
- **In the second step** the migration file importer component converts this information into Exchange format and places it where it is accessible to Exchange users

In addition to the Migration Wizard, Exchange also includes a number of other migration-related tools.

- **Archive importers** for Outlook 2000 users to use in importing archives and personal address books from Lotus cc:Mail, Microsoft, Mail, and other products
- **A Microsoft importer** for Lotus cc:Mail archives for users of cc:Mail
- **Exchange Application Services** for Lotus Notes for migrating Notes applications to Exchange
- **Active Directory Cleanup Wizard** for finding and taking care of duplicate accounts created during the migration process
- **Mailmig,** a command-line utility that allows batch processing

Exchange Server is, of course, far more complex than the illustrations in this chapter can show. It includes a multitude of management options presented through the MMC and its snap-ins, typically accessed either by right-clicking an object and making the appropriate choice on a shortcut menu or by adding or modifying information on an object's property sheet. Although these features have not been covered in this chapter, they will—where appropriate—be discussed later in this book.

CHAPTER FOUR

Exchange 2000 Installations

No matter how great or desirable they are, Microsoft Windows 2000 Server and Exchange 2000 offer nothing more than potential if they sit on the CD uninstalled. To realize their potential, they have to be used—planned for, deployed, and tested. Although the nuts and bolts of planning and installing Windows and Exchange are the purview of other (how-to) books, this chapter provides a toe-in-the-water overview of the issues and processes you need to consider. Because Microsoft Active Directory services is such an integral part of an Exchange 2000 deployment, this chapter provides an overview of Windows and Exchange installations. First, however...

Customer Concerns

The design of Exchange 2000 results in part from Microsoft's addressing two years' worth of customer concerns regarding Exchange stability, flexibility, and other issues. Overall, customers regard messaging and collaboration as

- **Critical to business**   for communication and teamwork
- **Potentially involving large investments**   in hardware, software, licensing, application development, and employee education
- **Pressured by the need to lower the total cost of ownership (TCO)**

In response to these concerns, Exchange 2000 is based on the three major design goals—messaging, messages, and messengers—listed in Chapter 1.

- **Messaging**   equates to performance issues—reliability, scalability, and flexibility—and cost reduction
- **Messages**   equates to Internet integration and openness to new approaches to workflow and collaboration
- **Messengers**   equates to "any time, anywhere" access to information

Individual features of Exchange 2000 that are designed to address these and other concerns include Active Directory integration (scalability), use of SMTP as the native messaging protocol (reliability and Internet integration), centralized administration based on the Microsoft Management Console (lowered cost of ownership), multiple message databases and active/active clustering (scalability and reliability), the new Web Store and XML support (Web integration), and new ways of communicating (instant messaging, wireless access, and chat services).

Of course, an organization's decision to implement a certain feature will depend on whether that feature exists in the version of Exchange being installed. To refresh your memory, the following features, mostly related to scalability and performance, are in the Exchange 2000 Enterprise Edition only:

- Unlimited storage (see Chapter 7)
- Multiple databases (see Chapter 7)
- Support for front/back-end deployment (see Chapters 7 and 8)
- Clustering (see Chapter 7)
- Chat (see Chapter 10)

Presence or absence of these features obviously affects adopting organizations. Decisions must be made as to what features complement business goals and how they affect the method, timing, structure, and testing of a Windows 2000/Exchange 2000 deployment. Such decisions are, however, just part of the planning that needs to be done about the method and timing of an Exchange deployment. Other—broader—issues include organization size, administrative model (centralized or decentralized), site and domain structure, and whether the Exchange deployment will or will not be 100 percent Exchange 2000. In some installations, Exchange will coexist with another mail system or with an earlier version of Exchange, if not permanently, then until all users and resources can be fully migrated to Exchange 2000.

This chapter covers the broader issues of deployment and leaves the details on Internet support, clustering, Internet integration, scalability, and other such features to Part II.

Centralized vs. Decentralized Administration

Here are two organizations: a hospital run by a single IT group that is responsible for planning, monitoring, and maintaining the network, as well as for setting goals, guidelines, and security policies; and a world-spanning enterprise that is a mélange of administrative groups, each of which manages the network, policies, and procedures of its own branch, unit, or department.

The hospital—like similarly managed organizations ranging from schools to chicken farms—is an example of centralized administration. The worldwide enterprise, on the other hand, is an example of distributed, or decentralized, administration, a more diffuse arrangement in which a core IT group is in charge of overall networking guidelines, but other individuals handle day-to-day administration of different groups.

Typically, as in these two deliberately opposite examples, a centralized administration model characterizes a small or medium-size organization that can depend on high-speed network links. The distributed model more likely describes a large or geographically dispersed organization with both high-speed links and slower WAN-type connections.

Common sense, of course, also tells you that organizations do not necessarily fit only one or the other of these models. An enterprise, say one with sizable bases in the Americas and Asia, can obviously be a composite of the two models, with administration centralized within each region but still distributed in relation to the organization as a whole. Still, the hospital and the global enterprise serve to illustrate the distinction between the two administrative models.

Administrative Groups and Routing Groups

One way Exchange addresses the needs of different organization administration is through the administrative and routing groups mentioned in Chapter 3. To provide administrative flexibility, and because the administrative structure and the physical network structure don't necessarily have much in common, Exchange 2000 uses these two new group types instead of the old site concept to group objects. Of the two, the routing group is closer to the concept of a site corresponding to earlier versions of Exchange.

Administrative Groups

An administrative group is used to bunch servers in a way that matches the structure of the organization. Administrative groups are designed to make permissions easier to assign and manage. Because child objects in an administrative group inherit the permissions applied to the group, creating administrative groups and adding objects to them can make permissions much easier to manage than having to apply those same permissions to individual objects.

An administrative group can include any of the following:

- Policies
- Routing groups

- Public folder trees
- Servers
- Conferencing
- Chat

Administrators also need to bear in mind that in mixed Exchange 5.5 and Exchange 2000 organizations, Exchange 2000 ensures that

- **Exchange 5.5 sites** appear as administrative groups in Active Directory services
- **Administrative groups in Active Directory services** appear as Exchange sites in the Exchange 5.5 directory

Routing Groups

A routing group is used to bunch servers in a way that reflects the physical network and hardware capabilities. Routing groups are designed as a way to define groups of servers with permanent, high-bandwidth connections and to support message passing between servers and groups of servers. The primary—indeed only—distinction between types of routing groups is

- **Intra-routing group communication messages** travel within the routing group in a single hop—that is, the sending and receiving servers in the routing group communicate directly
- **Inter-routing group communication messages** travel between routing groups, via bridgehead servers, through routing group connectors and often over slower or nonpermanent connections (The easiest connector to configure is the SMTP-based Exchange Routing Group Connector [RGC], but the SMTP Connector and the X.400 Connector can be used to connect to foreign messaging or X.400 systems.)

Using Administrative and Routing Groups

How do administrative groups and routing groups relate to centralized, decentralized, and mixed administration models?

- **A centralized administration model** is based on one or just a few administrative groups controlled by a central IT authority. Such a model may, however, include multiple routing groups, depending on network topology.

■ **A decentralized administration model** is based on a number of administrative groups—perhaps matching geographic regions or company divisions—that operate independently, control their own resources, and manage their own systems. As in a centralized model, these administrative groups may be under the authority of a central IT group, but that group is more concerned with setting policy than with system administration.

■ **A mixed administration model** is based on centralized control plus the assignment of specific aspects of the Exchange implementation to different administrative groups. For example, responsibility for routing or policies might be delegated to separate administrative groups, or different administrative groups might be responsible for separate geographic or organizational units. This mixed model is most likely to be used by large, widespread enterprises.

The following examples, all based on the same fictional business, show how centralized, decentralized, and mixed administration models might be used.

Centralized Administration

Suppose a coffee bean importer is based (where else?) in Seattle. The business is housed in a cluster of adjacent buildings, with separate departments for accounting, human resources, sales, and shipping/receiving. The business maintains a number of servers permanently connected by a LAN, all of which is under the control of the IT department. Although the servers in the LAN are physically organized into a number of routing groups, administration is still centralized because the IT department runs the show. The administration model looks like this.

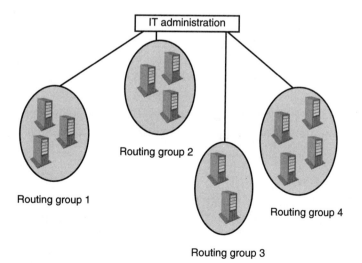

Distributed Administration

Now, suppose that a few years down the road the coffee importer has opened branch offices and distribution centers in other cities, say Los Angeles, Chicago, New York, and Washington, D.C. Each branch is administered by its own IT group, but collectively they still march to the policy drumbeat originating in Seattle. Now the administration model looks like this.

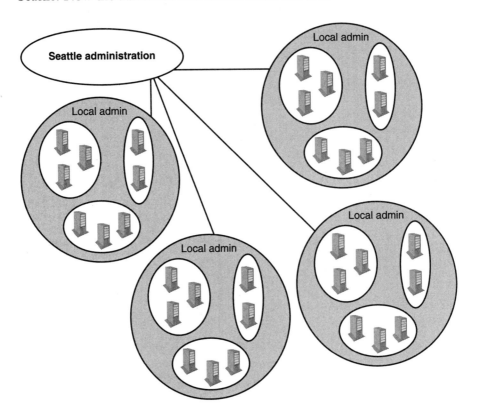

NOTE: As you can see, this administrative model closely resembles the Exchange 5.5 concept of sites. In fact, in a combined Exchange 5.5 and Exchange 2000 installation, this is the model implemented, with one administrative group and one routing group representing each Exchange 5.5 site.

Mixed Administration

Suppose that further down the road the coffee importer joins forces with a biscuit maker on the East Coast to caffeinate and fatten as many people as possible across the country. Although they now operate as a single company, the West Coast importer and the East Coast biscuit maker operate independently, even as they work toward the same business goals. Although a central IT group in Seattle maintained by the West Coast importer sets policies, the bean providers and the biscuit makers handle day-to-day network administration on their own. The entire (blended) company wants to ensure that it can depend on a single directory. This situation reflects a distributed administration model.

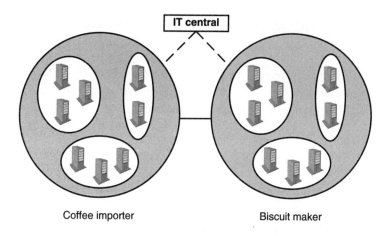

Here, the central IT group might take responsibility for the network backbone or for setting overall policy, but each division would be in charge of defining and administering local policies, as well as managing its own servers.

Sites, Domains, and Other Groups

So far, this book has described a number of different kinds of groups, some logical and some physical. Windows 2000 and Exchange 2000 present administrators with a wealth of such organizational building blocks—so many, in fact, that the distinctions between and among them might look a little fuzzy, especially because they can overlap one another (as sites and domains can) to provide administrative flexibility.

Before moving on to installation, migration, and coexistence issues, you might find a survey of major groupings in Active Directory services useful.

Active Directory services supports sites and domains that affect the entire directory. In addition, it supports organizational units used for creating logical hierarchies. And it supports one other concept, simply called *group*, that allows Active Directory objects to be lumped together for distribution or security purposes.

Sites

Active Directory sites are similar to but different from sites in Exchange 5.5 and earlier versions. Although they are based on groups of servers that are permanently linked by high-speed connections, sites under Active Directory services are now defined as collections of IP subnets. Not coincidentally, these subnets are still characterized by permanent, fast connections, but unlike earlier Exchange sites, they no longer represent administrative or namespace units.

Sites are used to organize servers in a way that helps Active Directory services use network bandwidth efficiently. This efficiency occurs in two areas:

- **Directing service requests from clients (where possible) to servers in the same site** Because client and server can count on a high-speed, permanent connection, such requests are handled quickly and efficiently.

- **Using directory replication** Although directory replication happens throughout an Active Directory forest, replication occurs between servers within a site—those most likely to need directory information—more often than it occurs between sites. Replication information thus spreads first to the servers that need it most and later to those less well-connected, which are also likely to be less in need of the information.

Domains

Active Directory sites group servers; Active Directory domains allow administrators to organize objects logically. As already mentioned in Chapter 2, a domain is a collection of computers that

- Have their own namespace

- Share a common directory database

- Have their own security policies and trust relationships with other domains

Although an organization can function perfectly well with a single Active Directory domain, the ability to group computers in multiple domains provides a number of advantages, especially to larger organizations. Through multiple domains, administrators can

- **Create a "top tier" hierarchy of domains** under which resources can be grouped into organizational units for ease of management, as shown in the following illustration

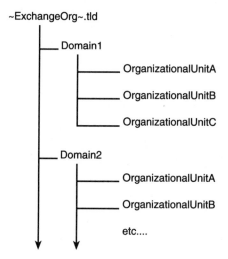

- **Segment the directory logically**   Because each domain stores only information about its own objects, multiple domains help organize and control publication of information in a way that suits administrative and management requirements

- **Apply policies governing access, configuration, and use**   on a domain-by-domain basis to whole groups of objects, yet retain the ability to apply individual policies to different domains, as appropriate

- **Delegate administrative authority**   to individuals within separate domains to reduce the burden on a single central administrative team

Organizational Units

Organizational units, as described in Chapter 2 and shown in the preceding illustration, are groups—actually, containers—within Active Directory domains. And, as mentioned, they are a means of collecting and organizing resources in a way that matches the organization's logical hierarchy. Organizational units can contain not only users, but also groups, computers, printers, folders, and other organizational units.

Unlike the groups described in the next section, organizational units can contain objects only from their parent domain. They are, more than anything, containers for sorting related objects for administration purposes, as shown in the following illustration, in which two "domains" organize chocolate candies (examples don't *always* have to be serious).

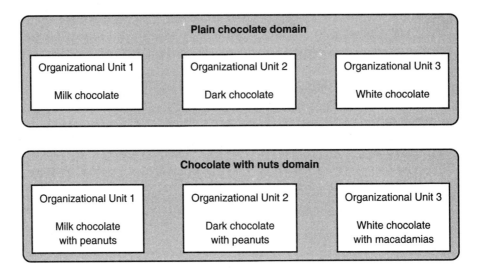

Active Directory Groups

Active Directory groups are similar to organizational units in the sense that they are management units. In this case, however, they enable administrators to group users, computers, contacts, and other groups for managing access to shared resources or to create e-mail distribution lists.

Active Directory groups fall into two categories: security groups and distribution groups.

- **A security group** the more far-reaching of the two, is used for assigning permissions for shared resources and for sending e-mail messages to all members

- **A distribution group** is strictly for sending e-mail to a group of users

Security and distribution groups, unlike organizational units, are associated with one of three different scopes, which define their membership and their relationship to the rest of the domain tree or forest. Basically, these scopes are defined as:

- **Universal scope** The group can include members from any Windows 2000 domain, can be included in other Windows 2000 groups, and can be assigned permissions in any domain in the tree or forest

- **Global scope** Group members must come from the same domain in which the group is defined, but can be put into groups in any domain and can be granted permissions in any domain in the forest

- **Domain local scope** Group members must be from a Windows 2000 or Microsoft Windows NT domain, can be included in other domain local groups in the same domain, and are assigned permissions only within the same domain

Although these definitions of groups and scopes are straightforward enough, keeping straight the interrelationships between the type of group, the scope assigned to them, and the mode in which Windows and Exchange are operating can be a challenge. By default, Exchange runs in mixed mode, in which Windows 2000 and Windows NT domain controllers can coexist in the same domain. In native mode (which you might recall is irreversible once a domain is switched over), the domain controllers must be Windows 2000 only.

A table is probably the most enlightening way to show you how group type, scope, and operating mode interact (see Table 4-1).

Active Directory Group Type, Scope, and Operating Mode

Mode	Universal Scope	Global Scope	Domain Local Scope
Native mode (Windows 2000 only)			
Can include:	Accounts, global groups, and universal groups from any domain	Accounts and global groups from the same domain	Accounts, global groups, and universal groups from any domain, plus domain local groups from the same domain
Can contain:	Both security groups and distribution groups		
Can be included in:	Other groups in any domain	Other groups in any domain	Other domain local groups only in the same domain

Table 4-1. *(continued)*

Relationship between Active Directory group type, scope, and operating mode.

Table 4-1. *continued*

Mode	Universal Scope	Global Scope	Domain Local Scope
Can be assigned permissions:	In any domain	In any domain	Only in the same domain
Can be converted to:		Universal scope, providing it doesn't belong to any other global group	Universal scope, providing it doesn't include another domain local group
Mixed mode (Windows NT plus Windows 2000)			
Security groups:	Can't be created	Can include accounts only	Can include accounts and global groups
Distribution groups:	Can include accounts, other distribution groups with universal scope, and other groups with global scope from the same domain	Can include accounts from the same domain and other global groups from the same domain	Can include universal and global groups from any domain, plus domain local groups from the same domain

See? It's not that simple.

Installation, Coexistence, and Migration

Exchange 2000 can be installed in a number of different situations:

■ **A new,** "pure" Exchange 2000 installation

■ **Coexisting** (probably temporarily) with an earlier version of Exchange

- **Coexisting** (perhaps permanently) with another mail system
- An **upgrade** to Exchange 2000 from an earlier version
- A **migration** to Exchange from another mail system

Installation and migration are mainly functions of the Microsoft Exchange 2000 Installation Wizard and the Microsoft Exchange Server Migration Wizard. Coexistence involves the Active Directory Connector (for earlier versions of Exchange) and connectors specific to other mail systems.

Decisions related to how, when, and even whether one of the preceding installations will work best for a particular organization depend, of course, on the organization's communication and collaboration needs. If the organization is small, localized, and reliant on one or a few servers, a pure Exchange 2000 deployment might be the answer. If users need to communicate regularly with other users on a "foreign" system, coexistence is obviously the way to go. If an earlier version of Exchange is up and happily running to everyone's satisfaction, migration to Exchange 2000 might be the ideal solution. And if migration is the approach to take, a small, centralized organization might find a single-step migration feasible, whereas a large, widely dispersed organization might find a phased changeover both desirable and necessary.

Each of these installation types carries with it the need to consider certain factors, such as directory replication, use of connectors, and coexistence of server versions, sites, administrative groups, routing groups, user data, and so on. The remaining sections of this chapter cover these considerations as they relate to different Exchange installation types.

NOTE: You can find detailed information on migrating to Exchange 2000 in the *Microsoft Exchange Server Planning and Installation* guide.

New Installations

The most straightforward type of installation is, of course, one in which Exchange 2000 is simply...deployed.

The Process

Before Exchange 2000 can be installed in a new or existing installation, Windows 2000 and Active Directory services must be running on the primary domain controller. Then, when the Exchange 2000 Installation Wizard is run, the administrator chooses to join or create an Exchange 2000 organization. This action

- Allows the administrator to specify the organization name
- Results in the setup program creating two default containers, the First Administrative Group and, under it, the First Routing Group

When setup is complete on this server, Exchange setup won't allow any other Exchange organization to be created.

What Happens

Behind the scenes during a new installation, the Exchange setup program automatically handles several tasks.

- **Upgrades** the Active Directory schema to the Exchange schema
- **Adds** the Exchange server to the Active Directory site in which it is located
- **Installs** and starts Exchange services

After installation is complete, the new Exchange server relies on Active Directory services for configuration and user information, and all the Exchange clients rely on Active Directory services for information derived through LDAP requests.

Exchange administration is now handled through the Exchange MMC console—except, of course, for resource management handled through the Active Directory Users and Computers console.

Coexistence

Installing Exchange 2000 into an existing mail-enabled organization introduces a few more variables and a number of considerations, especially those related to synchronizing and replicating the directory so that it remains a viable, up-to-date, and freely usable resource for the organization.

Coexistence can refer to two different types of Exchange installation. It can mean

- Coexistence with an earlier version of Exchange
- Coexistence with another mail or collaboration system

Each of these, obviously, has its own considerations.

Coexistence with Earlier Exchange Versions

Coexistence with earlier versions of Exchange also means coexistence, at least at some point, with the earlier version of Windows—Windows NT—on which they run. What does this mean? Not much as far as Exchange functionality is concerned.

Upgrading one server in an existing Exchange organization to run Windows 2000 server and Exchange 2000 doesn't affect the remaining Exchange servers—they continue to run as they always have. The most notable change is in the behavior of the Windows 2000 server, which now benefits from improved performance, plug and play, and Windows 2000 management tools. This continuity between the old and the new doesn't mean, however, that Windows 2000 and Exchange 2000 can be stuck willy-nilly into the organization. There are a number of considerations to bear in mind—significant ones—to maintain functionality and to ensure peaceful coexistence and a smooth upgrade later on.

The Directories

Because coexistence between Exchange 2000 and earlier versions is critical to the upgrade path, care has been taken to ensure that there is no loss of directory information. However, because the Active Directory services is administered through the MMC snap-in, changes made using the Exchange Administrator of earlier Exchange versions are not made directly to Active Directory services, but instead are propagated through Exchange replication via the Active Directory Connector.

Thus, the most notable *non*-change in upgrading a server in an Exchange organization to Windows 2000 is the fact that the older Exchange directory and the new Active Directory services directory won't be unified until the Exchange servers are upgraded to Exchange 2000, and the installation therefore will require connection agreements so that changes will be replicated between directories.

Administration

For administration, it's important to remember that each version of Exchange requires its own administrator—Exchange Administrator for the older version, Exchange System Manager for the newer one—with one exception:

- After Exchange 2000 has been introduced into the organization and all necessary connection agreements are in effect, user objects for both old and new versions of Exchange should be managed through the Active Directory Users and Computers console

Furthermore, although the complete messaging organization appears in both the Exchange 2000 System Manager and in the Exchange Administrator,

- Configuring an Exchange 2000 object in Exchange Administrator does *not* change the object, even though it appears to
- Conversely, Exchange System Manager won't make changes to any objects owned by previous versions of Exchange

In other words, to each its own, except where user objects are concerned. In that case, you'll need the Active Directory Users and Computers console all the way.

Installation Considerations

One of the most critical aspects of introducing an Exchange 2000 server into an existing Exchange organization is to ensure that at least one of the existing servers is running a specific version of Exchange: Exchange 5.5, Service Pack (SP) 3. The server running this release is the one to which the new Exchange 2000 server will connect, and it's particularly important for two reasons:

- **The Exchange 2000 setup program will use the Exchange 5.5 SP3 server to extract site information** so that it can map existing sites, on a one-to-one basis, to administrative and routing groups. Thus, if an existing Exchange organization includes sites named, say, North, South, East, and West, the setup program will map these sites to new administrative and routing groups using the same names.
- **The Exchange 2000 server and the Exchange 5.5 SP3 server will rely on a connection agreement,** established through an Active Directory Connector, to enable directory replication.

After this preliminary groundwork is taken care of, Exchange 2000 can be installed on a new server and joined to the existing organization. Briefly, preparing for this process involves the following steps:

- Ensuring that the computer on which Exchange will be installed is in a domain controlled by a Windows 2000 domain controller
- Running Active Directory services by upgrading an existing Windows NT domain controller or creating a new domain controlled by a Windows 2000 server
- Setting up connection agreements between each Exchange 5.5 site and Active Directory services

- Populating Active Directory services with information about Exchange 5.5 mailboxes, custom recipients, distribution lists, and public folders

After Active Directory services and Active Directory Connectors tie the organization together, the final recommended step before installing or upgrading to Exchange 2000 is to convert one or more (depending on the organization's topology) Windows 2000 domains to native mode, at least in certain circumstances. The need for this conversion lies in the way Windows 2000 and earlier versions of Exchange handle distribution lists and access to public folders. Exchange 2000 relies on Windows 2000 Access Control Lists (ACLs) for permission management, whereas earlier versions allow use of distribution lists for both sending mail and setting public folder permissions.

In brief:

- Exchange 4.0 and 5.*x* distribution lists can be nested and can allow membership from any Exchange site (For functionality, they are comparable to Exchange 2000 universal security groups.)
- In a mixed mode environment, objects from any domain can be included in a universal security group
- However, a universal group can be created and managed only within a native Windows 2000 domain

Hence, the conversion of at least one Windows 2000 domain to native mode is necessary in the following circumstances:

- The installation needs a place where Exchange 4.0 and 5.*x* distribution groups can be created and converted to operate within the Windows 2000 permissions model
- The organization relies on distribution lists nested in public folders
- The organization wants to use universal security groups, rather than deal with the continuous maintenance necessary in using either domain local or domain global groups (the two alternatives) for public folder access control

Thus, the solution to providing smooth back-and-forth interoperability between earlier versions and Exchange 2000 lies in the creation of a group management domain, a Windows 2000 domain controlled by a server operating in native mode.

Once established, this group management domain both takes in Exchange 5.5 distribution list information through an Active Directory connection agreement and also provides a centralized location for the creation and conversion of distribution lists from earlier versions of Exchange. The result: old-style distribution list functionality operating within Windows 2000 and its permissions model.

Administrative and Routing Groups

After Exchange has been installed on the first server, administrators must ensure that additional administrative and routing groups are created *before* Exchange is installed on other servers. The reason for creating these groups at this point is both simple and eminently practical. Even though servers are easily dragged and dropped between routing groups, they can't be moved from one administrative group to another when Exchange is running in mixed mode, as they could be before the entire organization was upgraded to Exchange 2000.

Coexistence with Other Systems

Coexistence with other mail systems means one thing: connectors.

As mentioned in Chapter 1, Exchange has always had the capacity to co-exist with other mail systems using connectors that act as "bridges" (not in the networking hardware sense) between the two mail systems.

Also as mentioned, connectors aren't one-size-fits-all software tools. They are as specific to individual mail systems as gateways are to individual network types (for example, gateways that connect mainframes and LANs). Exchange connectors can be put in place temporarily, before migrating all users from another mail system to Exchange, or permanently, as when an organization needs a means of connecting its Exchange users with a network that isn't and most likely won't be Exchange-based.

Whether temporary or permanent, Exchange connectors perform three vital functions:

- **Message transfer** (as expected)

- **Directory synchronization,** which ensures that directory information is propagated in both directions so that users of both systems can exchange mail

- **Calendar querying** (for Lotus Notes and Novell GroupWise), which enables users of both systems to coordinate meeting times and other such collaborative requests

Most importantly, connectors operate transparently so that users of each system continue to work in their own familiar messaging environment, but can communicate with users on the other, "foreign," mail system.

Exchange 2000 provides connectors for the following systems:

- Lotus Notes
- Lotus cc:Mail
- Novell GroupWise
- PC Networks
- A Free/Busy connector for Microsoft Schedule+

These connectors enable message transfer over LANs and over asynchronous and X.25 communications connections. Exchange can also be used with additional third-party connectors and gateways.

Upgrades and Migration

The Exchange documentation doesn't explicitly distinguish between an upgrade and a migration, at least in relation to coexistence between Exchange 4.0/5.5, other mail systems, and Exchange 2000. However, there's an implicit distinction between an upgrade—the path from an earlier version of Exchange to Exchange 2000—and a migration—the path from another mail system to Exchange 2000. That is the distinction to bear in mind in the following sections.

Upgrades

Enabling Exchange 2000 to coexist with an existing Exchange organization rather naturally segues into upgrading the entire organization from an earlier version to Exchange 2000.

There are three approaches to upgrading, referred to as in-place, move mailbox, and swing server. Each method has its advantages and disadvantages, especially in hardware capacity and availability and the amount of tolerable downtime. These advantages and disadvantages are detailed in the following sections and summarized in the table in the section "Upgrade Summary."

In-Place Upgrade

An in-place upgrade is the simplest type. It involves simply taking the server offline and then running the Exchange 2000 setup program.

An in-place upgrade does, however, require that

- The server must be running Windows 2000 and Exchange 5.5 SP 3, or these software packages must be installed ahead of time
- Existing hardware must be capable of running Exchange 2000
- Server downtime (longer than in the other methods) must be acceptable

An in-place upgrade offers two main advantages:

- It uses existing hardware
- It doesn't involve conversion of the existing information itore, because Exchange 2000 and Exchange 5.5 use the same database format

Upgrade by Moving Mailboxes

In situations where the existing server hardware is *not* capable of running Windows 2000 and Exchange 2000, the recommended option is the move-mailbox approach. This method is also recommended if mailboxes and public folders are stored on dedicated servers.

This method involves four steps:

1. Installing Exchange 2000 on a new server
2. Joining that server to the existing Exchange site
3. Moving mailboxes (and public folders) to the new server
4. Taking the old server or servers out of the picture

The method offers a number of advantages, including

- **The ability to move mailboxes** from Exchange 4.0 and later, to schedule the move for a convenient time, and to predetermine the number of users to be moved
- **The opportunity to upgrade hardware** at the same time
- **Slight inconvenience for the users,** who need only exit mail during the short time the mailbox is being moved and then log on after the move is complete
- **Reduced risk factors** involved because the Windows 2000 and Exchange 2000 installations don't occur on a working server and because not all users need be moved at the same time

■ **The existing Exchange server remains available**   as a backup
server if needed

The move mailboxes process looks like this.

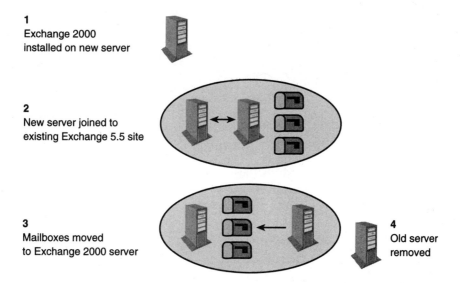

1
Exchange 2000
installed on new server

2
New server joined to
existing Exchange 5.5 site

3
Mailboxes moved
to Exchange 2000 server

4
Old server
removed

Using a Swing Server to Upgrade

The third upgrade option, using a "swing" server, is an extension of the move
mailbox approach, and involves three steps:

1. **Installing Windows 2000 and Exchange 2000**   on a new server
   and joining it to an existing Exchange 5.5 site

2. **Moving mailboxes**   from an Exchange 5.5 server to the new Exchange 2000 server

3. **Upgrading the recently "vacated" Exchange 5.5 server**   to Exchange 2000 and then repeating the process of moving mailboxes
   from another Exchange 5.5 server to the newly upgraded Exchange
   2000 server

The following illustration shows how the swing server upgrade builds upon
the move mailboxes upgrade process.

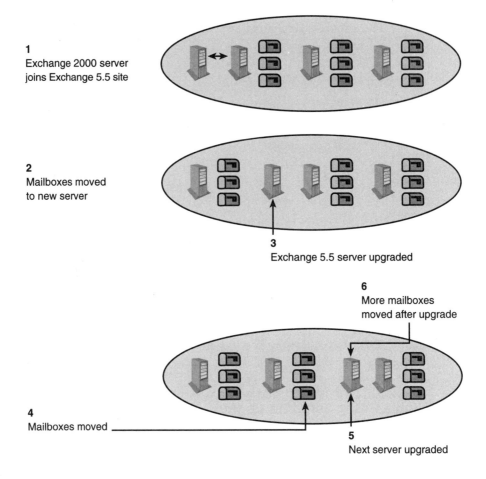

1
Exchange 2000 server
joins Exchange 5.5 site

2
Mailboxes moved
to new server

3
Exchange 5.5 server upgraded

6
More mailboxes
moved after upgrade

4
Mailboxes moved

5
Next server upgraded

Upgrade Summary

Table 4-2 summarizes the advantages and concerns or inconveniences associated with each of the three upgrade options.

Upgrade Options: Advantages and Concerns

Upgrade Option	Advantages	Concerns
In-place upgrade		
	Uses existing hardware	Server must be capable of (and already running) Windows 2000 and Exchange 5.5, SP 3
	Quick because no database conversion is needed	Downtime longer than with other options
Move mailbox upgrade		
	Can upgrade directly from Exchange 4.0 and 5.0	Requires new hardware
	User inconvenience limited to logging off and on	
	Slight downtime while mailboxes are moved	
	Risk minimized because upgrade doesn't take place on a working server	
	Existing server remains available if needed	

Table 4-2. *(continued)*
A comparison of in-place, move mailbox, and swing server upgrade options.

Table 4-2. *continued*

Upgrade Option	Advantages	Concerns
Swing server upgrade		
	Same as for move mailbox method, except that existing server remains available only through part of the process	Requires more up-front planning and more complex execution
	In addition, upgrade requires minimal investment in new hardware and retains service of existing hardware	

Migration

Although the move from an earlier version of Exchange to Exchange 2000 can be called a migration, it is probably more appropriate to use the term to describe the "journey" of an organization to Exchange 2000 from a different mail system.

The migration process, as you would expect, requires thoughtful planning to prevent three undesirable side effects: excessive downtime, data loss, and negatively affecting users.

In essence, migration itself involves a two-step process:

- **Copying and preparing existing data** (mailboxes, messages, and so on) for export to Exchange
- **Importing** that data into Exchange

Migration Tools

At the heart of migrating from another mail system to Exchange is the Migration Wizard, installed during Exchange setup. The wizard has two components: the source extractor, which does the work of copying data for export and putting it in a format that the wizard can use, and the migration file importer, which takes that formatted information, prepares it for use by Exchange, and then makes it available to users.

The Migration Wizard and some additional tools (also included with Exchange) make it possible to migrate to Exchange 2000 from any of the following:

- Lotus Notes 3.*x*, 4.0, 4.1, and Lotus Domino 4.5 and 4.6
- Microsoft Mail for PC Networks 3.*x*
- Lotus cc:Mail, database versions DB6 and DB8
- Novell GroupWise 4.*x* and 5.*x*
- Collabra Share 1.*x* and 2.*x*
- IMAP4-compliant Internet messaging systems
- LDAP-compliant Internet directory services

The Migration Wizard works either alone or in combination with third-party and other source extractors—for instance, source extractors for IBM PROFS, NetSys MEMO, and Digital ALL-IN-1.

In addition, Exchange includes the following specialized tools:

- **The Microsoft Importer for Lotus cc:Mail Archives** for importing archive files and private directories from Lotus cc:Mail

- **Microsoft Application Converter for Lotus Notes** for converting and synchronizing Lotus Notes application data with Exchange 2000

- **The Active Directory Account Cleanup Wizard** for cleaning up duplicate Windows 2000 accounts created during the migration process

Migration Considerations

It's easy enough to say that migration means something is extracted from one "box" and put into another, but that's a lot like saying that writing a novel means ideas are extracted from the imagination and put onto paper. A lot more goes on, and different mail systems will raise their own special considerations. For example, the migration from a mainframe environment such as IBM PROFS might cover issues and considerations ranging from internal and external connectivity (X.400, mainframe, gateways to LANs) to possible effects on mainframe performance, and even to the level of comfort and familiarity of administrators with server-based software. Likewise, in migrating from a server-based mail system to Exchange, administrators might need to allow for such factors as their users' learning curve or the extent and duration of maintaining connectors between the old and new mail systems.

There are, however, certain considerations to bear in mind in migrating from one mail system to another, among them

- **The possibility that duplicate accounts will be created,** either as the Migration Wizard compares existing accounts to those it's migrating or as it creates new accounts based on information from applications that originally created them

- **Ensuring that gateways or connectors are available** so that traffic can flow between the two systems while migration is underway

- **Determining whether traffic should be routed** through the existing system or through an Exchange connector or gateway

For these and other migration considerations, as well as strategies to deal with them, you should refer to the *Microsoft Exchange 2000 Server Planning and Installation* guide.

Phased Migrations

As for migration itself, there are two ways to go about the process: single-phase or multi-phase.

A single-phase migration simply moves everyone to Exchange in one fell swoop. This approach is probably best suited to small organizations, but it can also be used in a larger organization if the hardware and both client and server software are available and ready to go, and if the capacity exists to move all clients at once.

A multi-phase migration, on the other hand, is more likely to be needed when

- Users must be moved in groups, rather than all at once

- Hardware needs to be "recycled" as in the move mailbox or swing server options

- The organization wants to "test the waters" with a manageable group of users rather than toss everyone into the pond at the same time

A multi-phase migration, at least in larger organizations, is more typical than a single-phase migration. Note, however, that it involves ensuring that the two mail systems can coexist, and it requires more planning and anticipation of possible bottlenecks, routing issues, connection reliability, and so on. Again, these concerns are detailed in the *Microsoft Exchange Server 2000 Planning and Installation* guide.

PART II

UNDER THE HOOD

CHAPTER FIVE

Windows 2000 and Active Directory Services

Part 1 of this book dealt with more or less "global" Exchange 2000 concerns: where it came from, how it differs from previous versions, what it looks like, and roughly how it can be deployed in an organization. This chapter begins Part 2, which provides a closer, deeper look at the anatomy of Exchange 2000, starting with the foundation on which it depends: Microsoft Windows 2000.

Unless you slept through the previous chapters, you doubtless noticed that they consistently (perhaps too insistently) referred to Windows 2000 this and Microsoft Active Directory services that. Integration, integration, integration has been the buzzword throughout. Now it's time to examine how and why the Exchange 2000 integration with Windows 2000 and Active Directory services represents a fundamental change in Exchange itself.

Soul of a New Directory

Even though Active Directory services has its roots in the old Exchange directory, directory services now belong to Windows 2000. Some similarities remain—for example, both Active Directory services and the Exchange 5.*x* directories use distinguished names (more about that later) to identify objects. On the other hand, and most happily in terms of network efficiency, Active Directory services replicates objects on a per-property basis, updating only those properties that change, rather than replicating the entire object, as happened with the old Exchange directories. However, to start at A and work toward Z...

Directories and Directory Services

The goal of Active Directory services, as is the case with any directory service, is to organize and provide information about network objects—users, passwords, printers, and so on—to the network's users and administrators. This mass of information, usually just referred to as the *directory,* is a data store that can be replicated throughout the organization. The directory is, in effect, a big telephone book. *But* it's also one that would be of little use just sitting around on a server. To become useful, a directory requires a directory service that not only stores, but also makes directory information available to users. That service, for Windows 2000 and Exchange, is Active Directory services, and it's designed around the following features:

- **The data store, or directory,** without which Active Directory services would lose half of its name and devolve into a service with nothing to serve

- **A schema,** which keeps the directory from becoming a free-for-all by defining two basic sets of rules: one for the object classes that can be included (created) in the directory, and another for the attributes that can be assigned to those objects (The schema definitions themselves, by the way, are also stored as objects so that they can be managed just like other directory objects.)

- **A Global Catalog,** which is stored on each domain controller and contains both a complete replica of all objects in the host domain and enough information about every object in other domains to ensure that each object in the directory is findable, no matter which domain it calls "home"

- **An indexing and search mechanism,** which can be accessed through the Search command on the Windows 2000 Start menu, that enables administrators and users to find the information they need

- **A replication service** that takes care of copying and distributing directory information throughout the entire network (as mentioned earlier, on a per-property basis in Active Directory services)

Finally, for the benefit of its users, Active Directory services also offers a one-stop logon process made possible through its integration with the security subsystem in its Windows 2000 parent. And for the benefit of network administrators, this same security model offers easy, centralized management that addresses both user authentication at logon and object-based access control to network resources.

Domains, Trees, and Forests: A Recap

Active Directory services thus provides a means for administrators to manage network users and resources, and it provides a way for users to find one another. As you'd expect, it must therefore organize information logically. And so it does, both to make that information usable and to reflect the structure of the organization represented in its data store. As already described in Chapter 2, Active Directory services, or rather its directory structure, is made up of domains. Furthermore, closely related domains—those that comprise contiguous namespaces—link together in a parent/child hierarchy called a tree, and groups of trees can be gathered into one (possibly more) forests.

About Those Namespaces

The "DNS Integration" section later in this chapter deals with DNS integration and domain naming. However, because it's not possible to discuss domains, trees, and forests without also discussing their names, here's a brief refresher.

In terms of Active Directory services, a namespace refers to the names of the domains in a domain tree or forest. The naming parallels DNS conventions in that each domain name in a tree is unique, and domain relationships are easy to see because related names form branches on the tree. For example, the domain names *domain1.figtree.microsoft.com* and *domain2.figtree.microsoft.com* are unique and yet immediately show that they are related domains on the same (*figtree.microsoft.com*) tree—that is, they belong to a contiguous namespace.

Not all namespaces, however, are or even must be contiguous. A single organization could easily support both the domain tree used in the previous example as well as a second, separate tree with the domains *domain1.appletree.microsoft2.com* and *domain2.appletree.microsoft2.com*. In this case, *microsoft.com* and *microsoft2.com* would represent separate—noncontiguous—namespaces. Yet, because they both belong to the same organization, they could be related to one another as separate trees in the same forest.

Now, as for domains, the building blocks that make up trees and forests...

Domains

There are three ways to look at domains, all important: why they exist, how they're organized, and what they actually are.

Why domains? Domains perform two vital functions. First, they allow for logical organization of objects in the organization. Second, they represent units of replication through which information about the directory can be spread to other domains throughout the organization.

Although domains can include different numbers of servers and different numbers and kinds of objects, all domains are characterized by one feature, without which they can't be domains: All have at least one domain controller, a server that, thanks to Active Directory services

- **Stores directory information** specifically, the schema and configuration for the tree and the naming context (domain name structure) for its own domain
- **Manages user logons and authentication**
- **Manages access to the Active Directory directory and network resources**

Perhaps the easiest way of all to define a domain controller, however, is this: a server becomes a domain controller when Active Directory services is installed on it. The very act of installation is what turns an ordinary server into a domain controller.

Domain organization In terms of organization, domains in a tree are (not to push the woodsy motif too far) like branches. They can spread out, although they do so upside down and more neatly than real branches do. Growing downward from a first, or root, domain, a basic domain tree actually ends up looking like a stepladder.

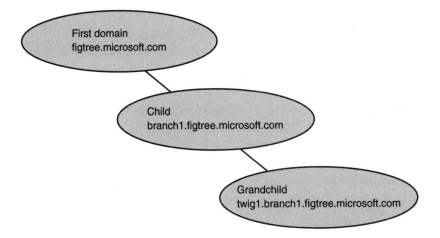

NOTE: The term *root domain* refers to the first domain in both a tree and a forest. To avoid confusion, the tree *root* in both the previous and the following illustrations is labeled *first domain*.

It's only when the first domain of the tree gives rise to child domains branching in multiple directions that the structure takes on a reasonably tree-like appearance.

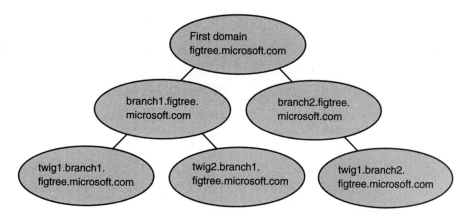

And, of course, at the highest level of organization, multiple trees representing separate, noncontiguous namespaces can be grouped together in a forest.

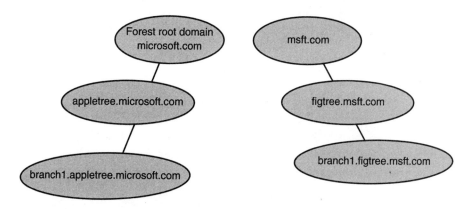

A forest, although it can contain trees representing noncontiguous namespaces, is actually held together by several features:

■ **The forest has a root domain,** the first domain created in the forest (*microsoft.com* in the illustration)

- **All the trees in the forest share** a common schema, configuration information, and Global Catalog
- **Transitive trust relationships** (described in the "Domains themselves" section of this chapter) are established between domains in trees and between trees in the forest

The root domain of a forest, by the way, is noteworthy for several reasons. Unlike other domains

- **Its DNS name** (for example, the real-life *microsoft.com*) is the basis for naming the entire forest
- **It can't be removed** without removing the entire forest
- **No other domains** can be created above it

It is, in fact, the *real* root of the organization.

Domains themselves Although administrators and users can view domains as tools that allow for organizing objects logically, Active Directory services also sees domains as security boundaries—organizational fences, so to speak. Administrators can use these security boundaries to

- **Group objects** to reflect the structure of the organization, irrespective of the underlying network topology
- **Define security policies** that are specific to individual domains and don't cross over into other domains
- **Delegate administrative authority** on a domain-by-domain basis
- **Ensure a high degree of scalability** overall, because each domain is self-contained in that it stores information only about its own objects, yet can and does share that information with other domains through the Global Catalog to provide applications such as Exchange 2000 with the ability to access the entire forest-wide directory

Finally, and once again relating to security, domains establish trust relationships with other domains. Earlier versions of Windows supported one-way trust relationships that extended only between two domains, as shown in the following illustration.

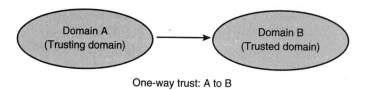

One-way trust: A to B

Such a trust relationship means that objects in the trusted domain (domain B in the illustration) could access resources in the trusting domain (domain A), but that the reverse is not true.

In contrast, Windows 2000 and Active Directory services support much more flexible transitive, two-way trusts that enable trust relationships to ripple through the tree-and-forest domain structure. This is how it works:

- When a child domain is created from a parent domain, Windows 2000 automatically establishes a two-way trust between parent and child, meaning that access requests can flow in both directions. This is the two-way part.

- The two-way trust established between parent and child is also, and again automatically, created as a transitive trust in which a domain trusted by the parent is also trusted by the child. In other words, as shown in the following diagram, if domain B trusts domain A, and domain C is created from domain B, then domain C automatically trusts domain A, and the trust relationship propagates up through the domain tree. (Note that the domains in the illustration are organized hierarchically, as in the DNS and Windows 2000 tree and forest model.)

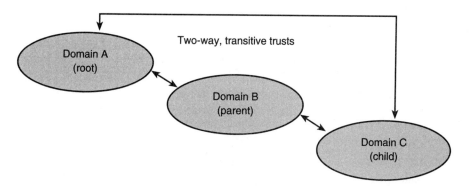

Two-way, transitive trusts

In a forest, the same type of trust relationships hold true between the root domain of the forest and the root domains of the individual trees, in that the root domain of each tree establishes a transitive trust agreement with the root domain of the forest. This is the mechanism that enables tree-to-tree trust relationships in the forest.

Organizational Units

Organizational units, new in Windows 2000, are objects—containers, actually—in which administrators can group users and groups of users, resources such as computers and printers, and shared folders within a single domain. Although organizational units are, as they appear to be, a mechanism for organizing users and resources to reflect the logical structure of the organization, they also exist to provide administrators with a means of grouping objects to make it easier to delegate administrative authority and apply group policies. Organizational units are essentially one step below domains in the Active Directory services hierarchy. They are a management tool, the smallest unit that can be assigned administrative authority or group policy, and they provide a means of organizing objects in a way that mirrors the structure of the organization. Furthermore, because organizational units can contain other organizational units, they can help minimize the number of domains that need to be created.

DNS Integration

DNS, as already mentioned in Chapter 2, is short for Domain Name System, the linchpin of the Internet. By now, even Net newbies are fully aware of DNS names, even though they may never realize that's what they're using when they access the World Wide Web through *msn.com,* go book browsing at *amazon.com,* or download software updates from *microsoft.com.* In each case, however, the "dot com" (or .org, .edu, .gov, .net, or .mil) is as much a giveaway as the cat's footprints on the kitchen counter.

Name resolution vs. a locator service   Although both the DNS popularized by the Web and the DNS integration in Active Directory services are based on the same naming structure and, in fact, both act to resolve names to IP addresses, there is a significant difference in what they do, as well as where and why they do it.

DNS is an Internet name resolution service that translates domain names to IP addresses. A DNS server resolves queries either by finding the needed information in directories stored on the server or by referring the queries to another DNS server that holds the required information. Once a DNS name has been resolved to an IP address, the name resolution service is complete. DNS as a name resolution service is not at all dependent on Active Directory services.

In contrast, Active Directory services, even though it uses DNS as a locator service, has a different objective. Active Directory services exists so that Active Directory services clients, through the use of LDAP, can send queries to Active Directory servers and receive in return the information they seek about objects in the Active Directory database. Where DNS comes into play is in enabling clients to find Active Directory domain controllers by sending a query to their configured DNS servers for the names and IP addresses of the Active Directory domain controller or controllers in their domains. Thus, DNS is a vital link in a chain that leads the client to an Active Directory server to be able to access and use the information and services provided by Active Directory services. The following illustration shows how DNS serves different objectives when used as a name resolution service and as an Active Directory locator service.

(a) DNS name resolution

(b) DNS as an Active Directory locator service

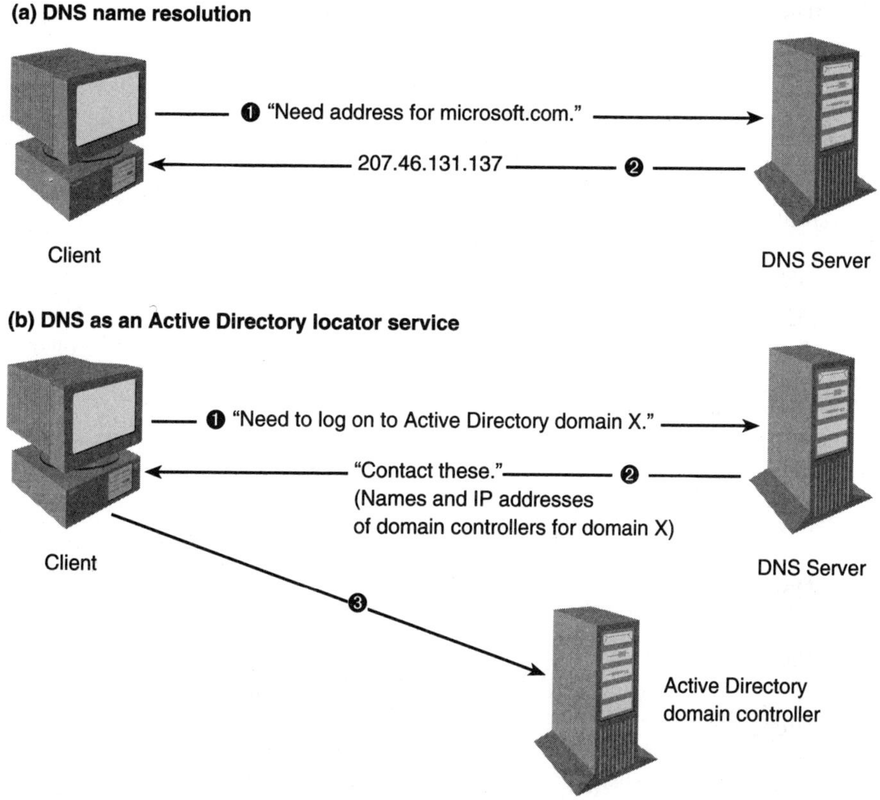

LDAP   Another important factor to bear in mind about DNS integration is that it's closely tied to LDAP, which clients use to actually send their queries to Active

Directory servers. Under Active Directory services, LDAP runs as a service—a program or process that performs system functions that enable other software to work—on the domain controller for each domain. The LDAP service is assigned an IP address, and when an Active Directory client contacts its DNS server to log on to the network, the DNS server returns the IP address of the LDAP service on the client's domain controller. In effect, the DNS server sends the client the "bottle" into which it can stuff the Active Directory queries it sends out onto the network "sea."

As for LDAP itself, it's a protocol—a set of "rules" that enable communication between two network entities—that runs over the ubiquitous Internet-based TCP/IP protocol. In effect, it defines the way in which clients can access a directory to request information about resources and about each other. One of the great advantages of LDAP is that clients don't have to know the particular domain where the individual or resource resides.

A "slimmed down" version of the X.500 Directory Access Protocol (DAP), LDAP was developed at the University of Michigan and provides for the same type of hierarchical tree that DNS does, though in this case the hierarchy is based on the following terminology:

- A root
- Countries (actual countries) below the root
- Organizations within countries
- Organizational units within organizations
- Individuals within organizational units

Directories based on this structure can be distributed and synchronized across multiple directory servers, but in keeping with the LDAP focus on "lightweight," the servers take responsibility for referring queries to other servers when necessary. Thus, a client requesting information doesn't receive a "sorry, not here" response, but rather a "try over there" when the server it contacts doesn't have the information required.

Essentially, LDAP is simpler and faster to use than the "heavyweight" X.500 DAP. Because it's an Internet standard, it also provides for interoperability with other directory services. Active Directory services supports both version 2 of LDAP, which allows read-only access to a directory database, and version 3, which allows both read and write access.

Active Directory Services and DNS: similarities and differences   Although Active Directory services integrates the DNS naming convention and hierarchical structure, it's important to understand that it's *not* DNS itself. Even though Active Directory domains and DNS domains can use identical names, and Active Directory services computers are assigned DNS names, Active Directory services and DNS don't represent identical namespaces. In other words, the following tree can represent both DNS domains and nodes and Active Directory domains and computers.

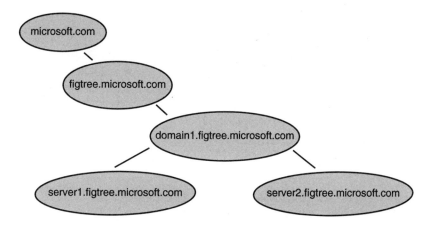

However, in the real world, the two exist as different namespaces because

- **They exist for different reasons**
- **They manage different types of information,** in the case of DNS, the names of DNS servers and nodes, in the case of Active Directory services, Active Directory domains and objects

NOTE: In a way, the Active Directory services structure picks up where the Internet DNS leaves off—but only to a certain extent, because Active Directory servers have DNS names and can legitimately be DNS hosts as well. If all this sounds a bit confusing, just remember that the definition of a namespace is "a bounded area within which a name can be resolved to the object it represents." In the case of DNS and Active Directory services, the objects in the namespaces are accessed differently and serve different purposes. Therefore, appearances to the contrary, the namespaces are different.

Domain Names, User Names, and Object Names

Given the fact that Active Directory services relies heavily on DNS and domain names, it must follow that Active Directory services must go by certain rules where names are concerned. And so it does. In actuality, however, Active Directory services understands not only domain names and namespaces, it also understands a plethora of other names. In addition to the DNS naming system, Active Directory services also recognizes (and sometimes even generates) special names for directory objects, such as user accounts and groups. In all cases, names exist to uniquely identify the object they represent. In working with Active Directory services, you encounter, among others,

- **DNS names,** including fully qualified domain names, or FQDNs
- **User-based names,** especially the logon-related user principal names, or UPNs, and UPN suffixes
- **Security-related security principal names and security IDs,** or SIDs
- **LDAP-related distinguished names, relative distinguished names, and canonical names**
- **Object-based globally unique identifiers,** or GUIDs

These names are described in the following sections.

The DNS naming convention and fully qualified domain names By now, it probably isn't very easy to find a networking professional who doesn't know that the Internet DNS is a hierarchy of domain levels arranged as follows:

- **A root domain,** sometimes shown as "" (for a null value) and indicated in fully qualified domain names as a dot (.) at the end of a complete domain name sequence—*microsoft.com.*, for example
- **A group of top-level domains,** or TLDs: .com, .org, .edu, and so on
- **Individually owned (second-level) domains**
- **Subdomains** within individually owned domains
- **Host computers** within subdomains

The dividing line between the external Internet and internal network domain and host names comes between the top-level domain and the individual domain, as shown in the following example.

NOTE: Once again, to respect the ownership rights of real Internet domains, the abbreviation .tld (for top-level domain) is used in place of .com and the other real top-level domains.

Domain Name System	Example domain names	
Root	.	External: the Internet
Top-level domain	*.tld*	
Individual (second-level) domain name	*topdog.tld*	
Subdomain	*shepherd.topdog.tld*	Internal: the individual
Host name	*rin-tin-tin.shepherd.topdog.tld*	organization

User principal names and suffixes   Within this DNS structure, Active Directory services recognizes two types of user-based names, the user principal name and the user principal name suffix. These names are used at logon and are based on IETF RFC 822, titled "Standard for the Format of ARPA Internet Text Messages," a document intended to standardize the syntax for text messages sent in the envelope/content format typical of electronic mail systems.

At any rate, the user principal name, or UPN, and its suffix are essentially the two parts of an address joined by an @ sign. The principal name is the user's account (logon) name and the suffix is the part that follows the @ sign—the part that identifies the domain in which the account resides. For example, in the account name *joannew@microsoft.com, joannew* is the principal name and *microsoft.com* is the suffix.

By default, the UPN suffix is the same as the account's domain name, as in the preceding example. However, the UPN suffix does *not* have to be a valid DNS name because it's used only within Windows 2000 and its domain structure. As a result, in cases where an organization's domain tree is extensive and runs to many levels, administrators can simplify matters for themselves and for their users by assigning alternative suffixes. For example, if the default UPN and its suffix in the preceding example were something like *joannew@partridge.peartree. microsoft.com,* the administrator could change the suffix to peartree, bogusname, or the more logically compelling *microsoft.com.*

Security principals and security identifiers   In addition to providing access to directory information, Active Directory services manages user accounts and access to network resources. To help with this, Windows 2000 defines a security principal. Although the term tends to suggest some type of conceptual security mechanism or safeguard, it's actually a name for any user, group, or computer account on the network, to each of which Windows 2000 automatically assigns a unique security identifier, or security ID (SID). This security ID,

117

rather than the account name, is used internally by Windows processes in managing permissions and access to resources.

The security ID is unique to each account created. That is, if an account created for Jane Doe is deleted and then re-created under the same name, the old and new accounts will have different security IDs, and the new account won't automatically assume the rights assigned to the old account.

LDAP-related distinguished names and relative distinguished names In Exchange 5.5, the directory service (now moved under the Active Directory services banner) created a unique distinguished name for every directory object. This name, which continues to be used under Active Directory services, is the basis for routing messages throughout the organization and serves not only to identify the object itself but its position in the domain hierarchy as well.

Although distinguished names are based on the same elements (user name, domain, and so on) as DNS names and UPNs, they are more detailed and are associated with two-letter abbreviations called LDAP attribute tags that identify their various components. In Windows 2000, these tags and what they mean are:

- **cn for common name**   the name of an object in the user class
- **ou for organizational unit**   the name of an object in the organizational unit class
- **dc for domain component**   the names that identify objects in the DNS domain name class

For example, the distinguished name for a user named Hdumpty in the WallSitter organizational unit, which is part of the *microsoft.com* domain, might look like this:

cn=Hdumpty,ou=WallSitter,dc=microsoft,dc=com

As can be seen here, the distinguished name thus includes the full path from the object to the domain root. What is not as obvious, however, is that the distinguished name also happens to include a relative distinguished name, or RDN. An RDN is the actual name—the attribute—of the object represented by the LDAP attribute tag (usually cn) in a distinguished name. Thus, although cn could refer to any of dozens or thousands of common names, in the example above the common name Hdumpty uniquely identifies one object alone. In Active Directory services architecture, each RDN is stored in the Active Directory database along with a reference to its parent object. So, for example, the entry for Hdumpty would point to its parent object, WallSitter.

Distinguished names are based on X.500 naming conventions and in two cases, *cn* and *ou,* the abbreviations match X.500 naming exactly. However, X.500 does not include a dc component and does include two single-letter abbreviations, *o* for organization and *c* for country. Where these are concerned, the X.500 *o* and Active Directory services *dc* are more or less comparable; *c* is X.500-only and is not supported in Active Directory services.

Comparison of X.500 and Distinguished Names

X.500	Distinguished Names
Cn	Cn
Ou	Ou
o	Dc
c	No equivalent

Table 5-1.
X.500 and Distinguished Names.

Canonical names   Even though Active Directory services uses distinguished names to enable LDAP clients to access the directory and retrieve information about directory objects, it's important to note that the two-letter abbreviations—cn, ou, and dc—don't themselves appear in Active Directory services management tools. Instead, these tools display names in what is called canonical format which, essentially, combines the DNS naming format with distinguished names minus the LDAP attribute tag.

Although both distinguished names and canonical names contain the same elements, there are some immediately obvious differences between the two.

- **Distinguished names**   begin at the left with the object name and move progressively higher up the hierarchy until reaching the root at the right. **Canonical names** reverse the order, beginning with the domain-name information at the left and ending with the object name at the right.

- **Distinguished names**   are built of object names, abbreviations, equal signs, and commas. **Canonical names** use the DNS domain-name format plus forward slashes between objects.

119

Thus, the canonical name for Hdumpty in the preceding section would appear as

microsoft.com/WallSitter/Hdumpty

Globally unique identifiers, or GUIDs   Globally unique identifiers or GUIDs (pronounced "goo-ids") are, as their name suggests, global in scope and unique in identifying objects. They are, in fact, 128-bit numbers assigned to objects at the time of their creation. GUIDs are required, unchanging, and unchangeable. They exist to provide applications with a constant, permanent means of referencing objects even if their distinguished name or canonical name is changed, or the object is moved from one part of the hierarchy to another.

How It Works

A rose by any name is still a rose, and a network object—whether known by its UPN, distinguished name, canonical name, GUID, or security ID—is still a network object. It exists out there somewhere. And Active Directory services exists to identify it, authenticate it, provide access to it, and allow it to access permitted resources whenever necessary. So how, at least superficially, does Active Directory services go about doing that?

Domain Controllers

Domain controllers are at the heart of Active Directory services in that a domain must contain at least one domain controller before it can be an Active Directory domain. In addition, Active Directory services must be installed on a server before it can be a domain controller, and the Global Catalog must reside on a domain controller, although not every domain controller need host the Global Catalog.

Every domain controller does, however, store three types of directory information: the schema, configuration information, and data. These three categories are known as naming contexts or directory partitions and are the basis for replicating information across the forest.

The schema   As you might recall from Chapter 2, the schema is a kind of blueprint for the actual entries in the directory. Not only does it define the types of objects that can be created in the directory, it also defines the attributes those objects can have. That is, it's the schema that "allows" an object named *user* to be created in the directory and that allows the *user* object to have attributes such as first and last names, telephone extension, and so on.

In effect, the schema is a template for the directory. It applies to the entire forest and is replicated to every domain controller in the forest.

Configuration information   Configuration information, in some ways the least intuitive of the three types of directory information, describes Active Directory services itself, including aspects such as the domain structure and replication topology—the connections over which directory information is replicated among domain controllers. The configuration information partition is also used for information storage by applications that are aware of Active Directory services.

Configuration information represents metadata (data about data) and applies to all domains in the forest. During replication, configuration information, like the schema, is replicated throughout the forest.

Data   The data partition, the easiest of the three partitions to understand, contains all the objects in the domain. Like the Seattle or Chicago white pages, this is the "telephone book" for its domain and, like the white pages, it's specific to that domain. Domain data is replicated to every domain controller in the domain, but is not distributed to other domains. However, a partial replica that includes the most-often searched object attributes, does get transferred to the Global Catalog so that domain controllers throughout the forest can find and make use of this domain-specific data.

The Global Catalog

The Active Directory Global Catalog, which (in Exchange 2000) replaces the global address list of earlier versions, is something like a souped-up data partition in that it stores and replicates both the complete object data for its own domain as well as the partial replicas for all other domains in the forest. It is, essentially, the "master" directory for the entire forest.

By storing key information about all the objects in the forest, the Global Catalog performs two primary, and very important, functions:

- **It makes information about the entire group of users available to domain controllers**   so that users can log on to the network. Without the Global Catalog, the user would be able to log on only to the local computer.

- **It makes forest-wide searches for users and resources available to clients,**   no matter which domain hosts the information they seek.

By default, the Global Catalog is created on the first domain in the forest, but it doesn't have to exist on only one server. Administrators can configure other Global Catalog servers as well, with their number and locations depending on the organization's logon requirements and need to service requests for directory information. In terms of optimum network performance, the domain controller for a site should also be a Global Catalog server so that it can handle forest-wide queries. This ideal, however, should be tempered by two additional factors:

- Numerous Global Catalog servers in numerous domains can mean increased network traffic as directory information is replicated throughout the forest.

- Unless a domain contains only one domain controller, the Global Catalog should not be hosted on the same server that acts as infrastructure master. The infrastructure master is the server responsible for finding outdated object information, requesting the updated version from the Global Catalog, and then replicating the corrected information to other domain controllers in the domain. If both the Global Catalog and the infrastructure master are on the same machine, the infrastructure master won't function.

To ensure that the Global Catalog is kept complete and up to date, domain controllers in a domain replicate *all* objects in that domain, along with partial replicas, to the Global Catalog server. If other Global Catalog servers exist, they then replicate the partial replicas among themselves.

Replication

As for replication itself...in all cases, replication means duplication of the directory, among domain controllers and to the Global Catalog. How replication actually takes place depends on when it occurs, as well as on whether it happens within or between sites.

Replication when and as needed   To allow administrators needed flexibility, Windows 2000 supports the ability to manually configure replication connections and to force replication over a connection when necessary. Left to its own devices, however, Windows 2000 Server is designed to automatically optimize replication based on

- Evaluating which connections are used and using the most efficient ones

- Using multiple replication routes to promote fault tolerance

- Replicating only changed information rather than entire objects to reduce replication costs

To ensure that only needed changes are replicated and that the same change doesn't travel to a domain controller more than once over different routes, Active Directory services and its domain controllers keep track of both how many changes are made to the directory and by whom.

For instance, each domain controller keeps track of the number of changes it makes to its own directory, as well as the number of changes it has received from other domain controllers with which it exchanges replicated information. Thus, a domain controller can check its directory and, if necessary, request that a laggard domain controller send an update.

Similarly, as changes are made to the directory, Active Directory services keeps track of which attributes change for an object and, clever thing, notes whether that change was made by a client (in which case the change must be replicated) or whether it made the change itself while updating the directory. Another domain controller contemplating replication can thus check to see who made the change and base its own replicate/don't replicate decision on what it finds.

Replication within a site When replication is left up to Active Directory services, it occurs often and automatically within a site to ensure that directory information is as current as possible. (A site, remember, is a group of servers with permanent, high-bandwidth connections that belong to the same IP subnet). In this situation, all directory objects plus the schema and configuration data are replicated among however many domain controllers there are in the site. Basically, this is a share and share alike situation, even if one of the domain controllers is also the keeper of the Global Catalog.

The simplest form this type of replication takes occurs in a site consisting of a single domain with more than one domain controller. Graphically, the replication paths can be illustrated as follows. (The broken line indicates schema and configuration data; the solid line represents domain object data.)

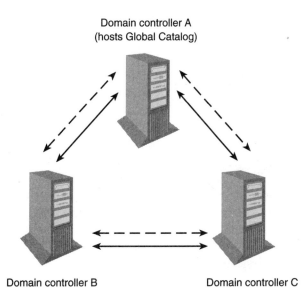

Domain controller A
(hosts Global Catalog)

Domain controller B   Domain controller C

Not all organizations, of course, are made up of single sites and single domains. Some are more complex and involve multiple domains. If the domains still exist within the same site, however, the basic replication pattern is the same, with one added factor: the schema and configuration data, as well as partial replicas of the domain data, must now be passed between domain controllers hosting the Global Catalog. Now, the situation looks like the following. (Again, the broken line represents schema and configuration data and the solid line represents domain data. The added wavy line represents partial replicas.)

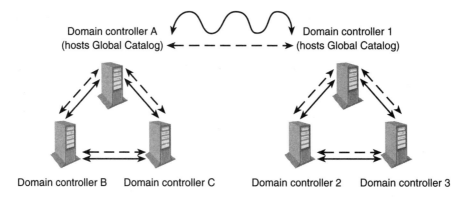

Domain controller A (hosts Global Catalog)   Domain controller 1 (hosts Global Catalog)

Domain controller B   Domain controller C   Domain controller 2   Domain controller 3

Replication between sites   When a forest contains multiple sites, as across a WAN, those sites are said to be connected by site links—low bandwidth or unreliable connections. These connections are not automatically created, but must be entered, along with information about availability, replication frequency, and cost, through the Active Directory Sites and Services console. Armed with this information, Active Directory services then can determine which connection to use, and when (as in time of day) to transfer replication information. Like trust relationships, site links are transitive, so if sites A and B are connected and B and C are connected, site A can also communicate with site C.

In transferring directory information, administrators can use either of two Internet protocols, IP or SMTP.

- **The IP protocol**   can be used both within a site and between sites.

- **The SMTP protocol,**   which requires a certification authority (CA) for encrypting directory information, is intended for use with mail-based sites that are not connected to the rest of the network. SMTP can be used only for replication between sites or domains. It can't be used for replicating within a site.

The preferred method of connecting sites is to pass replication information between bridgehead servers, which then pass the information on to other domain controllers in their respective sites. It's also possible, however, to configure other domain controllers so that they, too, can transfer replication information between sites. Replication between sites can be graphically illustrated as follows. (The solid line represents the site link, the broken line represents within-site connections, and the bridgehead servers are shaded.)

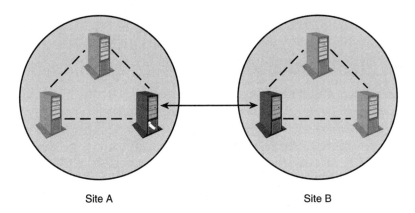

Site A   Site B

Now, before going on to see how Active Directory services affects Exchange, there is one more topic to consider: domain mode. (Actually, there is much more that can be said about Active Directory services, but this *is* a book about Exchange.)

Domain Mode

As mentioned in Chapter 3, Active Directory services can operate in either of two modes: mixed mode or native mode.

Mixed mode is the default and is needed when a domain is mixed-vintage, depending on both Microsoft Windows NT 4.0 servers and Windows 2000 servers. Although a Windows 2000 server can be introduced into a Windows NT domain and the two versions of the operating system coexist quite peacefully, Windows NT does put some constraints on Active Directory services. In particular, it limits the directory to 40,000 objects and requires the domain to function as if it were a Windows NT 4.0 domain. In a mixed-vintage domain, a Windows 2000 domain controller acts, and is seen by backup Windows NT domain controllers, as the primary domain controller (PDC) required by Windows NT domains.

In contrast, when a domain is switched to native mode, meaning that all domain controllers are running Windows 2000 Server, the Windows NT limitations disappear. Scalability moves up from 40,000 objects to the ability to support millions of objects. In addition, the domain can now support the richer group creation and nesting capabilities of Active Directory services. The only drawbacks, if such they are, to native mode are that switching to native mode is *irreversible* and that the domain can't include any Windows NT domain controllers (although Windows NT servers are perfectly acceptable, and clients don't need to be upgraded).

Windows 2000 and Exchange

Where Exchange 2000 is concerned, the principal effect of Windows 2000 is (what else) the complete and seamless integration of Exchange with Active Directory services. Instead of having to rely on its own directory, Exchange now relies on the logon, security, object creation, management, and replication capabilities of Active Directory services.

However, while Active Directory integration is the most profound and visible change in Exchange 2000, Windows 2000 actually affects Exchange in three additional ways. These are:

- **The directory,** of course
- **Transport,** in particular support for enterprise-level messaging
- **Name resolution,** meaning a shift from the earlier NETBIOS-based WINS name resolution to DNS

The Directory

Earlier versions of Exchange depended on a separate directory database for storing information such as mailboxes and public folders. This "separateness" was primarily because the Windows NT Security Accounts Manager (SAM), the database containing user account and password information, was not meant to include detailed user information, such as telephone numbers. In fact, the only connection between the Exchange database and the Windows NT security database was a link between mailbox objects in Exchange and the user's primary Windows NT account.

Now, because Active Directory services is capable of holding a rich store of information about user accounts, security, and messaging, the separate Exchange directory is no longer needed. A single directory can now support not only both network logons and directory searches, but also centralized management and one replication mechanism that satisfies the needs of both Windows and Exchange. In effect, Exchange has done away with the need for a separate "telephone book" of its own and now assumes that all of its directory-related needs are neatly stored and readily available in Active Directory services.

Object Name Changes

Although integration with Active Directory services represents a clear and natural evolutionary path for Exchange and Windows, the very fact that Active Directory services is both new and the sole source of directory information means that the terminology familiar to users of earlier versions of Exchange has undergone some evolution of its own. In particular, pre-Exchange 2000 objects, although they have equivalents under Active Directory services, are now represented by different object classes and different names. To wit, Exchange 5.5:

- **Mailboxes** are now **mail-enabled users,** meaning that they are security principals and are able to send and receive mail. They also have SMTP addresses, which can be generated based on fields in the directory (as dictated by the administrator).

- **Custom recipients** are now **mail-enabled contacts.** These, too, have SMTP addresses.

- **Distribution lists** are now **mail-enabled groups.** This can get a little sticky conceptually, because Active Directory services recognizes two types of groups, security and distribution, but group type and scope—domain local, global, and universal—are determined by the domain mode. (For a refresher on this, refer back to Chapter 4.) However, one great benefit of Active Directory integration is that Active Directory security groups can automatically function as distribution lists, too, and thus make group administration essentially do double duty in both Windows 2000 and Exchange.

- **Public folders** are now...**public folders.** However, even though they are mail-enabled objects, they are created through the Exchange Management console rather than the Active Directory Users and Computers console.

Address Lists and Address Books

Address lists are, of course, every e-mailer's stock in trade, not only for addressing messages, but also for finding people, setting up meetings, and sending out mass mailings—sometimes dumb ones—to whole groups at a time. But even though users have the ability to search address lists and even use them as the basis for generating personal address books, it's up to administrators to manage the master lists for the organization and to create custom lists that serve the needs of certain groups of users. To help in this task, Exchange 2000 supports two basic types of address lists, known as default address lists and custom address lists.

Default address lists   Default address lists are simple for administrators because they require no work whatsoever. Based on certain predetermined object attributes, default address lists are generated during setup and are automatically available to users. Altogether, Exchange creates four default lists based on the following attributes:

- Contacts
- Groups
- Users
- Public folders

And, like earlier versions of Exchange, it creates a Global Address List (GAL), which is identical to the global address list in earlier versions of Exchange and includes all recipients: mailbox-enabled and mail-enabled users, groups, public folders, contacts, and resources.

Custom address lists   Unlike the default address lists, which gather and group addresses from throughout the organization, custom address lists enable administrators to create specialized, rule-based address lists to help users view the organization from certain useful perspectives—for example, by region or by department. Custom address lists are obviously far beyond the abilities of any (current) software to generate because they require administrator smarts. However, their actual creation requires only that the administrator

- Open the desired address lists node under Recipients in the Exchange System Manager
- Right-click the node and choose New (address list)
- Name the new list and specify the filter rules that will determine list membership

Address lists and address book views   Note that Exchange 2000 address lists replace the address book views of Exchange 5.*x*, which were also used by administrators to create specialized address lists based on field groupings. There is, however, compatibility with Exchange 5.*x* address book views, in that these earlier views are migrated to Active Directory address lists when a server is upgraded, and updates to the migrated, newly transformed address list are made through the Active Directory Connector. However, in organizations running both Exchange 2000 and Exchange 5.*x*, it's important to bear in mind that travel is in one direction only—that is, new Exchange 2000 address lists and updates to existing Exchange 2000 address lists don't travel back for replication in the older Exchange 5.*x* directory.

Transport

Underlying Active Directory services, indeed all Windows 2000 network functionality, are the transports that carry not only directory data, but also messages, queries, files, and all other information between and among network users.

The very act of installing Windows causes base Internet protocol stacks to be configured as part of the operating system. Among these are the SMTP (discussed further in Chapter 8) and NNTP protocols so valuable to Exchange users. Once installed and configured, these stacks can then be used by Windows and components that need their services. In terms of Active Directory services and Exchange, for instance, the fact that SMTP is available means that directory information can be replicated over SMTP, if necessary, rather than over the IP protocol, with its attendant use of remote procedure calls (RPCs). To gear itself up to enterprise-level messaging, Exchange 2000 extends the protocol stacks by adding increased functionality and routing capability during installation.

Name Resolution

Exchange without a network and a uniform means of resolving resource names would be about as useful as a post office without mail carriers and a standardized format for addressing letters. For example, "Jane, somewhere in New York" would never succeed in sending mail to "Joe, somewhere in Seattle" (although she just might manage to send a letter to "Santa, at the North Pole"). Similarly, Exchange clients rely heavily on Windows 2000 networking capabilities and protocols, and on the ability of Windows 2000 to resolve names to directory objects.

DNS is, of course, the primary Windows 2000 name resolution service for mapping DNS names to IP addresses. Permeating Windows 2000, it's used for logon and other functions, as well as the traditional "get me to the Internet" or "please find this computer" types of client queries. However, because not all clients and software understand DNS and because previous versions of Windows relied on a different name resolution technique known as WINS (Windows Internet Name Service), Windows 2000 provides support for both DNS and WINS.

WINS exists to help resolve NetBIOS (NETwork Basic Input/Output System) computer names, such as "host-a." It does so by maintaining a WINS database that maps names to IP addresses. DNS and WINS work together to resolve names, as follows:

1. A client sends the request to its preferred DNS server.

2. The preferred server contacts other DNS servers (root, top-level domain, and so on) as necessary to resolve the various parts of the DNS domain name.

3. If the last DNS server contacted can't completely resolve the name, for example, *host-a.microsoft.com,* it then separates the first part (before the first period) of the DNS name and sends that to a WINS server.

4. The WINS server resolves "host-a" to its corresponding IP address and sends the result back to the DNS server.

5. The DNS server then sends the IP information back to the preferred server.

Windows 2000, Exchange 2000, and Business

Whether an enterprise is large or small, elimination of the Exchange directory and integration of Active Directory services affects both scalability and cost reduction. On the scalability front, Active Directory services effectively creates a single, unified directory that handles users, groups, resources, permissions, network logon, and so on, for organizations ranging from single-server, single-site businesses on up through enterprises spread across numerous domains, sites, and servers. This same unified directory also, at least in theory, lowers cost of ownership through centralized administration and MMC and its snap-ins.

In addition, Exchange itself, especially in its enterprise form, offers features that emphasize improved scalability and the capacity to handle the needs of enterprise-class organizations and information-oriented businesses, such as ISPs (Internet service providers) and ASPs (application service providers). Briefly, these features include

- **Message databases** that can be split across more than one physical database

- **Active/active clustering**

■ **The ability to distribute services** across multiple servers for greater scalability

■ **Support for front-end/back-end configuration** in which Internet access protocols can be managed separately, on a different server, from back-end databases

More detail on these features appears later in the book, especially in Chapters 7 and 8.

Information Storage and the Web Store

Think of the Web Store as a new, cool feature of Exchange 2000—or rather, think of it that way as long as you bear in mind that it both is and is not an actual feature. It's a "feature" in the sense that Exchange is what makes the Web Store happen. It's not a "feature" in the sense that the Web Store is nowhere to be found in the Exchange user interface.

Well, great…. The Web Store is, and yet the Web Store isn't. Is this book turning into some kind of metaphysical view of the glories of Exchange? Is it going to tease you with one of those "when is a *blank* not a *blank*" types of questions? Nope. The whole point of the yes-it-is/no-it-isn't description of the Web Store is simply this: The Web Store is a *concept*, one that needs Exchange 2000 to turn it into something real that users can see and use. So, even though the Web Store is closely tied to Exchange, it's not a feature in the same way that MMC, ADC, and other Exchange components are features.

Because the Web Store exists as both a concept and a real-life information repository, this chapter is divided into two major parts. The first part, titled "The Web Store Concept," describes the idea of a Web Store—what it is, what it can contain, and how it affects the organization, its administrators, and its end users. The second part examines the Exchange technologies, such as the information store and file system, that contribute the functionality that makes the Web Store actually happen.

The Web Store Concept

To understand why the Web Store concept came into being, think back over the past few years. Has networking changed? Have users' needs changed? Has there been some kind of shift in the way people communicate? In the way they use and access information?

Of course. It's called the Internet—actually, not so much the Internet as the World Wide Web—the cyberspace universe of open Internet standards, URLs, HTTP, TCP/IP, as well as, increasingly, the Web-oriented multimedia kaleidoscope of animation, video, text, and sound.

Evolving Communication Needs

These days, everything is the Web. It's the Web that drives seemingly daily developments in access (wireless, handheld), information delivery technologies (streaming media, real-time chat), development tools (XML, ASP), and so on. The computing world is much different now than it was even a few short years ago, and people's approach to communicating and collaborating has similarly evolved. Instead of the plain-text e-mail of "old," people now routinely

- Use rich formatting, including color, in their messages
- Embed live links that take the recipient to specific Web pages
- Attach documents, images, sound, and video files to their mail
- Alert the recipient to their cleverness with animated dancing hamsters, massive graphic signatures, and other extraneous byte hogs
- Use e-mail clients such as Microsoft Outlook to handle calendars, meeting requests, contact and to-do lists, and notes to themselves, as well as to post messages and opinions in special-interest public and semi-public folders

In other words, e-mail (the first and perhaps foremost collaborative product for most people) has come a long way.

New Needs, New Approaches

So how does this evolution (revolution?) in communications relate to the Web Store? Obviously, the "Web" in its name is a dead giveaway. First of all, Web standards, such as TCP/IP and HTTP, are increasingly the same standards used not only on corporate Web sites, but also in corporate intranets, so a strong Web foundation is a necessity, and the Web Store (through Exchange) provides that foundation.

Resting on this base of Web protocols and technologies is the Web Store concept itself. This concept is, simply put, Microsoft's approach to making information—of all kinds—available to users (to quote the company) "anytime, anywhere, and from any device." The Web Store thus combines Web technologies with Exchange database features, such as transaction logging, single-instance storage, and flexible property management, to provide a reliable, scalable, easy-to-use, Web-based solution to information storage and management.

Because of the Web Store concept, people can access, create, change, and store information in one place, and they can do so with client software ranging from any Internet-capable e-mail application to browsers such as Microsoft Internet Explorer and applications such as Microsoft Office.

Who Needs the Web Store

The impetus for developing the Web Store wasn't, of course, development for its own sake. Rather, the concept grew as a means of meeting the needs of an increasingly important group of people—knowledge workers. They are the folks who must rely heavily on information access and management in their jobs and who must be able to communicate and collaborate freely. And the solution to their communication and collaboration needs is unified messaging—the "anytime, anywhere" ability to access information of any kind when and as needed, and with any device ranging from a PC to a wireless telephone. This is the accessibility embodied in the Web Store concept.

What the Web Store Provides

The Web Store is built in large part on Internet technologies, and its relationship to the Internet is two-pronged. First, of course, there is the continuing, extensive integration of Internet protocols and technologies into Exchange itself. Second, because Exchange supports the Web Store, and the Web Store forms the basis of Microsoft's unified messaging platform, changes to Exchange's information store architecture are what make the Web Store possible. Through this Internet integration and approach to unified messaging, the Web Store helps eliminate barriers to communication and collaboration by providing the organization with a *single* repository for information that can include

- E-mail
- Documents
- URLs
- Voice-mail messages
- Streaming media
- Business applications
- Workflow applications
- Calendaring

And more.

Features of the Web Store

In the main, the Web Store offers features related to the Web, the Web, and the Web. That is, most everything that supports a working Web Store is Internet-related: Internet protocols including HTTP and the up-and-coming XML, streaming media files, and Web-oriented programming through use of OLE DB, WebDAV, ADO, and so on. These features are intended both to lower administrative costs and to make information access, document management, and collaboration easier and more productive for end users.

In a nutshell, the following sections outline what the Web Store offers. Note that they are meant to be an overview. The actual technologies and protocols are described later in this chapter and in Chapter 9, "Internet Integration." (And, of course, they're defined in the glossary at the end of the book.)

Streaming Media Files: .stm

The richest and most visible feature of the Web Store is its ability to support streaming media—voice, audio, video, and other types of multimedia. Thanks to this capability, users can now find numerous new ways to make their e-mail even more creative.

As mentioned earlier, e-mail is no longer a simple matter of exchanging plain text with someone else. It's now as much a way of collaborating as it is communicating. This book, for example, though printed on paper, relied on electronic communication and collaboration. Text, graphics, and page proofs were transferred by modem between Redmond, Washington; San Diego, California; Davenport, Iowa; and Victoria, British Columbia, Canada, as were the inevitable queries, requests, and authorial excuses. If the Web Store had been in place, no doubt voicemail messages would have been part of the mix as well.

Even so, this book was one of the less multimedia-rich uses of Exchange. There are certainly other instances where sound and video would be, if not necessary, then highly desirable: for example, music or film clips being worked on by advertising agencies; voicemail to and from a salesperson almost constantly on the road; or slide shows being saved into a Microsoft NetShow file by a consultant or educator.

To support such capability, the Web Store is designed to store multimedia files as MIME content in a new type of Exchange store known as an .stm file, which exists as a companion to the Exchange standard rich-text .edb file.

Because the .stm file exists, multimedia content delivered by client software using non-MAPI protocols such as HTTP, SMTP, and IMAP4 can be popped directly into the .stm file as a stream of MIME data *without* first needing to be converted to a MAPI-acceptable format. Because this content goes directly into the .stm file, the Web Store minimizes file conversions and the associated risk of introduced errors; it also helps improve network performance. In addition, because streaming media becomes just another type of data, the data doesn't require any special management from administrators.

Content Indexing and Searching

The Web Store is designed to provide an organization with a single repository for documents as well as e-mail and other messages. Given such flexibility, however, one question soon arises, at least in the user's mind: How can I find what I need?

The answer is in the Web Store's indexing, which allows searches for

- **Key message fields,**   such as sender, recipient, and subject
- **Document properties,**   including advanced searches for properties such as author, data, or department
- **Document content,**   including attachment text

As you would imagine, such indexing requires considerable amounts of processing time and power. To make searches fast as well as accurate, Exchange does the following:

- **It indexes searchable text**   before searches are executed
- **It merges the results of two searches,**   one for document properties using an ESE (Extensible Search Engine) index, and the other for terms in a full-text index, as shown below

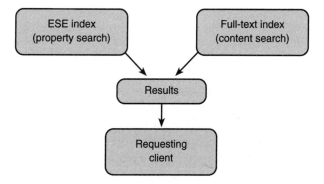

Where full-text indexing is concerned, note that this does *not* mean that every word of every copy of every document is indexed. Exchange, as explained in Chapter 1, relies on single-instance storage, so a document used by many people is indexed only once.

HTTP

On a less visible though no less important level, the Web Store also supports a number of Internet-related protocols and features. So, as would be expected, it supports the HTTP that, along with TCP/IP, pretty much defines the Web. HTTP is, of course, the set of rules used by client and server in retrieving Web pages. In effect, the client sends a request to a Web (or intranet) server that basically says "please send this page" whenever a user types an URL or clicks an embedded link. The server then looks for the page and either sends it back to the client or, if there is a problem, sends a "can't do it" along with a response explaining why.

HTTP is also the most significant feature of the Web Store in that every file object deposited in the store is associated with a unique URL. In other words, the Web Store, through HTTP, ensures that any object can be found and retrieved through its URL.

This URL identifies the hierarchical path to the item and takes a form like one of the following:

- For a file in a public folder, the format is

    `file://./server/domain/publicfolders/filename`

- For a file in a user's mailbox, the format is

    `file://./backofficestorage/dnsname/MBX/username/inbox/filename`

NOTE: The prefix in each case is *file://.* not *http://.* In the case of the user's inbox, *backofficestorage* is a specific identifier that refers to a Microsoft BackOffice storage share name that is automatically mapped to drive M: on the computer running Exchange. This share becomes accessible to users when they map a local drive to BackOfficeStorage.

WebDAV

Although its name doesn't indicate any relation to HTTP or, for that matter, even hint that it's a protocol, WebDAV (Web Distributed Authoring and Versioning) is an extension of HTTP version 1.1. Currently an IETF (Internet Engineering Task Force) draft standard, WebDAV is designed for file-system-like operations (such as copy and move) over the Internet and corporate intranets. As its name indicates, WebDAV defines methods for document tracking and management (versioning) and so is valuable in situations requiring collaboration and shared access to information. WebDAV is designed for use in situations where data is stored on a server but accessed by, and used on, the client.

In terms of Exchange, WebDAV is the means by which users gain access to the Web Store—access that can be had from any Internet client, that is, browser software. The following illustration shows the Web Store as it looks when rendered into HTML and displayed by a browser.

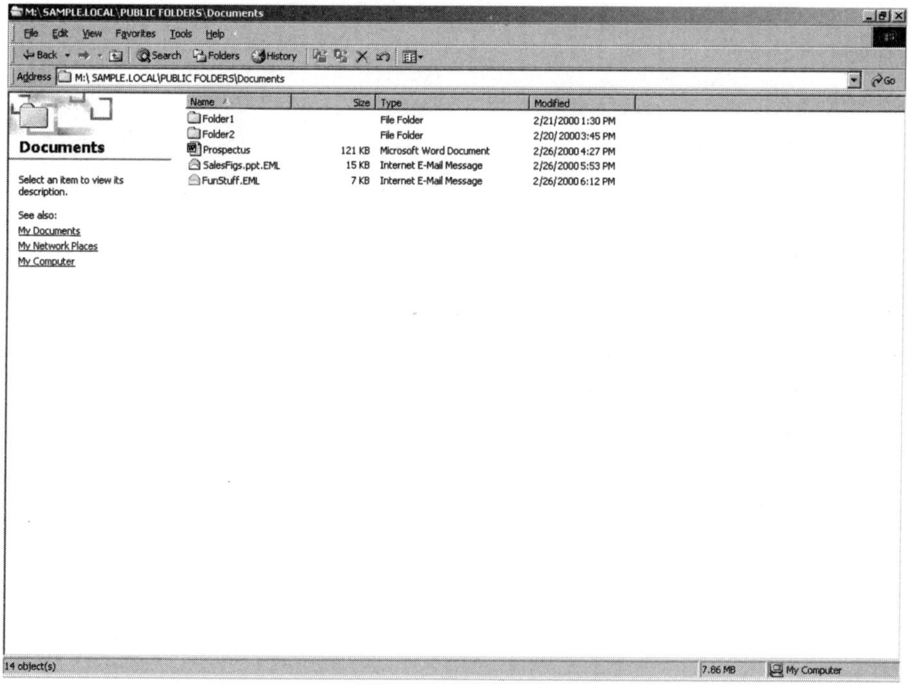

HTML

The venerable HTML is the common language of the Web. Like the symbols used by editors and proofreaders, it's the set of codes that Web designers use for telling any browser software how they want their work to be displayed: "this is a title, this is boldface, this is red," and so on.

A World Wide Web Consortium (W3C) standard, HTML has evolved through several iterations and is now at version 4.0, which emphasizes internationalization and accessibility as well as supporting tables and forms, style sheets, and scripting and multimedia options.

The Web Store includes built-in support for HTML versions 3.2 and 4.0. It automatically provides HTML 3.2 views of objects, rendering them in familiar folder/document graphics based on properties promoted to the store for each item. These properties, because they are included in the store, can also be used in queries.

For browser software that is based on HTML 4.0, such as that included with Internet Explorer 5.0 and Microsoft Office, the Web Store offers more functionality, including support for the object-oriented Dynamic HTML that enables more interactivity and responsiveness in Web pages.

XML

XML, the eXtensible Markup Language, is a developing Internet standard (currently a recommendation to the W3C). Like HTML, XML is a means of indicating how a Web page is to be displayed. Unlike HTML, however, XML is also a means of describing and defining the data itself. For example, XML allows an item to be tagged as a fax number, last name, e-mail address, and so on. In this respect, XML enables Web developers to both make data look pretty *and* give it meaning, so that XML-enabled programs can process the actual content of the XML document.

Because the Web Store (naturally) supports XML, information not only can be standardized for presentation, it can also be accessed by developers who create applications that need to work with the data in the store itself.

Programming Support

And speaking of XML and its metadata orientation, what of programming support in Exchange? It's there in a number of ways, including support for Web development using Active Server Pages (ASP) and through a number of APIs that provide programs with a means of accessing and controlling Exchange objects. Here, briefly, are some of the features of interest to developers.

Win32 The Microsoft Win32 file-system APIs work in concert with Exchange's new Installable File System (IFS), which provides access to the Web Store.
Through Win32 and IFS accessibility

- Administrators can share Web Store data just as they share documents on a file server

- Applications based on the file system can be ported to the Web Store

- End users can rely on tried-and-true methods of accessing Web Store contents

ADO ADO, or ActiveX Data Objects, provides programmers with a rapid-development tool for accessing Web Store data. Like the more powerful and involved OLE DB described next, ADO supports access to SQL Server. Unlike OLE DB, however, it is designed as an easy-to-use API for high-level development in Active Server Pages and languages including Visual Basic, Visual Basic for Applications, and Visual Basic Scripting. ADO, again like OLE DB, enables access to the store through the item's URLs.

OLE DB OLE DB is a Common Object Model, or COM-based API. Like ADO, it's designed to enable applications to access data. Unlike the easy-to-use ADO, OLE DB is the low-level COM cornerstone for accessing, storing, and retrieving data records. The vehicle for accessing the store itself is an OLE DB provider that is installed when Exchange server is installed. OLE DB is the method of choice for COM-based system-level development that requires either powerful performance or access to SQL Server features that can't be gained through ADO.

CDO CDO, or Collaboration Data Objects, is the API designed for development of collaborative applications—messaging, calendaring, contact management, and so on. Designed to support rapid development in C++ and Visual Basic, CDO can also be used with Visual Basic Scripting Edition, Java Script, and Java. CDO is installed as part of Exchange Server and includes a library of workflow services that allow for development of workflow and tracking applications based on transacted, synchronous events (the ability to process events as they occur).

Web Store events As mentioned above, workflow applications can be designed to respond to events as they occur. Three types of Web Store events can occur:

- **Synchronous,** in which processing occurs as conditions occur to trigger the event

- **Asynchronous,** in which processing occurs after the fact, in response to an event that has occurred

- **Transport,** in which events are triggered in response to the arrival of SMTP and NNTP messages

Benefits for the Enterprise

Different Web Store technologies address the needs of three distinct groups of individuals: administrators, users, and developers. However, there is also the enterprise as a whole to consider, and it too benefits from the Web Store.

These benefits—stemming from the features described in preceding sections—are in the areas of file system services, database services, and collaboration.

- **File system services support,** which includes
  - ❑ The ability to read from and write to documents through client software such as Microsoft Office
  - ❑ The ability to store streaming media including both audio and video

141

❑ Access to a flexible data model in which data can be stored hierarchically in folders and can also be mixed within folders that can hold multiple types of data

■ **Database services,** which provide for more sophisticated queries than can be handled by file system services, support both the ability to include different types of data in the repository and the ability to present consistent views to the end user. For querying, the Web Store supports such functionality as ActiveX Data Objects (ADO) scripting, SQL queries and transactions, and full-text indexing for information retrieval.

■ **Collaboration,** which includes such tasks as contacts, calendars, and both group and real-time (chat-type) teamwork, is supported by a development platform that allows developers to use such familiar tools as Microsoft FrontPage and Visual Studio. For instance, as mentioned earlier, Microsoft Collaboration Data Objects (CDO) are installed as part of Exchange and can be used to create numerous collaborative applications that handle such tasks as filtering messages and bulk e-mails, scheduling and setting appointments, tracking workflow, and routing documents.

The Web Store and Administrators

From an administrator's point of view, the Web Store provides benefits in three main areas: administration and cost concerns, scalability and reliability issues, and security and integration with Microsoft Windows 2000.

Administration and Costs

Because the Web Store represents a single location for storing information of all kinds, administrators benefit from single-seat administration in the following two main areas:

■ **Lower operating costs** because the Web Store centralizes management, backup, and restore operations in a single storage engine

■ **Easier training and reduced training costs** because of the need to learn how to manage and maintain one rather than several different types of servers (file, mail, and so on)

Scalability and Reliability

As described later in the "Storage Groups and Multiple Databases" section of this chapter, Exchange and the Web Store address scalability by supporting the ability to spread storage across more than one database. This kind of distribution pays a significant scalability dividend in allowing the Web Store to grow into a potentially gigantic virtual database, while simultaneously keeping each separate database small enough to manage, back up, and recover easily and quickly.

Furthermore, because databases can be separated like this, administrators gain management flexibility of two kinds, each with its own advantages:

- Administrators can maintain separate databases to meet the needs of different groups of users

- Alternatively, administrators can distribute group data across the databases on multiple servers

Maintaining separate databases offers group-by-group control over configuration—folder size (in terms of storage limits), length of time data remains in the store, and so on. However, it also tends to concentrate group-specific information in the same place and thus can affect the group's functions if the server or the database fails. Distributing a group's data across multiple servers lessens disruption to any group's operations in the event a particular server or database happens to fail.

Distributing databases also, and obviously, helps ensure the reliability of the Web Store, because other databases can continue functioning while a failed database is being restored to service. The Web Store also supports reliability in several other ways important to securing critical information:

- **Write-ahead transaction logging** ensures data integrity by guaranteeing that information can be recovered and restored from the logs, even if an interruption occurs before the data has been written to disk

- **The ability to replicate folders and their contents** provides for copies of the data to exist on other servers and, in addition, allows for load balancing across servers

- In the enterprise version of Exchange 2000, **support for active/ active clustering** ensures that control over Web Store data can be shifted from a failed server to a functioning server if necessary

Security and Integration with Windows 2000

The Web Store blends with and extends Windows 2000 security. It allows control over permissions at the item and field level, so administrators can control a user's ability to access, change, or delete even individual items. Furthermore, by relying on Windows Access Control Lists (ACLs), the Web Store enables administrators to apply permissions once to both the Web Store and shared files controlled by Windows 2000.

Microsoft Windows 2000 Integration

The Web Store is designed for optimal management within the Microsoft Windows 2000 environment. It can fully leverage Microsoft Active Directory configuration information while fully supporting the security settings enabled by Windows 2000 ACLs. Administrators already familiar with Windows 2000 administration will find it easy to support and manage the Web Store, because many of its concepts are the same. The Web Store is fully integrated with Windows 2000 security and file system infrastructures, and supports management through Active Directory services and the Microsoft Management Console.

The Web Store and Knowledge Workers

For knowledge workers, the benefits offered by the Web Store can be summed up in two words: higher productivity. This potential increase in productivity (the actual increase varies with employee dedication) is based on making mail, documents, and collaborative applications easier to find and use.

A Choice of Clients

One obvious contributor to higher productivity stems from the fact that users no longer need to fire up a particular application to access information because the Web Store is accessible from a wide range of clients, including

- Microsoft Outlook
- Any Internet e-mail or bulletin board client
- Windows Explorer
- Any Web browser that supports HTML—especially version 4.0

Figures 6-1 and 6-2 show the Web Store as it can be accessed from Microsoft Outlook and by using Microsoft Outlook Web Access.

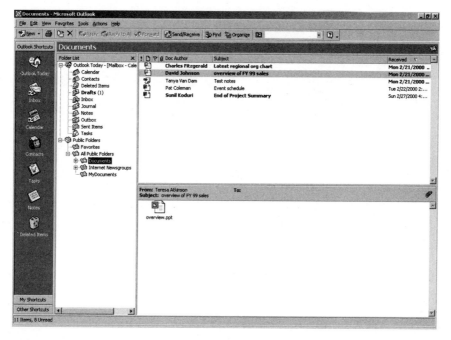

Figure 6-1.
The Web Store accessed from Outlook.

Integration with Microsoft Office 2000

Using the Web Folders feature in Office 2000, users can gain access to Web Store servers and, as a result, open and save documents to the Web Store directly from Office applications, such as Microsoft Word. All that's needed is a server URL for the application to follow "home," so to speak. Figure 6-3 shows a Web folder being accessed through the File | Open command.

Little more needs to be said.

Document Property Storage

Whereas the Web Store's support for multiple clients and its integration with Office 2000 make content easy to access, its ability to store Office document properties helps make it easy for users to find and sort through the information in the Web Store database.

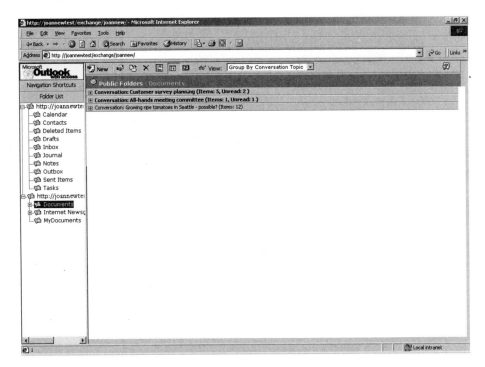

Figure 6-2.
Using Outlook Web Access.

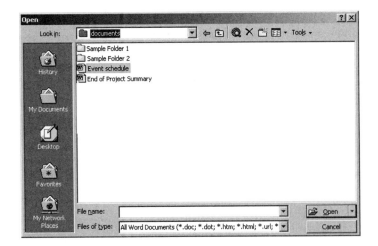

Figure 6-3.
Accessing a Web Store folder through the File | Open command.

This capability, referred to as property promotion, means that users and applications can define and save custom properties, such as author, document description, or recipient. Because these properties are stored with the documents and can be viewed from Microsoft Outlook, they can later be used as the basis for searching and sorting documents—just as sender, subject, date received, and other criteria can currently be used as the basis for searches in Outlook. Figure 6-4 shows a view of custom properties as displayed in Outlook.

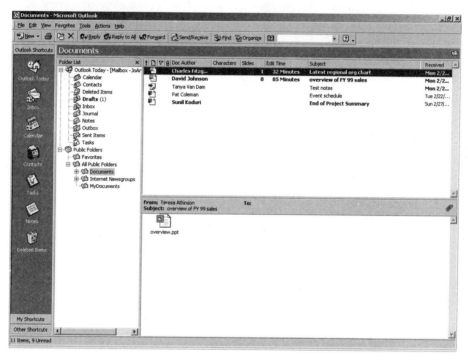

Figure 6-4.
Custom properties in the Outlook client.

Exchange Technology That Makes It Happen

The Web Store is, of course, the Exchange 2000 information store—Web-oriented, remarkably accepting of different types of information, and highly accessible in terms of both client software and ease of use. The preceding sections in this chapter have described the protocols, APIs, clients, and file types it deals with. Now it's time to turn to the technologies that actually make it happen, the foundation on which concept becomes reality.

Exchange 5.5 vs. Exchange 2000

The Exchange 5.5 information store was characterized by a number of features.

- **It was a single-instance store** in which only one copy of a message was kept, even if copies were sent to multiple recipients; this method of storing data was designed to optimize storage
- **It was divided into two core databases,** one public and one private
- Because it was capable of handling up to 16 terabytes of information, **it was more or less without size limits,** depending on the capacity of the hardware on which it was kept
- **It was transacted,** meaning that, to manage information both quickly and efficiently, incoming data was temporarily held in a transaction log file before being written to the actual database

Like the Exchange 5.5 store, the Exchange 2000 store is also a single-instance, transacted store. And it is capable of handling massive amounts of data. However, Exchange 2000 introduces a number of improvements that make it both better and more reliable. The changes include

- **Storage groups,** which support multiple databases
- **A streaming file type,** .stm, for MIME content
- **An installable file system** that supports the Web Store
- **Active/active clustering** for high availability and fail-safe support for mission-critical systems
- **Front-end/back-end servers** that allow for hosting client access protocols separately from the data store
- **Multiple public folder trees** for easier navigation and better administrative control

■ **Internet-based client access**

■ **Content indexing** to support faster and more advanced searches

The following sections provide a look at those features not already covered in this chapter.

Storage Groups and Multiple Databases

As already mentioned, Exchange supports multiple databases that can be distributed across a number of different servers. One primary reason for this change in Exchange 2000 is the time required for recovery in the event that a server fails. For example, under earlier versions of Exchange, recovery was an offline and potentially time-consuming process. Because information was stored in two databases (public and private), specific mailboxes or public folders couldn't be recovered individually. As a result, although Exchange itself was capable of hosting large numbers of users on a single server, organizations found that there were, in effect, practical limits based on the amount of time it could or would take to restore information if the server failed.

Storage Groups

To address this shortcoming, Exchange 2000 supports up to 90 separate databases per server. All databases run under a single process, STORE.EXE, but can be mounted and dismounted individually, so recovery of one can take place without affecting the performance or accessibility of the others.

Although they can be managed individually, these multiple databases aren't like sheep in a pasture, each running off and doing its own thing. Instead, one to six databases are "herded" together as a storage group, which is defined as one instance of the Extensible Storage Engine, or ESE, (the "shepherd") plus the transaction logs ("sheepdogs") for the databases in that group. (Note that ESE is the new name for the Joint Engine Technology, or JET database engine.)

Altogether, a single server can (though it's not recommended) host 15 storage groups of six databases each, for a total of 90 databases, plus one additional storage group reserved for recovery purposes. In the Exchange Management console, storage groups appear under their servers. By default, Exchange creates one storage group called First Storage Group, as shown in the following illustration.

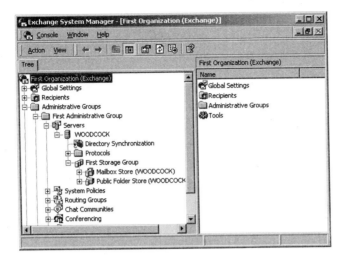

Additional storage groups can be created by right-clicking the name of the server in the tree and choosing Storage Group from the New submenu. The dialog box for creating a new storage group looks like this.

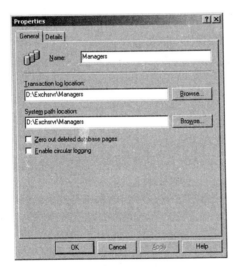

Note the circular logging check box in the illustration. Circular logging saves disk space by overwriting transaction log files once their contents are written to disk. The alternative is the default, sequential logging, which provides more of a fail-safe capacity in that more data—beyond the last backup—remains available for recovery.

Uses for Them All

Ninety databases. That's a lot. What would they hold and how would they be distributed? The most obvious possibility, of special value to ISPs and similar organizations that host multiple companies or other independent groups, is to assign each company or group its own gaggle of databases. Doing this has three primary benefits:

- It keeps each group's data completely separate from the others

- It makes it possible to back up and restore databases independently

- It allows the administrator to assign different storage and data-retention policies to each group

Along the same lines, within an organization, administrators might want to assign separate databases to individuals (executives, say) or groups of individuals. This type of distribution allows for rapid recovery, but it also increases demands on server memory, especially if the assignment is based on one mailbox per database. Generally speaking, although such a distribution can be managed if necessary, the number of databases assigned to individuals should be limited as much as possible.

Practical Considerations

As a general rule of thumb, each database created requires a minimum of 10 MB of memory. (Memory is a more significant consideration than disk space.)

Performance can be improved by hosting the transaction log files on a separate drive. Note also that because transaction logs contain files that haven't yet been written to the database or databases proper, the logs are critical to accurate data recovery and so should be protected from failure through a mechanism such as RAID (Redundant Array of Independent—or Inexpensive—Disks). Bear in mind that the database or databases plus the transaction log *together* mirror the current state of affairs in the system, because information is written *first* to the transaction log and *later* to the database.

Data Storage and Access

In addition to its new policy of spreading the database wealth among servers, Exchange 2000 offers a number of improvements or enhancements in terms of the data store and access to it.

The Streaming Store (.stm)

As mentioned earlier in this chapter, in the section "Streaming Media Files: .stm," Exchange 2000 now provides native support for a more efficient, Internet-oriented multimedia experience for users in the form of streaming files, which are given the extension .stm and are designed to store MIME content directly. (MIME, if you need a refresher, is the acronym for Multi-Purpose Internet Extensions, and is designed to allow e-mail messages to contain different types of data files, including video, audio, and graphics.)

.edb and .stm files   Each Exchange 2000 database includes both the standard, rich-text (.edb) file and an .stm file for streaming Internet content. This division is seen in both public and private stores, so both mailbox and public folder databases consist of both an .edb and an .stm file, as shown below. (Priv1.edb and Priv1.stm are assigned by default to the First Storage Group.)

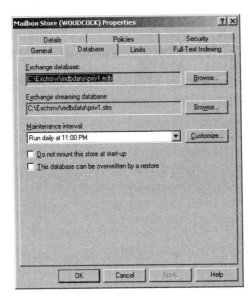

MIME, MAPI, and data conversion   Exchange 2000 supports a streaming store as a response to the complexity and resource demands of earlier versions, which stored all data as MAPI (Messaging API) properties within the rich-text (.edb) database. For example, an incoming SMTP message would be handed to the information store, which would then convert MIME data to MAPI and hold the message for delivery in the .edb file. When the recipient called for the message, the once-converted data would be converted again, this time back to a MIME stream.

To avoid the extra work and potential for error caused by the double conversion, when Exchange 2000 receives data through an Internet protocol, it bundles MIME data directly into the .stm file without conversion. Furthermore, if it receives a "deliver the message" request from an Internet client, it streams the content directly to the client without converting the information at all. The only time conversion takes place—and this is called deferred content conversion— occurs when a MAPI client, such as Outlook 2000, requests delivery. In that case, the store converts the MIME data to MAPI, just once, and delivers the data to the client.

In terms of security, however, it's important to note and remember that STORE.EXE locks the streaming file during normal operation. Although direct file access is not possible, security measures should be in place to guarantee that the database itself remains secure and that users can't see the files directly.

Internet Support

Internet support, in terms of URL access, WebDAV, and Internet-based clients, was covered earlier in the "Features of the Web Store" section of this chapter. It's also important to note that Exchange's information store supports both NNTP (Network News Transfer Protocol) and SMTP (Simple Mail Transport Protocol) which, together, enable users to view and participate in USENET newsgroups as well as send e-mail. In terms of server capability, note that public folders can be promoted to newsgroups and that Exchange 2000 can scale to deal with more than 50,000 newsgroups and a million daily posts.

Multiple Public Folder Trees

In yet another change from earlier versions, Exchange 2000 now supports the ability to host multiple public folder trees, or top-level hierarchies (TLH). This capability, rooted (no pun intended) in Exchange's support for multiple databases, is the basis for two significant changes in the way public folders are handled (by Exchange) and set up (by administrators).

- Whereas earlier versions of Exchange replicated public folders throughout the organization, Exchange 2000 replicates each tree to a single public folder store per server

- Because of this more limited replication, administrators can now restrict selected sets of public folders to individual servers for better control

Who can see them Although multiple public folder trees are eminently creatable, they aren't all necessarily visible to users. Which trees a user sees depends on which client and protocol that person is using.

- **POP3 users**   see none at all

■ **IMAP, MAPI, and WebDAV users** see the main public folder tree—the one installed with Exchange that contains their primary public store

Additional public folder trees are accessible as file repositories through applications and the Installable File System, when the folders are mapped as network drives.

What they can do In addition to holding group-specific or content-specific sets of information, public folders in Exchange 2000 have one additional, very public use: hosting Web sites. Because of the Web Store concept and the fact that Exchange now includes .stm files, Web pages can be placed in public folders for viewing from clients' browsers. Web sites implemented in this way provide better performance than when pages are served from a file system, and they can also be replicated—if need be—in other public folders.

Front-End/Back-End Servers

Also new in Exchange 2000 is a split between the databases and client access protocols. Whereas STORE.EXE managed both in earlier versions of Exchange, Exchange 2000 hands protocol management to IIS (Internet Information Services), which is part of Windows 2000. Within IIS, it runs as a service and makes use of Windows 2000 features, including security and Active Directory services.

Because there is now a distinct separation of store management and protocol management, Exchange 2000 can provide administrators with the ability to deploy front-end servers that handle client access and back-end servers that handle the databases themselves. Although MAPI clients connect directly to the back-end server because they can't use the front-end, other clients (such as IMAP4) go through the following process:

1. The client connects to the front-end server.
2. The front-end server, using the same protocol the client uses, sends the client's request to the back-end server.
3. The back-end server returns the requested data.
4. The front-end server returns the data to the client.

On the surface, separating activity into a front-end/back-end architecture might not seem particularly efficient or effective. However, this type of arrangement offers a number of benefits related to performance and scalability, all of which are tied to the front-end server, which

- Can cache protocol command verbs, such as LIST, to ensure fast access

- Handles client authentication through Active Directory services

- Can "read the client's mind" by anticipating commands (based on what past Internet clients have requested) and having the information ready and waiting in advance

The Installable File System

The Installable File System, or IFS, is yet another new feature in Exchange 2000. Its reason for being is integration. Its purpose is to turn the Exchange store into a home for data belonging to any application. It is, in short, designed to be a one-stop document mart, an all-around repository that turns folders and their contents into objects that can be accessed as file shares.

IFS exists to provide users with a means of finding, accessing, and directly writing information to the .stm file from standard applications such as Internet Explorer and Microsoft Office. In this sense, it actually *is* the Web Store, especially when considered along with such features as content indexing, Web (HTTP) support, and the store's ability to save custom document properties as a matter of course. Through the combination of IFS and these additional features, users gain the ability to perform sophisticated searches and to access documents with applications and Web clients.

Structurally, the IFS folder hierarchy resides on drive M: on the computer running Exchange. This drive corresponds to the domain name (for example, *sample.local*) and can be shared out as a network drive. Once this drive is shared out, users can then access shared resources by mapping their own local drives to folders or their mailboxes in the IFS hierarchy. Within this hierarchy, IFS contains two default folders: \Public Folders and \Mbx (mailboxes).

- **The public folders and their contents** can be listed and viewed with (shades of the DOS command line!) standard file-system commands, including Dir, Copy, and Delete

- **Mailboxes,** although individually invisible, can be accessed by users with permissions by specifying the path to a specific mailbox

Clustering

The last, though far from least, technology to mention here in relation to the Web Store is clustering—the active/active grouping of servers (explained below) as a means of ensuring high availability, reliability, and data integrity. Although clustering, along with Exchange's support for multiple databases, provides obvious benefits to the Web Store and its contents, it's a Windows 2000 feature that affects a number of Exchange services, including chat and conferencing. As such, this section provides a glimpse of clustering as it relates to Exchange and the information store. A more detailed description follows in Chapter 7, "Scalability and Reliability."

To begin with, clustering is the practice of grouping servers in such a way that, even though they're separate, independent computers, they appear to the network as a single unit. They work cooperatively to ensure that, if one fails, another is ready to take over and continue offering service.

In the Windows 2000/Exchange 2000 world, clustering has been implemented in two different ways:

- **In Exchange 5.5,**   the first version in which this feature was supported, clustering was of the active/passive variety, meaning that Exchange Server could be running on only one node at a time. In the event of failure, the passive node would take over.

- **In Exchange 2000,**   clustering is active/active, meaning that Exchange services can run simultaneously on all the servers in a cluster. If one fails, another takes over the failed server's responsibilities, as well as continuing to handle its own.

Nodes and Virtual Servers

Within a cluster, servers can be grouped in clumps of two, three, or four. Each of the servers is known as a *node* and is connected both to the other servers in the cluster and to a shared storage device. Furthermore, each node can run one or more virtual servers, as shown in the following illustration.

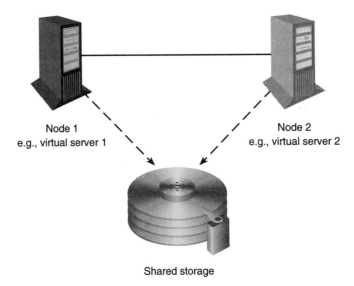

Node 1
e.g., virtual server 1

Node 2
e.g., virtual server 2

Shared storage

To the client, a virtual server is as real as a physical server, in that it has a unique name and IP address. Unlike a physical server, however, a virtual server isn't associated with specific hardware. Thus, if a problem occurs on the virtual server's host node, the virtual server can be moved to another node in the cluster and clients can—once the move has occurred—continue to access the server using the same name.

Resource Groups

In terms of Exchange, storage groups can be assigned to the cluster as resource groups. (Storage groups, you'll recall, are made up of one instance of the ESE transaction logging system, up to six databases, and the transaction logs for those databases.) These resource groups, although they "belong" to individual virtual servers, actually reside on the shared storage medium. Thus, if one (or more) of the virtual servers in the cluster are running on a node that fails, it (or they) can be moved temporarily to one of the healthy nodes in the cluster. The result: high availability for Web Store messaging, as well as for chat and other Exchange services.

And there you have it. The concept of a Web Store; the Internet protocols, clients, APIs, and standards that make it work; and the Exchange 2000 information store, databases, and features that support it. This is the new face of Exchange, designed to unify messaging and make information and collaboration readily available to the knowledge workers who drive large parts of the world's economy.

CHAPTER SEVEN

Scalability and Reliability

The emphasis of Exchange 2000 on scalability and reliability has been mentioned numerous times so far, typically in sentences such as "this [new] feature enables Exchange to scale up to X users" or "this [new] feature provides for high reliability." But while sentences scattered here and there can provide an overall favorable impression of scalability and reliability, it's also helpful to be able to jump directly to a section of the book that focuses on these issues.

NOTE: Much of this chapter deals with features that are included in the Enterprise, but not in the Server version of Exchange 2000.

Overall, the Exchange 2000 features that contribute to scalability and reliability include:

- **Multiple databases,** which reduce backup and restore time, as well as extend both scalability and reliability

- **Active/active clustering,** which focuses on improved reliability and accessibility for the end user

- **Load balancing,** which represents another form of clustering—one focused on distributing traffic across multiple servers rather than (as in active/active clustering) concentrating on safeguarding accessibility in case of server failure

- **Distributed configuration architecture,** which allows for partitioning services onto multiple servers and, in the process, allows Exchange to scale up to match the needs of ISPs, large-scale enterprises, ASPs, and the like

- **The Web Store (see Chapter 6)** which, through its reliance on storage groups, multiple databases, clustering, and native MIME storage, offers both scalability and reliability combined with Internet integration and rapid delivery of streaming media files

■ **Use of Microsoft Windows 2000 security (see Chapter 5),** which addresses centralized management along with reliability (in the security sense)

As you can see, some of these areas have been covered in previous chapters and need little additional description. Their mention here is primarily to reinforce their importance as contributors to Exchange 2000 accessibility, scalability, and reliability. The primary focus of this chapter is the first four items: multiple databases, clustering, load balancing, and distributed configuration.

Multiple Databases

The multiple databases in Exchange, with their ability to support a possible, though not recommended, 90 databases in 15 storage groups per server, obviously contribute enormously to the product's ability to scale up to handle the messaging needs of millions of users. There are, equally obviously, good and not so good ways to arrange these databases to maximize performance and ensure safe, reliable backup and recovery.

Single-Instance Storage

Exchange 2000, like Exchange 5.5, relies on single-instance storage to minimize the amount of disk space required to hold messages sent to more than one individual. Because of its multiple databases, however, Exchange 2000 implements single-instance storage with a bit of a twist. A message is stored once, even if sent to dozens of people, *if* those people's mailboxes are in the same database. If the mailboxes aren't in the same database, however, the message is sent to each necessary database or, if the databases inhabit different storage groups, to each database and the transaction log for each storage group.

Exchange 2000 implementation is thus still single-instance storage, in that each database receives a single copy. But instead of one copy stored in one large mail store, the Exchange 2000 approach is what you might call "multiple single-instance storage" (no, that's not a real term). That's because the same message can be copied once to a number of databases and transaction logs, depending on how many storage groups are involved and on how the recipient mailboxes are distributed among their databases.

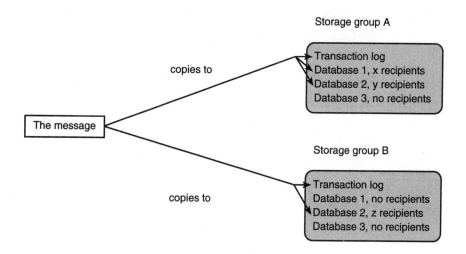

Transactions and Transaction Logs

To ensure fault-tolerance and the ability to recover message stores even after a server crash or other severe failure, Exchange 2000, like earlier versions, relies on transactions recorded in a transaction log file. To Exchange, a transaction is a set of changes—inserts, deletions, updates, and so on—made to the database on disk. To guarantee the integrity of the database, however, a transaction is defined as an all-or-none proposition. That is, all of the changes in the transaction must be completed, or none will be recorded. So, before any transaction is committed to the database, Exchange ensures that the entire set of operations, recorded in the transaction log, can be "replayed" and reconstructed if necessary.

As for the transaction logs themselves, their size varies depending on how backup and restore are configured, but Exchange 2000 (or rather the Extensible Storage Engine [ESE]) sets aside 5 MB per log file and creates a new log file each time the old one reaches 5 MB. (The old one is not deleted, however, unless circular logging is turned on.) The ESE also handles the movement of transactions into the databases.

In essence, transaction logs serve as the failsafe intermediaries between memory and the database or databases on disk. As transactions flow into Exchange, they are first cached in memory. To ensure no loss of data, transactions are then written to the transaction log files and later, when time permits, they are committed from the logs to the databases in which they belong.

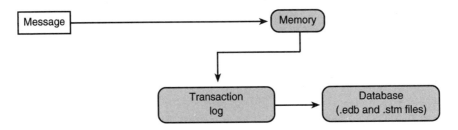

This architecture provides Exchange with several benefits.

- **It contributes to speed in sending messages,** because writing to log files is quicker and less complex than writing to the actual databases.

- **It ensures that all messages can be recovered even after a power outage.** Even messages that had not been committed to the database before the outage can be fully recovered, because the transaction log plus the database provide a complete record of all transactions up to the moment of failure.

- **It enables recovery on a database-by-database basis,** because each transaction is associated with a database ID, even though all databases in a storage group rely on a shared transaction log.

Log and Data Drives

In Exchange 2000, each storage group of one to six databases relies on one set of transaction log files and a single instance of the ESE transaction logging system. Because the transaction logs are really the only means of reconciling data in memory with data in the databases, they are as crucial as the databases themselves in guaranteeing the smooth and successful operation of a messaging system based on Exchange Server. As such, Microsoft recommends certain practices in setting up and managing the transaction logs and databases.

For transaction logs:

- **Protect the drives against hardware failure** through a means such as disk mirroring (RAID) to insure against possible data loss.

- **Keep the transaction logs and databases on separate drives** for optimum performance and to isolate the log files from failures that affect the databases.

■ **Maximize performance** by making the number of transaction log drives per server equal to the number of storage groups, and place each transaction log set on a separate spindle.

■ **Always format the file system for Microsoft NTFS 5.0.**

■ **Leave circular logging turned off.** Circular logging is a holdover from days when disk space was at a premium. It allowed log files to be maintained at a fixed size by overwriting their data once it had been committed to disk. Circular logging has two major disadvantages:

❑ It allows information to be restored only to the last full backup rather than to the last transaction.

❑ It doesn't allow for incremental or differential backups, both of which require complete transaction logs. (An incremental backup copies changed transaction log data since the last full or incremental backup and deletes the transaction log files. A differential backup copies changed transaction log data since the last full backup and doesn't delete the transaction logs.)

For database drives:

■ **Help ensure accessibility, reliability, and scalability with clustering** (described in the next section). Clustering allows for backup nodes (servers) to take up the slack if the server for one of the storage groups in the cluster happens to fail.

■ **Address data security.** Although more than one storage group can be housed on a single drive, the data is extremely valuable. To help protect it, provide fault tolerance in the form of RAID striping with distributed parity or striping (writing across multiple disks) and mirroring (duplicating data on separate disks). Additional security, if supported by the RAID controller, can be provided by online spares or "hot" standby disks.

Clustering

NOTE: Clustering requires either Windows 2000 Advanced Server or Windows 2000 Datacenter Server.

Although Exchange 2000 supports clustering, the feature itself belongs to Windows 2000—specifically, either Windows 2000 Advanced Server or Windows

2000 Datacenter Server. As a Windows feature, clustering is installed through the operating system's Configure Your Server utility.

The Cluster Itself

As explained in Chapter 6, a cluster (also known as a server cluster) is a group of computers, with shared storage, that work together as if they were a single unit. Each computer in the cluster is called a node. These nodes make online resources available to users without the users ever knowing, or needing to know, that the host is one of several computers in the cluster. Windows 2000 Advanced Server supports two-node clusters; Windows 2000 Datacenter Server supports four-node clusters. A typical two-node cluster looks like the following illustration.

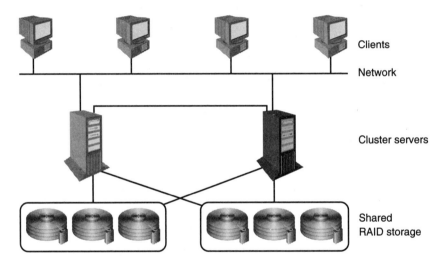

To coordinate their activities, nodes in a cluster send messages to one another. These messages, in turn, are controlled by clustering software, which falls into two categories.

- **The Cluster service** is the cluster's administrative and maintenance software, so to speak. It is a set of components that runs on each node and takes care of both ordinary and extraordinary chores related to keeping the cluster going. On the ordinary level, it handles communication between nodes. On the extraordinary level, it takes charge of restarting failed applications when necessary or, in more dire circumstances, distributing the workload from a failed node to the other members of the cluster.

- **The Resource Monitor,** in contrast, is resource-oriented software. Like the Cluster service, it runs on each node, but instead of facilitating communication between nodes, it passes requests between the Cluster service and the resources (resource DLLs, actually) hosted on the node. Thus, when the Cluster service needs something from a resource, the Resource Monitor passes the request to the appropriate resource. Conversely, when a resource needs to send information to the Cluster service, the Resource Monitor guarantees delivery.

Even though they both run on each node, the Resource Monitor and the Cluster service are separate processes for two important reasons:

- First, so that the Cluster service and its vital functions are protected from resource failures.

- Second, so that the Resource Monitor itself can act as a failsafe for the Cluster service. It is designed to take all resources and affected groups offline if the Cluster service fails on one of the cluster nodes. Thus, the Resource Monitor provides backup support within backup support, all with reliability in mind.

Virtual Servers and Resource Groups

Within the cluster, programs and services run on virtual servers—logical devices that can be hosted by any node and that users connect to just as they would to physical servers. Each virtual server has its own name and is associated with a unique IP address, which is published and managed by the Cluster service.

These virtual servers represent resource groups. A resource group is defined as a set of resources that can be

- Managed by the cluster

- Brought online and taken offline as a unit

- Hosted, or "owned," by only one node at a time

Resource groups are moved to another node as a single unit, and each resource group is associated with two cluster-related policies:

- The server it should run on
- The server to which it should be moved in case of failure

Thus, if the server hosting a resource group—a virtual server to Windows 2000—happens to fail, the Cluster service takes care of two operations:

- Moving the group to a new, functional node in the cluster
- Reassigning the IP address of the resource group's virtual server to the new node, so that clients can connect as they did before, even though the server's resources are now hosted on a different machine

Clustering and Exchange

To Exchange, clustering is a means of supporting high availability and mission-critical operations such as NNTP newsfeeds and the information-store databases that hold Exchange messages and Web Store content.

As mentioned in Chapter 6, the big change from Exchange 5.5 (the first version to support clusters) is the switch from active/passive to active/active clustering. Whereas Exchange 5.5 could run on only one node in the cluster and the fallback node was essentially redundant (in terms of Exchange) until needed, Exchange 2000 services can run on all nodes in the cluster, and thus all nodes can participate in serving the needs of users in the enterprise.

In Exchange 2000 clusters, the basic resource unit (and the unit that is moved in event of failure) is the virtual server. The virtual server, in turn, is responsible for the resources (storage groups) kept on the cluster's shared physical storage. Thus, if the node hosting the virtual server happens to fail, the actual storage groups remain on the physical disk, but the virtual server is moved to a new node and the Cluster service reassigns the virtual server's IP address to operate from the new node.

Nodes and Storage Groups

Because Exchange services can and do run on more than one computer in the cluster, it's important to ensure that each of the nodes has the ability to take on the extra workload it must if one of the other nodes fails. Essentially, this means following the rule that there should be one less storage group per node than there are nodes in the cluster. In other words

- **In a two-node cluster,** each node should have one storage group defined
- **In a four-node cluster,** each node should have three storage groups defined

In addition

- Servers in a two-node cluster should run under 50% load
- Servers in a three-node cluster should run under 66% load
- Servers in a four-node cluster should run under 75% load

Load Balancing

Load balancing, the ability to distribute requests across multiple servers, is a feature related to and capable of being used with both clustering and the front-end/back-end distributed architecture described in the "Distributed Configuration" section of this chapter.

Like clustering, load balancing—or rather the Network Load Balancing service—is a feature of Windows 2000 Advanced Server and Datacenter Server. In a way, load balancing is clustering, but in another, significant way, it's not.

- **Network Load Balancing is clustering** in that it relies on a group of servers—up to 32 of them—to distribute workload
- **Network Load Balancing is not clustering** (as described above) in that it exists to distribute incoming traffic across the servers in the cluster, rather than to provide failover service if hardware or software on one node in the cluster happens to fail

In other words, the Network Load Balancing service emphasizes high performance and scalability, as is needed by World Wide Web and e-commerce servers. The failover type of server clustering is primarily designed to provide reliability and unbroken accessibility, typically to databases such as the Exchange stores and, of course, those handled by Microsoft SQL Server.

On the other hand, even though load balancing clusters and server clusters have different objectives, they can be used together to provide the advantages of both, as shown in the following diagram.

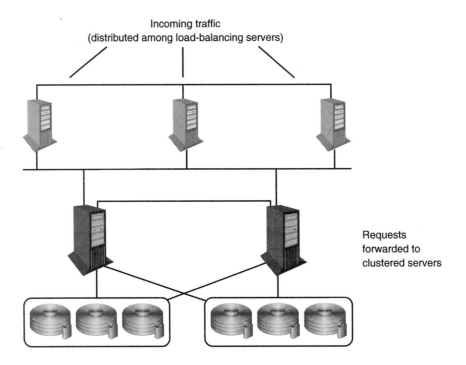

Network Load Balancing Service in a Nutshell

Windows 2000 Network Load Balancing service is designed to grab incoming TCP/IP traffic and distribute it evenly across the servers in a load-balancing cluster. The cluster is assigned a single IP address (or a set of addresses if the host is multihomed, that is, connected to multiple networks). To clients, there's no difference between the hosts in the cluster and a single server—except when a host fails or is taken offline. In that case, load balancing redirects traffic to working hosts and, because the client will typically retry when a connection is lost, the end user experiences no more than a second or two of delay until a working server responds.

Within a cluster, all the host servers belong to the same IP subnet, and all "listen in" on requests arriving at the cluster's primary IP address. As the requests arrive, the host servers map clients by packet information, including IP address and port, and thus determine which host gains the honor of servicing the request.

Distributed Configuration

Distributed configuration in Exchange 2000 refers to its support for subsystems— directory, protocols, and information store—to be placed on different servers. Thus, a bank of front-end servers can be dedicated to the tasks of handling incoming client connections, and back-end servers can be dedicated to the job of managing the databases the users need. Not surprisingly, this ability to spread the load across multiple servers accounts for the capacity of Exchange to scale upward to meet the needs of millions of users. Assigning authentication and, if used, Secure Sockets Layer (SSL) encryption and decryption to the front-end servers enhances performance of the network by eliminating such processing from the back-end servers.

This same separation of powers also contributes to the reliability of Exchange. The vital components are no longer locked onto one or a few servers, and component failures can thus be isolated from one another and corrected without affecting the entire system. In addition, because directory services—now a Windows 2000 function—need not be hosted on each Exchange server, distribution also contributes to flexibility in implementation.

Distributed configuration is especially visible in Exchange support for front-end/back-end servers. It allows separation of Exchange databases from the Internet access protocols that can come knocking on their server doors. As described in Chapter 6, access protocols are now handled by the Windows 2000 Internet Information Service (IIS)—specifically, INETINFO.EXE—and are thus no longer part of the information store managed by STORE.EXE.

"Epoxy"

On the surface, the need to enable two pieces of software (INETINFO.EXE and STORE.EXE) to communicate and coordinate their activities might seem less efficient than the approach taken by Exchange 5.5. After all, Exchange 5.5 included Internet protocols such as POP3, NNTP, and IMAP as part of STORE.EXE.

In actuality, Exchange 2000 and IIS manage just fine, thanks to a special queuing layer known as EXIPC (formerly, "Epoxy"), which works with STORE.EXE and INETINFO.EXE and enables them to swap information rapidly and thus provide fast protocol-to-store access.

Creating a Front-End Server

Creating (or un-creating) a front-end server is a simple matter. All it takes is a single checkbox on the server's properties sheet...

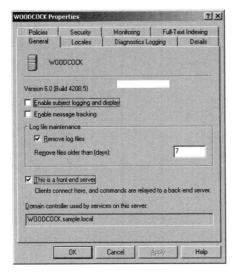

...and either a reboot of the system or a restart of the POP, IMAP, and HTTP services.

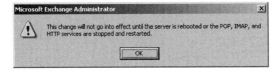

Routing Requests to the Back-End Server

Exchange makes it possible for users to connect to multiple front-end servers through a unified namespace. These servers invisibly provide access to back-end database servers. Because Exchange provides this capability, it (and its administrators) must also provide some means of ensuring that

- Users are connected to the correct back-end servers
- The incoming traffic is distributed evenly across the front-end servers

There are three ways to accomplish this. In order of preference, they are:

- **Use of Windows 2000 Network Load Balancing service**
- **Round-robin DNS,** which loops through server IP addresses as they are passed out to clients in a rotating, fixed order—in other

words, the order 1, 2, 3, 4 becomes 2, 3, 4, 1, which becomes 3, 4, 1, 2, and so on

- **Statically mapping the server name to the client**

Front-End/Back-End Servers and Outlook Web Access

Microsoft Outlook Web Access, as you might recall, is installed by default as part of Exchange. Though not as full-featured as the standard Microsoft Outlook client, it is a valuable means of providing access through browser software in a number of different situations.

- To suit the needs of roaming and remote users

- To support users of UNIX, Macintosh, and PCs that lack enough memory or hard disk storage for the standard Outlook client

- To provide a simple but effective cross-platform messaging solution to organizations that don't require much beyond basic e-mail, scheduling, and collaboration capability

- To deliver extranet functionality to vendors and other external users

Outlook Web Access can be installed and run on a single server. But it is also tailor-made for front-end/back-end server support involving multiple servers, if for no other reason than implementing a distributed architecture allows users to access their mail through a single namespace. Administratively, this approach also ensures that servers and mailboxes can be moved without affecting the URL used to access them, and Outlook Web Access itself can be scaled to meet the needs of an expanding organization.

Front-end/back-end configuration with Outlook Web Access involves the following:

- **An Exchange virtual server,** which is listed in the tree under the HTTP protocol folder in the Exchange Management console

- **A hostname for the server,** which forms the first essential part of the URL used to access user mailboxes

- **A maildirectory** (named *exchange* by default), which follows the host name and is also essential for accessing user mailboxes

- **A userid for each user,** which is the user's alias and serves to identify him or her to the system

Thus, internal (intranet) users accessing their mailboxes through a browser would type the URL as

```
http://hostname/exchange/userid/
```

Users connecting from outside, over the Internet, use the same basic format, but replace the host name with the organization's domain name.

```
http://domain.com/exchange/userid
```

And finally, to access public folders—by default placed in the *public* portion of the virtual server's folder hierarchy—users omit the mail directory but include the path to the particular folder they want.

```
http://hostname/public/foldername
```

Note that in a mixed environment that includes both Exchange 5.5 and Exchange 2000 servers, public folders can be accessed only on Exchange 2000 servers with Outlook Web Access, even though the feature also exists in Exchange 5.5. In addition, to ensure that servers don't become overloaded, Microsoft recommends distributing traffic either through use of Network Load Balancing or through round-robin DNS. Of the two, Network Load Balancing is more reliable, because round-robin DNS doesn't automatically allow for forwarding requests sent to a nonfunctioning server.

CHAPTER EIGHT

Information Flow and Routing

Networks, large and small, have two features in common. They move information from place to place, and they provide storage for that information when and as necessary. The information might flow from client to server, server to client, server to server, or client to server to a network device such as a printer. At some point on this route, the storage required might be permanent (for network-resident information) or temporary (for information as it travels from source to destination). Regardless, all networks move and store information. Message flow and routing determine when, where, and how that information gets moved from place to place.

A Myriad of Destinations

Where Exchange is involved, some information—such as directory replication data—passes only between servers. However, even though transferring such information is crucial, such transfers are secondary in the sense that they are needed to support the larger objective of Exchange: moving messages and other data from clients to the information store and from there to their intended destinations.

Of course, any given message could be destined for a host of locations, both within and outside the network. At one extreme, for example, a message might end up no further away than the office next door, even though the information itself must travel over the network from the sender to the Exchange server and then to the recipient. But even if the route itself is hardly a straight line, if both of these Exchange clients are in the same domain and on the same server, such next-door delivery is relatively simple. Exchange merely needs to log the message, check the directory, and pop the message directly into the recipient's mailbox.

At the other extreme, however, a message might need to be delivered to numerous recipients in different buildings, organizations, cities, or countries.

Almost certainly, these recipients' mailboxes would be housed in different databases, and even those users in the same Exchange organization could well have mailboxes residing on different servers. Furthermore, the recipients themselves could be scattered throughout multiple domains and domain trees. Mail delivery in this situation is a more complicated matter. It can involve different protocols as well as routing based on connectors, multiple hops, and temporary queuing until a scheduled, nonpermanent connection can be established for delivery—say, from one country to another.

Simple or complex, direct or indirect, Exchange is responsible for both routing and delivering the mail.

Message Flow and Message Routing

There are, when you think about it, two different aspects to message transfer in Exchange. There is the movement—the flow—of messages through Microsoft Windows and Exchange, and there is also the movement—the routing—of messages from server to server.

- **Message flow** in Windows and Exchange involves such features as built-in support for SMTP by the operating system and Exchange, as well as their built-in support for other Internet protocols, including IMAP4, POP3, and NNTP. Within Exchange itself, message flow also involves routing, queuing, categorizing, and communication between protocols and the information store.

- **Message routing** from server to server, on the other hand, involves routing groups, connectors, and link state tables. It might also involve the hosting of the Exchange protocol, storage, and directory subsystems on separate servers (the front-end/back-end division of services described in Chapter 7).

This chapter covers both types of message transfer.

Message Flow

Much ado has already been made, both here and in Microsoft white papers and documentation, about the tight integration of Exchange and Windows 2000. This integration is most extensive where Microsoft Active Directory services is concerned, but it also affects other areas, including clustering, administration, and security.

Integration also has an effect on message flow, although in this area the connection between Windows and Exchange might be better described as a partnership than as integration. In other words, integration is highly visible in areas such as the complete reliance by Exchange on Windows 2000 for Active Directory services, cluster management, and security. But where messaging is concerned:

- Even though Windows 2000 installs core Internet protocol stacks, including SMTP, for handling tasks such as replication and basic messaging, it is Exchange 2000 that extends these stacks to boost functionality to the levels required by enterprise-class messaging, message transfer, and collaboration.

- Even though Windows 2000 runs Internet protocols as part of the Internet Information Service, or IIS process, it is Exchange that takes advantage of IIS to support front-end/back-end hosting that allows scalability up to millions of users.

Separation of Powers: IIS and the Information Store

As mentioned in Chapter 7, Internet protocols were built into the information store in Exchange 5.5 primarily to ensure rapid access to messages. In Exchange 2000, these protocols, including SMTP, POP3, IMAP4, and NNTP, have been removed from the store and are handled separately by Internet Information Services 5.0, the IIS process.

Within Windows 2000, IIS runs as a service, making use of other Windows services, including security and, of course, Active Directory services. IIS is included in Windows to support tasks related to the World Wide Web, such as site creation and management. However, because it now contains SMTP, NNTP, and other Internet protocols formerly included in the Exchange information store, IIS is also needed by Exchange for message routing and the instant messaging described in Chapter 10.

Although Internet protocols are now separate from the information store and, in fact, are handled by a completely separate service, message flow in Exchange 2000 does not suffer. Both protocols and store can depend on rapid communication, thanks to the new Exchange queuing layer, the Exchange Interprocess Communication layer, or EXIPC ("Epoxy") introduced in Chapter 7. Situated between IIS and the information store, EXIPC serves as an intermediary between the two, as shown in the following illustration.

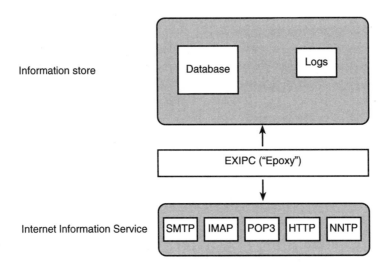

EXIPC relies on protocol DLLs on both the IIS and information store sides, as well as on shared memory and pairs of queues to create protocol-specific communication pathways between IIS and information store processes. Acting somewhat like reserved lanes on a freeway (carpool or bus lanes, for example), these pathways are what enable high-performance information exchange. A closer look at these links between EXIPC, IIS, and the store—illustrated by one protocol, SMTP—is shown in the following illustration.

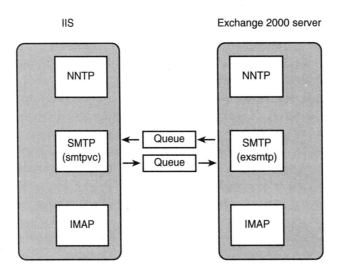

SMTP

SMTP is now the native transport in Exchange 2000, and SMTP message flow in Exchange begins with message flow in Windows 2000 Server—specifically, with Windows listening in at port 25 (the default) for incoming SMTP mail.

Advantages of SMTP

Recall that SMTP runs in Exchange 2000 as a peer to X.400 and is, in fact, the default transport for traffic routing both within and between sites. Although X.400 is still used to connect Exchange computers with X.400 messaging systems, SMTP is the primary messaging protocol in Exchange 2000, for two reasons:

- SMTP has replaced X.400 over the past few years as a standard messaging protocol throughout the world. Thus, the use of SMTP as the primary protocol ensures that Exchange can interoperate well with both the Internet and other messaging systems.

- SMTP, along with the Exchange 2000 elimination of reliance on remote procedure, calls for intra-site communication and the new distinction between routing groups and administrative groups, provides for more flexibility in deployment. Deployment can now be based on administrative needs rather than on bandwidth availability.

SMTP from the Administrator's View

Although SMTP message flow happens invisibly, the Exchange Management console displays the SMTP servers that actually show the results of all the queuing, routing, and delivery required. These servers are the tools administrators use for configuring, viewing, and managing SMTP and its mail queues and message delivery.

SMTP Virtual Servers

At the heart of SMTP mail delivery are its virtual servers. Virtual servers are defined as single instances of the SMTP protocol service and, by default, each physical server hosts one virtual SMTP server. A physical server can be configured to host multiple virtual servers, but note that

- **Each virtual server is multithreaded** so multiple virtual servers on a single physical server are generally configured to support different messaging services or authentication needs, rather than to increase scalability.

■ **All virtual servers on a physical server must belong to the same routing group.** A single physical server can't cover more than one routing group.

Whether a physical server hosts one or more than one virtual server, each virtual machine is defined and distinguished by its own name, as well as its own configuration information, including IP address, port number, access settings, and message limits. The server is, by default, named Default SMTP Virtual Server, but it's easy to change the name to something more expressive with a right-click and the Rename command.

NOTE: To view a virtual server, open the Exchange Management console and then expand, in turn, the Servers node, the Exchange server on which the virtual server resides, and then the Protocols and SMTP nodes under the server name.

As shown in the following graphic, each virtual server includes three components: domains, current sessions, and the queues used for message handling and delivery.

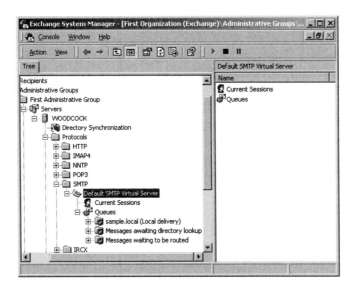

The virtual server The virtual server itself is, of course, the primary SMTP component. It's the one through which administrators set and control such parameters as IP address, logging format, access restrictions, number of concurrent connections, message size, number of recipients per message, and directory used for "bad mail" (messages whose destination can't be determined and which thus provoke a non-delivery report, or NDR). The following illustration shows the Properties sheet and some of these items for the default SMTP server installed by Exchange.

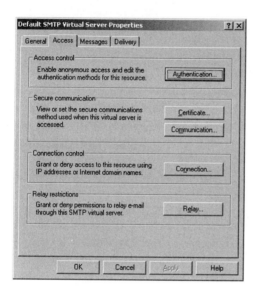

Current sessions The Current Sessions node under each virtual server displays information about users. This information includes user, source location, and connection time for each session. Right-clicking the Current Sessions node also allows the administrator to use the Terminate All command if necessary.

Queues SMTP queues include pre-categorizing and pre-routing queues, as well as queues for messages to be delivered. Some queues, such as the one for delivery to the local domain, are static. Queues for outgoing mail, however, are dynamic, depending on where the messages are to be delivered. Administrators can administer both queues and the messages within them, and can also use queues as a means of resolving bottlenecks and other problems related to message flow in the organization.

Directories   (Although the term *directories* is used in this section, the objects of attention here are collections of messages, not Active Directory services information. Think of these directories as file folders.)

The Exchange Management console doesn't display directories the way it displays domains and queues, but directories are nonetheless critical to message processing and delivery. Each time an SMTP virtual server is created, Exchange creates a folder for it. This folder is given the name *vsi* followed by a number. Thus, the default SMTP virtual server is assigned folder vsi 1, and folders vsi 2, vsi 3, and so on are assigned to additional virtual servers. Each vsi folder holds three default directories for its virtual server. These are:

- **Badmail,**   for undeliverable messages. These are the messages that prompt the SMTP service to return the message to the sender along with an NDR. If the NDR can't be delivered, the message is sent to Badmail purgatory.

- **Pickup,**   for outgoing RFC 822-formatted messages created as text files. Messages in this folder are picked up by SMTP and sent on for delivery.

- **Queue,**   for messages that can't be delivered immediately. SMTP attempts to resend messages in the Queue directory at designated intervals.

SMTP Configuration Options

For each SMTP virtual server, administrators can control a number of options, which fall into the four broad categories identified by the tabs on the server properties sheet. These categories are:

- General
- Access
- Messages
- Delivery

The General tab   The General tab covers properties of the server itself—its identity in terms of port number and IP address, the type of logging (the same as other IIS services) for messages handled by the server, and both the number of concurrent connections and the timeout period for each connection.

The Access tab The Access tab (shown in the illustration on page 179) covers properties related to security and message relay. This is where, for example, administrators can restrict access to the SMTP port by

- Requiring authentication

- Associating a certificate with the server

- Allowing (and disallowing) connections from specific computers, as identified by IP address, subnet, or domain name

In addition, the Access tab offers control over e-mail itself. Although the Windows 2000 SMTP server restricts message relay to authenticated users, administrators can use the Access tab to extend service to additional users through specification of, again, IP addresses, subnets, or domain names.

Conversely, the Exchange default allows anyone to relay messages through the SMTP server because Exchange installations are typically intranet rather than Internet. This behavior, however, opens the door to junk mail and spoofing (pretending to be someone else, or rather, someone else's computer). To give administrators control over such nuisances, the Access tab can be used to set up the virtual server to disable message relaying from any but a known host, as identified by its IP address, group IP address, or domain name.

The Messages tab Because SMTP server resources are so valuable, messages and message sessions have, by default, the following size and scope limits:

- Message size: 2048 KB

- SMTP session size: 10,240 KB

- Messages per connection: 20

- Recipients per message: 64,000

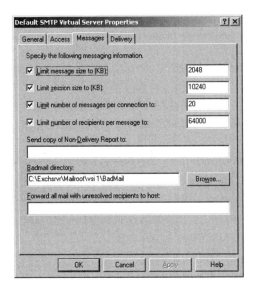

Messaging needs, however, vary with the organization, and so administrators can adjust these default values to customize Exchange performance and functionality. One organization, for example, might find it necessary to reduce the number of recipients per message to maintain optimal network performance.

NOTE: If the number of recipients exceeds the number allowed, the Exchange routing engine generates multiple copies of the message. For example, if 100 recipients are allowed and a message is addressed to 200, the routing engine would send one copy to the first 100 allowed individuals, and a second copy to the remaining 100 recipients. All recipients, however, would be listed on both copies.

Similarly, because additional connections are opened when the number of messages exceeds the number of connections, another organization might need to adjust the number of messages per connection to optimize network load or compensate for restricted bandwidth.

Finally, the Messages tab is also the place where administrators can specify the Badmail directory, tell Exchange whether and where to forward undeliverable messages, and where to send NDR reports.

The Delivery tab   Message delivery is, of course, the reason SMTP exists in the first place. Delivery is not, however, a simple process of sending bits or bytes to a port and assuming they'll arrive as intended. Although SMTP does attempt to deliver a message immediately, there are times when a connection is down or the network experiences some temporary problem. The Delivery tab allows administrators to configure the server to handle such circumstances. Among the options on this tab are the ability to specify—for both local and remote deliveries—the number of delivery retries and the delay and expiration periods before Exchange sends an NDR to the sender.

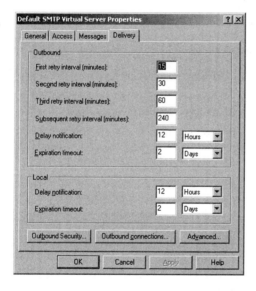

The Delivery tab is also where administrators can set authentication and encryption requirements for outgoing connections to other SMTP servers and define both the number of connections and timeout (in minutes) for outbound connections.

And, finally, advanced properties on the Delivery tab allow for the following:

- **Setting the maximum number of hops**   (to prevent messages from looping through the system) before an NDR is issued.

- **Setting a masquerade domain,**   a domain name that replaces the local domain name on the Mail From line in the SMTP protocol.

■ **Identifying a smart host** which is a remote server that, as described in the "Reaching Other Systems" section of this chapter, both receives all outgoing messages from the SMTP server and takes responsibility for delivery.

■ **Enabling reverse DNS lookup** on the addresses of incoming messages to verify the identity of the message sender.

Inside SMTP

Although administrators are not involved in the actual—electronic—message packaging, routing, and delivery, it certainly doesn't hurt to know what goes on inside the SMTP engine.

Exchange Extensions to SMTP

The basic SMTP support installed as part of Windows 2000 is designed to enable the operating system and other products to take advantage of a known transport for tasks such as replication (Windows) and document notification (Office 2000). When Exchange is installed, it

■ **Adds a secondary store drive,** DRVIIS.DLL, which provides for message pickup and "drop off" through communication with the information store by way of EXIPC

■ **Installs a routing engine** designed to enhance routing capabilities with link-state information (near real-time next-hop information about server availability) that allows cost-effective, efficient delivery between routing groups

Exchange also extends SMTP functionality in several areas, including

■ **Additional command verbs** that support transmission of link state information between servers

■ **An advanced queuing engine** that manages message-delivery queues

■ **A message categorizer** (a plug-in component of the advanced queuing engine) that determines where messages are to be delivered and, additionally, expands distribution lists

Inbound Message Flow

All told, Exchange uses SMTP for three functions: as a protocol for client messages, for routing messages from server to server, and for exchanging replication and other information, as mentioned earlier.

The various SMTP components are the pieces required to ensure a smooth, reliable flow of messages. Essentially, these components work together as follows for incoming messages:

1. When a message arrives, the IIS SMTP server creates an envelope for it—a message structure called IMAILMSG.

2. On successful receipt of the message, the SMTP server writes both the envelope and the message to disk, in a Queue directory, with the help of the NTFS store driver.

3. The message is then handed over to the advanced queuing engine, which places the message in a pre-categorizing queue (PreCatQueue) and then sends it on to the message categorizer.

4. The message categorizer determines where the message is to be delivered and, if necessary, expands the message's distribution list. After determining whether the message should be sent to the local store, the Message Transfer Agent (for non-SMTP delivery), or the SMTP engine, it returns the message to the advanced queuing engine.

5. The advanced queuing engine places the message in a pre-routing queue (PreRoutingQueue) until its delivery route can be determined and sends the destination to the routing engine.

6. The routing engine now responds with a next-hop identifier for the message's destination (or the next stop in a multiple-hop destination).

7. Finally, armed with destination information from the message categorizer and routing information from the routing engine, the advanced queuing engine sends the message on for delivery.

   ❑ If the destination is a local domain, the Exchange store driver (on the store side of EXIPC) picks up the message and delivers it to the information store or, if so instructed by a custom application, to a drop directory specified by the administrator.

❑ If the destination is remote, the message is passed along to SMTP for outbound messages or handed to the Message Transfer Agent for delivery.

Outbound Message Flow

Outgoing messages follow somewhat the same "route" as inbound messages, at least where the message categorizer and advanced queuing engine are concerned. The initial steps differ, however. Briefly, this is what happens:

1. The client submits a message to the information store.

2. The information store moves the message to a SendQ folder and informs the store driver.

3. The store driver picks up the message, constructs an IMAILMSG envelope, and hands it off to the advanced queuing engine.

4. At this point, the advanced queuing engine goes through the steps of sending the message to the message categorizer and routing engine to determine where and how the message should be delivered.

5. If the message is destined for the local store, it is now placed in the local delivery queue and delivered.

6. If the message is to be delivered to another server, it is placed in the appropriate queue for its destination identifier and linked with a connection to the next hop on its journey.

Message Routing

Understanding message flow within Exchange and Windows enhances understanding of the reliability, flexibility, and performance of these products. But although message delivery can begin and end with the local store and a single Exchange server, it often—perhaps usually—doesn't. Other servers, other mail systems, and even the Internet come into play. All told, Exchange messages can be routed from sender to receiver

■ On the same server

■ In the same routing group

■ Between routing groups

■ To a server outside the Exchange organization

This section of the chapter begins with an overview of these four delivery methods. The remaining sections then describe when multiple routing groups are needed, the types of connectors used in delivering mail outside a single routing group, and the new Exchange 2000 use of link state information for propagating network status and delivery information between routing groups.

Delivery on the Same Server

Routing, or rather delivery, when both the sender and the recipient are on the same server is a simple affair: client to server to recipient by way of the recipient's mailbox in the local store. The process can be diagrammed as a straight line from A to B, with a transfer from sender to recipient taking place at the Exchange server, as shown in the following illustration.

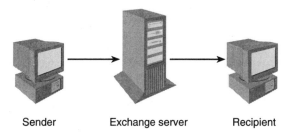

Sender   Exchange server   Recipient

Delivery in the Same Routing Group

When the message sender and the message recipient are on different Exchange servers, but still within the same routing group, the delivery process becomes more involved, in that a second server, the recipient's mail server, becomes part of the process. An additional difference is related to the protocol used to send the message: If the recipient's mailbox resides on an Exchange 2000 server, SMTP is used; if the recipient's mailbox is on an Exchange 5.5 server (in an installation still running in mixed mode), the older remote procedure call method is used.

In either case, however, message transfer is still a straight-line, point-to-point communication between the sending and receiving servers, as shown in the following illustration.

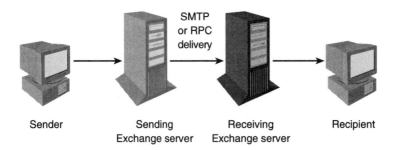

Delivery to a Different Routing Group

When the sender and recipient are in different routing groups, message delivery becomes yet more involved, in that the actual route might require multiple hops through intervening routing groups between the sending and receiving servers.

When an Exchange server needs to deliver a message to a different routing group, it does so in three steps:

1. It determines that the recipient is, in fact, in a different routing group.

2. It consults link state information and identifies a route for delivery.

3. It sends the message to the connector linking it either to the receiving routing group itself or to the next routing group in the path it has identified.

> NOTE: Exchange 2000 supports three routing connectors: Routing Group Connectors, SMTP Connectors, and X.400 Connectors. To keep from wandering off the "how Exchange routes messages from A to B" path, these connectors, as well as information on the link state database, are described later in the chapter in the sections "Connectors Linking Routing Groups" and "Link State Information."

In terms of actual delivery, if the sending server has been configured as a routing server, it has the ability to open a connection to the next routing group and send the message directly to a routing server in that group.

Message delivery between routing groups is shown in the following illustration.

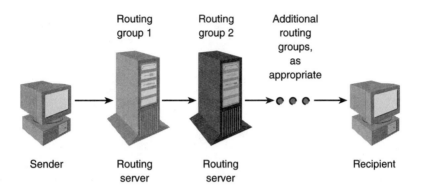

Delivery Outside the Organization

Message delivery outside the Exchange organization is similar to delivery to another routing group, in that a connector is needed as a "pipeline" to the other server. In this case, however, even though the message might travel from one routing group to another, its destination lies in another organization or on a foreign messaging system. When it sends messages outside the organization, Exchange Server follows these procedures:

1. If it doesn't find the recipient listed in Active Directory services, it resolves the address by finding a connector that can be used to transmit the message.

2. It then sends the message to a routing server in the same routing group.

3. The routing server then either sends the message over the appropriate connector or, if the connector is in a different routing group, sends the message to the other routing group.

4. When a routing server receives the message, it transfers the message to the server hosting the connector being used for transmission.

This last form of delivery is shown in the following illustration.

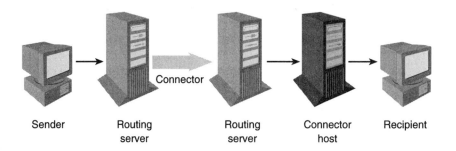

Single vs. Multiple Routing Groups

Routing groups in Exchange 2000 are the topological equivalent of the Exchange 5.5 site concept, in that each routing group represents a collection of well-connected servers that can communicate over fast, permanent, and reliable connections. Message transfer is point-to-point, with each server able to transfer information directly to another server in the group.

Although network reliability is the most important criterion in defining a routing group, it's not the only one. There are three additional factors that apply to any routing group. All of the servers in the routing group must

- Be part of the same forest

- Be linked by permanent SMTP connections

- Be able to communicate with the server designated as routing group master (As described in the "How It's Used" section of this chapter, this is the server in charge of tracking and propagating link state information within the group.)

Because Exchange assumes that all servers within a routing group do rely on high-speed, permanent connections, Exchange 2000 doesn't attempt to optimize use of network bandwidth.

So, when does an organization need one routing group, and when does it need more than one? Obviously, if the organization includes only a single group of servers and those servers can rely on reliable, high-bandwidth, permanent connections, one routing group is all that's required. If, however, any of the following factors apply, multiple routing groups may become necessary:

- Network connections don't provide the connectivity required

- Problems often afflict the underlying network

■ A multi-hop path rather than a single-hop path is required for message transmission

■ Message transmission must be scheduled between different locations

■ Routing group structure controls client connections to public folders

Connectors Linking Routing Groups

Exchange relies on connectors to route messages reliably and efficiently, both within and outside the organization. The primary (preferred) means is the Routing Group Connector which, as the name states, connects two routing groups. Exchange 2000 does, however, also support an SMTP Connector and an X.400 Connector, both of which also provide connectivity to non-Exchange systems or (in the case of the SMTP Connector) to the Internet.

Routing Group Connectors

Routing Group Connectors are more or less the bread-and-butter pipelines that Exchange relies on for linking routing groups. These connectors are both efficient and easy to set up. Although the base transport is SMTP and these connectors consult the (new) link state database for routing information, in other respects Routing Group Connectors resemble the Site Connectors used in Exchange 5.5. In fact, a Routing Group Connector can be used to connect an Exchange 2000 routing group with an Exchange 5.5 site and, when used, will automatically revert to using the Message Transfer Agent and remote procedure calls when it determines that it's transmitting to the non-Exchange 2000 site.

Within a routing group, a Routing Group Connector can be configured to use zero, one, or multiple bridgehead servers (the servers that actually handle transmission of messages between routing groups). Differences between these approaches are as follows:

■ **If no such server is designated,** all of the servers in the routing group act as bridgehead servers for message transmission.

■ **If one bridgehead server is defined,** all mail flows through it and the administrator thus has control over such aspects of messaging as tracking and archiving.

■ **If multiple bridgehead servers are defined,** the routing group gains in two areas: load balancing and stability. With multiple servers defined, if one goes down, Exchange can always find and use a server for message transmission.

Where configuration and use of Routing Group Connectors are concerned, administrators have the ability to control

- Connection schedules
- Message priority (high, normal, or low)
- Message size limits

Finally, as already mentioned, Routing Group Connectors are easy to set up. Although they are unidirectional and must be configured in pairs (inbound and outbound), the Exchange System Manager can automatically configure the required second connector when the first is set up. The following illustration shows the window used in creating a new Routing Group Connector.

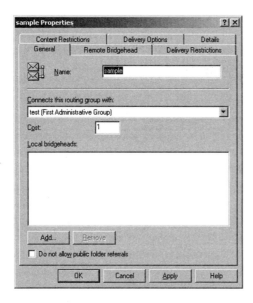

SMTP Connectors

Both Routing Group Connectors and SMTP Connectors obviously use SMTP as the transport protocol. So why does Exchange offer both, even though either one can be used to connect routing groups? There are several answers, based on a number of differences between the two connectors.

Overall, even though Routing Group Connectors are the preferred (and recommended) method for linking routing groups, SMTP Connectors can be used for

- Connecting an Exchange organization with SMTP-compatible but non-Exchange systems, as well as with the Internet.
- Connecting independent Exchange forests within an organization.

■ Creating more finely tuned connections between Exchange routing groups. SMTP Connectors can, for example, allow TLS encryption and authentication of remote domains before message transmission. It is also possible to configure an SMTP Connector to retrieve mail at specified times from a queue held for delivery on a remote server.

Reaching other systems   Unlike Routing Group Connectors, SMTP Connectors rely on either a DNS mail exchanger (MX) record or a smart host for message transmission.

A mail exchanger record, used in sending messages to a non-Exchange system, points Exchange to one or more servers in the foreign system. Given this information, the SMTP Connector can then connect and send mail to the server or servers identified in the record.

As for smart hosts...as shown in the following illustration, one of the options available in configuring an SMTP Connector is the ability to designate a smart host by its fully qualified domain name or by its IP address. This smart host is a remote server to which the Exchange server can transmit messages intended for a particular remote domain or routing group. Essentially, the smart host acts as a relay station, in that the Exchange server sends mail to the smart host and it, in turn, takes responsibility for using DNS to send the mail on to its destination.

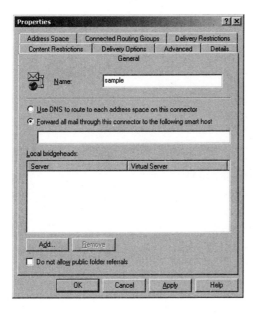

Specifying a smart host eliminates the DNS lookup that would otherwise be performed on all outgoing mail addresses.

MAPI and mail going to non-Exchange systems   Within or between Exchange organizations, Microsoft Outlook (that is, MAPI) clients can rely on Rich Text Formatting (RTF) to include advanced formatting, as well as message options including calendar and task information. Exchange supports RTF by default by encapsulating RTF in a form known as Transport-Neutral Encapsulation Format, or TNEF. This encapsulated formatting is then included with the message as a MIME attachment called WINMAIL.DAT and sent over SMTP to the destination server. If the destination server is an Exchange server, it uses the RTF attachment to render the content correctly for the message recipient.

When such an encapsulated message is sent outside the Exchange organization, however, the information encapsulated in WINMAIL.DAT may not be readable, and other attachments included with the message might be lost.

Exchange 5.5 and the SMTP Connector   The Exchange 2000 SMTP Connector is comparable to the Internet Mail Service in earlier versions. In fact, in systems upgraded from Exchange 5.5, the Internet Mail Service is turned into an SMTP Connector, and Internet Mail Service address spaces are added to a single SMTP Connector. Although it's possible that not all information will transfer over, the Exchange upgrade log will provide details on any such "lost" information.

X.400 Connectors

Like the SMTP Connector, an X.400 Connector can be used to link two Exchange routing groups. Unlike either the Routing Group Connector or the SMTP Connector, the X.400 Connector is also used to link an Exchange routing group with an X.400 messaging system.

Using an X.400 Connector between routing groups can be desirable in two situations:

- When X.400 is the only connectivity available
- When there is very little bandwidth available between the two routing groups

When an X.400 Connector is used between routing groups, one bridge-head server in each routing group provides the communication link.

Before an X.400 Connector can be established, however, an X.400 transport stack needs to be configured. There are three choices, depending on which underlying protocol is being used:

- **A TCP/IP X400 transport stack,** if the connector will be running over TCP/IP—as, for example, when the connector is used over the Internet

- **An X.25 X.400 transport stack,** if the connector will be running over X.25

- **A Dynamic RAS X.400 transport stack,** if the connector will be relying on Remote Access Service and a dial-up modem

Communicating with Other Mail Systems

In the real world, or at least the online version of it, two facts hold true: First, *everybody* loves e-mail; second, *not* everybody uses Exchange. Furthermore, because people rather messily refuse to limit their electronic communication to only those who use the same mail system, it's up to Exchange to offer ways for people to communicate with whomever they choose.

So, of course, Exchange supports mail over the Internet, as can be seen from its use of SMTP as a native transport. And, it supports communication with X.400 systems. And, for those who rely on other mail systems, Exchange supports connectors to

- Lotus Notes

- cc:Mail (which Lotus recently decided not to continue developing but which remains a player in the e-mail universe)

- Novell GroupWise

- Microsoft Mail

Link State Information

Now, after all this description of connectors and routing groups, it's time to take a fairly detailed look at the database that makes message routing and delivery economical and efficient: the link state table.

What It Is

To begin with, however, what's a link state? It sounds important, but at first glance the name doesn't really describe much about what it does. But that's just at first. When you examine the two parts of its name separately and then combine them, everything becomes crystal clear.

Whenever multiple routing groups are configured in an organization, those routing groups rely on *links* over which they route messages. There's part of the name. Now, each link can be in either of two *states*: UP (available) or DOWN (unavailable). Put the two together, and you have a term that describes the status of the connection between routing groups. The only part of its duties that its name doesn't mention is that this information on routing connections is near real-time, that it resides in a database table, and is propagated to all of the servers in the messaging system.

Why It's Needed

Exchange 2000 implements link state tables to provide all servers in the system with the vital information that allows them to determine

- The cheapest route to delivery, in terms of the *cost* associated with each link in the route (Cost here doesn't represent a financial value, but rather a preference that enables the system to determine the most efficient route. The lower the cost, the more desirable the route—kind of like "on a scale of 1 to 10, with 1 being the best....")

- Whether any link in a proposed route is not functioning

This information, or rather the link state tables that contain the information, is based on a link propagation protocol known as the link state algorithm, or LSA. This algorithm is, in turn, based on the Open Shortest Path First (OSPF) algorithm used by network routers. Unlike OSPF, however, which runs at the very low network level of the OSI model, the link state algorithm operates at a higher level and is thus freed of reliance on the network infrastructure and low-level protocols.

Because the link state algorithm takes responsibility for telling the entire messaging system the current state of (link) affairs, it ensures that

- Each Exchange server has access to the information it needs to determine the best, most reliable route to a destination instead of simply sending a message along a route that, potentially, could include a nonfunctioning link

- Messages do not "ping-pong" between servers, because each server is aware of alternate or redundant links, as well as their current state (UP or DOWN)

- Message looping—hop after hop after hop around the system—doesn't occur

How It's Used

Link state information is most valuable in an Exchange messaging system that includes a number of routing groups with multiple available paths between and among them. At the heart of this system (mail delivery-wise) is a special server in each routing group that has been designated the routing group master. This master

■ **Receives and keeps track of link state information,** for example, a "link down" message from a server in its routing group

■ **Propagates that information to the other servers in its routing group**

Non-master servers are required to send new link state information to the master immediately, and the master in turn takes care of broadcasting that information to other servers. The method of propagating link state information depends on whether the information is being transmitted within or between routing groups.

■ **Within a routing group,** the information moves between the routing group master and the other servers over TCP port 3044.

■ **Between routing groups,** information travels through TCP port 25 over SMTP and is transferred ahead of any messages waiting for delivery.

As for the link state information itself, it's gathered and distributed in two ways:

■ **Within a routing group,** servers report link state information to the routing group master and the master, in turn, immediately sends that information to the other servers in the routing group.

■ **Both within and between routing groups,** servers transferring messages over SMTP compare link state information through an Exchange 2000 SMTP command verb that enables them to compare link state information and to update it as well. In addition, where X.400 Connectors are used to connect routing groups, the X.400 protocol has been extended in Exchange 2000 to enable the connectors to update link state information—either as messages are transferred or through periodic polling.

Finally, when links go down, what happens? This is the sequence of events:

1. To start, before a link is actually listed as nonfunctional, the server attempting to send a message over the link retries three times at one-minute intervals.

2. If, after those three tries, a connection still can't be made, the link is tagged as DOWN and the server notifies the routing group master.

3. The routing group master, in turn, immediately notifies all the other servers in the routing group.

4. The bridgehead server in the routing group calculates an alternative route to the message's destination.

5. The link DOWN information is propagated to the bridgehead server in the routing group that will receive the message and attempt to send it over the alternate route.

6. The bridgehead server in this routing group contacts its routing group master and informs it of the problem.

7. This routing group master, like the one in the group that originally noticed the problem, spreads the word to all servers in its group.

8. The link DOWN status is propagated to succeeding routing groups along the route to the message's final destination.

9. Meanwhile, back at the original routing group, the bridgehead server continues to try and connect over the down link every 60 seconds. When a connection is finally made, the bridgehead notifies its routing group master, and the routing group master notifies its servers that the link is once again available for use.

And that ends this overview of message flow, both within Exchange and to potentially every part of the world. If any part of Exchange can be considered its heart, the architecture, protocols, and supporting software described in this chapter must be it. They are, after all, what make Exchange a messaging and collaboration tool for organizations ranging from small businesses to enormous enterprises.

C H A P T E R   N I N E

Internet Integration

To at least some extent, this entire book has been about Internet integration in Exchange 2000. That's as it should be, of course, because the Internet isn't only part of the computing world; it's becoming increasingly important in communication and commerce. And, in terms of protocols, transport, and access, the Internet lies at or near the heart of Exchange 2000. Thus, it's only natural that Exchange 2000 not only recognizes the Internet, but also makes it part and parcel of its own architecture.

But for the most part, the threads of Internet technology running through the preceding chapters have to do with the fundamentals of the Internet itself. SMTP and X.400, for example, are the universal "transports" that underlie Internet communications, just as HTML is—and XML is becoming—the universal "language" of client access.

But there's more to the integration of Internet technologies in Exchange. Exchange also supports NNTP, IMAP4, and POP3 for Internet-based news and e-mail. It supports WebDAV as an Internet-oriented authoring and collaboration tool. And it supports Microsoft Outlook Web Access, often abbreviated OWA, as a browser-based means of accessing e-mail, public folders, and even calendars.

This chapter begins with an overview of the Internet in terms of networking models and protocols in general. Later sections cover POP3, IMAP4, NNTP, HTTP, WebDAV, and OWA in detail.

Internet Protocols

Where the Internet is concerned, there are protocols and then there are protocols. In other words, although the word *protocol* is used to describe all of the standard (and nonstandard) methods that enable computers to communicate with one another, there can be vast differences between protocol A and protocol B in terms of what they do and the way they do it.

For example, both IP and HTTP are Internet protocols, yet IP works quite closely with the network hardware because its job is to sort, route, and deliver packets of data. On the other hand, HTTP works at a much higher level and never gets "down and dirty" with actual data packets. Instead, it helps client software to access the Internet and assumes that it can rely on lower-level protocols, such as TCP and IP, to do the actual sending and receiving for the client.

These and other differences in the ways protocols function—as well as the ways in which they interact—are based on the responsibilities outlined for the various layers defined in networking models such as ISO/OSI and TCP/IP.

Networking Models: An Overview

Networking models, as you know, are conceptual aids designed to help humans visualize, make sense of, and keep track of the many interdependent processes involved in enabling one application to communicate with another across a network. Essentially, a networking model slices communication into layers, beginning at or slightly above the network hardware itself and moving steadily upward through higher levels of abstraction to the application software. At each level, the model defines certain responsibilities that must be handled by the protocols that do the actual work required at that level. This section briefly describes the two models most relevant to modern-day networking, the classic ISO/OSI (International Organization for Standardization/Open Systems Interconnect) reference model and the TCP/IP networking model.

The ISO/OSI Model

In the networking world, the longtime standard is the ISO/OSI model, the seven-layer confection shown in the following illustration. (The model doesn't actually sit in limbo, of course; it's illustrated in the "space" between client and network just to reinforce its role in mediating between the two.)

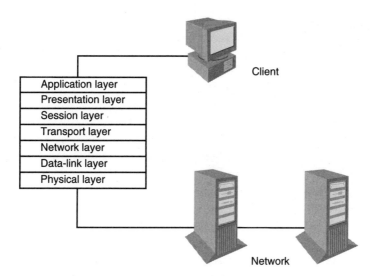

Starting from the top, these are the tasks assigned to each layer.

■ **Application layer**   provides network access to applications

■ **Presentation layer**   ensures that both sender and recipient used the same data format (e.g., ASCII), and also takes care of any encryption or compression required

■ **Session layer**   establishes the communication session

■ **Transport layer**   ensures that information isn't lost or duplicated; essentially, it takes responsibility for quality of service

■ **Network layer**   addresses and routes messages

■ **Data-link layer**   packages data in frames, controls the flow of frames, acknowledges transmission, and retransmits if necessary.

■ **Physical layer**   defines the hardware (for example, pin assignments) and transfers data as a serial bit stream

As can be seen, each layer in the ISO/OSI model builds on the layers below it. What isn't so obvious, however, is that protocols operating at each layer rely on the protocols above and below them. So, for example, a network-layer protocol is able to concentrate on its job alone and simply assume that the layers above and below it will handle their jobs without problem and without fail. This compartmentalizing and reliance on protocols in other layers is essential to a working protocol stack (a set of interoperating protocols) built on any networking model, including the ISO/OSI model.

The TCP/IP Model

Although the ISO/OSI model is a classic networking standard, the TCP/IP networking model more closely reflects the Internet, in that it's the basis for building a TCP/IP protocol stack. A TCP/IP stack is, after all, what defines the Internet and now, with the increasing business reliance on intranets, what enables communication between servers both within organizations and around the world.

Like the ISO/OSI reference model, the TCP/IP model attempts to describe networking in terms of a series of layers—once again, to modularize networking to make the concept of networking easier to understand and to implement. Unlike the ISO/OSI reference model, however, the TCP/IP model is generally considered to include four, rather than seven layers, as shown in the following illustration.

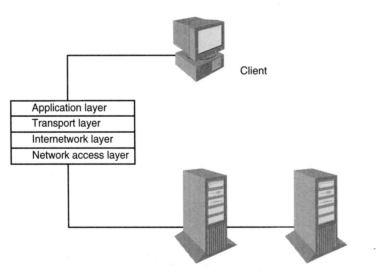

TCP/IP-based network, for example, the Internet

These four layers and their areas of responsibility can be defined as follows:

■ **Application layer** provides applications with network access and ensures standard and mutually comprehensible means of representing data

■ **Transport layer** establishes connections or virtual circuits and ensures end-to-end delivery

■ **Internetwork layer** routes messages

■ **Network access layer** transmits data frames and interacts with the physical network

As you can see, TCP/IP layers don't match the ISO/OSI model layer for layer. For instance, the TCP/IP internetwork layer has no equivalent in the ISO/OSI model, and the ISO/OSI physical layer lies outside (or beneath) the scope of the TCP/IP model. In other respects, however, the layers in the two models can be roughly matched in terms of the tasks handled at different levels, as shown in the following illustration.

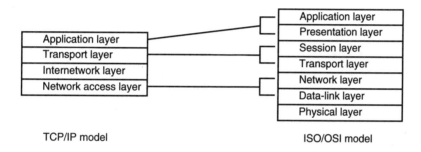

TCP/IP model   ISO/OSI model

TCP/IP Protocols

The TCP/IP model is, of course, the design for a working TCP/IP protocol stack. In this respect, it's comparable to a set of engineering blueprints for the design of the (sigh) much overpublicized "information superhighway." In this analogy, the protocol stack itself could be considered to represent...well, not so much the infrastructure (the physical network) of the Internet as the highway's traffic regulations and rules of the road. After all, the protocols aren't physical in nature, but they are indeed the means that enable packets to travel reliably from start to destination, negotiating roadblocks and detours when necessary, but without having to deal with general mayhem.

The TCP/IP stack itself includes a number of protocols that work on the application, transport, and internetwork layers:

■ **At the application level** are such well-known and widely used protocols as SMTP and POP (Post Office Protocol), both used for e-mail; FTP, which is a long-time standard used for rapid file transfer; and HTTP, which is, of course, the protocol that browsing software relies on for delivering Web pages over the Internet.

- **At the transport level** are two protocols: TCP and UDP (User Datagram Protocol). Both of these protocols mediate between the application layer and the internetwork layer. TCP, however, is a *connection-based* protocol (it establishes a connection between sender and receiver), and it takes care of retransmitting data if necessary. UDP, on the other hand, is a *connectionless* protocol (packets can travel over different routes between sender and recipient) and is also considered *unreliable* because it doesn't verify that data is transmitted accurately.

- **At the internetwork layer** is the IP protocol, another connectionless protocol like UDP. IP, however, is responsible for routing rather than delivering data. In determining routes, IP compares sending and receiving addresses and consults a routing table (roughly, a "map" of servers and their locations) to determine where to forward messages.

Below the internetworking layer, the TCP/IP model doesn't attempt to define its own protocols. Instead, at the network access layer, it relies on established transports such as the Ethernet, Token Ring, FDDI, and ATM and, beneath those, on hardware standards such as RS-232C for communications.

Internet Protocols, Exchange, and IIS

TCP/IP and, by extension, the TCP/IP networking model underlie messaging and data transfer in both Microsoft Windows 2000 and Exchange 2000. Exchange and IIS (Internet Information Service), however, also support protocols designed to provide specific services for end users:

- **POP3 and IMAP4** for remote e-mail access over the Internet
- **NNTP** for Internet-based newsfeeds

These protocols, like SMTP, are integrated into IIS to improve both scalability and administrative flexibility.

POP3

POP, the Post Office Protocol, comes in three versions: POP (the original), POP2 (which requires SMTP), and the newest, POP3 (which doesn't require SMTP). All versions of POP exist to enable client computers to retrieve mail from a remote server—usually, though not necessarily, over a TCP/IP connection.

The reason Exchange supports POP3 is also the reason POP came into being in the first place: to give roaming or resource-poor client computers a means of temporarily connecting to a mail server so that they can download messages being held for them. (This business of accessing a central mail repository, by the way, is where the "post office" part of the protocol's name comes from.)

Simpler and less capable than IMAP4, POP3 was defined in 1988 in RFC 1081. It was designed specifically to provide e-mail access to machines that couldn't maintain permanent connections to a messaging system. POP3 supports only message download. It doesn't provide for sending mail, but assumes that mail sent by the client is handled some other way. In the case of an Exchange client, that way is provided by SMTP, over which messages are routed either to the Exchange server itself or to another SMTP server, as the recipient address dictates.

POP3 is based on about 10 core commands designed to enable the client to download all of its mail for later, offline, use. In this respect, POP3 is simple and relatively inflexible, although that same simplicity also befits its rather limited goal in life. Essentially, a computer running a POP3 client, such as Microsoft Outlook or Microsoft Outlook Express, connects remotely to a POP3 server, downloads its mail, and then disconnects from the server. With Exchange, a POP3 client has the ability to download some rather than all of its mail, but because POP3 itself is limited to accessing only the user's mailbox, clients don't have the ability to view and use items in public folders.

IMAP4

IMAP4 is short for Internet Message Access Protocol 4 or, sometimes, Internet Mail Access Protocol (version 4). IMAP4 is similar to POP3 in that it enables remote or roaming users to connect to the Exchange information store. It's different, however, in allowing users to access their mail without downloading to a specific workstation. So, for example, people whose jobs or activities require logging on from different computers can use IMAP4 to check their e-mail from any location without having to download a little bit here, a little bit there. And, of course, the ability to leave messages neatly bundled in one accessible location on the server means that users on the move don't have to deal with multiple "piles" of mail on different computers. IMAP4 is more capable and flexible than POP3 in other respects, too. In Exchange 2000, for example, IMAP4 clients can

- Search e-mail by keyword while messages are still stored on the server

- Access public folders

- Access more than one e-mail folder

- View message headers before downloading

- Download specific messages

- Download only part of a message, such as an attachment

- Flag read and unread messages

IMAP4 is, however, like POP3 in supporting message downloads, but not specifying a means of sending messages. For that, it too relies on a mail transfer protocol such as SMTP.

POP3 and IMAP4 in Exchange 2000

In terms of Exchange 2000 and IIS, both POP3 and IMAP4 display the following features:

- The ability to run on a virtual server, complete with its own name, authentication, or message formatting

- The ability to run separately from the mail service in a front-end/back-end configuration

Front-end/back-end benefits In the case of both POP3 and IMAP4, the benefits of front-end/back-end separation of services are concentrated in two areas:

- **Ease of use and administration** Clients can use a single server name, such as IMAPserver, to connect to the front-end server, and this server will then pass their requests to however many back-end servers house the organization's user mailboxes. Thus, instead of having to map users to specific back-end servers, administrators can give clients a single POP3 or IMAP4 "open sesame" and leave the job of load balancing to hardware or software. In addition, the front-end/back-end configuration allows mailboxes to be moved from one back-end server to another without affecting the client's ability to connect through the front end. And this configuration allows for scaling upward by adding more servers as demand grows—again, without affecting clients.

- **Reduced server load** Where Secure Sockets Layer (SSL) connections are used, the job of handling encryption and decryption can be left to the front-end server. Because encryption and decryption place high demands on processing, turning these tasks over to the front-end server means that communication between front end and back end can then take place without the encryption overhead.

Mailbox management   Because of the integration between Exchange 2000 and Windows 2000, POP3 and IMAP4 mailboxes are managed within Microsoft Active Directory services. In addition, when the Exchange System Manager is installed, the Active Directory console gains a set of extensions that allows for creation of Exchange mailboxes when user accounts are added to the directory.

NNTP

Whereas POP3 and IMAP4 are used for remotely accessing e-mail, NNTP (the Network News Transfer Protocol) facilitates posting, distributing, and viewing news and group discussions between NNTP clients and news servers. Specified in RFC 977, NNTP is the Internet standard through which people throughout the world gain access to the thousands of special-interest forums represented on the widely accessed communal news and bulletin boards known as USENET.

Newsgroups and newsfeeds   At the heart of NNTP are two concepts: newsgroups and newsfeeds.

- **A newsgroup**   is a collection of messages posted by individuals interested in a particular subject. These posts are submitted through the Internet and distributed by USENET, which acts as the collection point and disseminator of newsgroup articles on all subjects. To impose structure on this welter of interests and information, newsgroups are hierarchically ordered into categories, such as recreation and computers. Because those categories are themselves so broad, they are further broken down into subcategories (and sub-sub-subcategories), such as PC-based computer games and recreational music makers interested in guitars.

- **A newsfeed**   is essentially a specified collection of newsgroup articles that are "fed" by one server to another through USENET. Newsfeeds travel from server to server in one of two ways:

  - ❑ **As a push newsfeed,**   in which one server periodically delivers information to another

  - ❑ **As a pull newsfeed,**   in which one server periodically contacts another to draw articles from it

No matter whether the information is pushed or pulled, newsfeeds must be enabled on both the sending and receiving sites. To participate in newsfeeds, a site must establish an account with a USENET provider, such as UUNET or MCI, and submit a list of the newsgroups to be included in the newsfeed. The server responsible for either pushing or pulling the information determines newsfeed timing.

The NNTP Service

NNTP support is built into Windows 2000 as the NNTP Service. A replacement for the Internet News Service in Exchange 5.5, the NNTP Service takes care of sending and receiving all NNTP-based news between client and server and between server and server. The NNTP Service supports a number of content formats, including MIME, HTML, GIF, and JPEG.

As built into Windows 2000, the NNTP Service supports the creation of news and discussion groups on stand-alone servers. When Exchange 2000 is installed, the NNTP Service is enhanced with the ability to

- **Support newsfeeds** through interaction with other NNTP servers and thus provide users with access to USENET newsgroups

- **Support a master/slave arrangement** by which clients access a "farm" of servers in which newsfeeds received by a master server are propagated to subordinate (slave) servers for improved scalability and fault tolerance

The following illustration shows the NNTP Service and its relation to both clients and USENET servers.

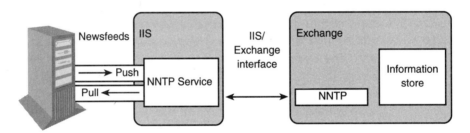

USENET server

NNTP server configuration NNTP, like the other Internet protocols, is configured to run on one or more virtual servers. By default, the server communicates through TCP port 119 (the port typical for NNTP servers) and SSL port 563. Just as with SMTP virtual servers, each virtual server on a physical server must have unique IP address and port numbers. By default, each virtual server accepts as many as 5,000 connections from other NNTP servers, but administrators can adjust this number to suit server resources and typical server workload.

For each virtual server, Exchange provides for access, settings, and control of newsgroups by way of the Virtual Server Properties sheet (shown in the following illustrations).

Briefly, the tabs on the Virtual Server Properties sheet allow for the following:

■ **General tab:** configuration options including IP address, port, number of connections, and so on

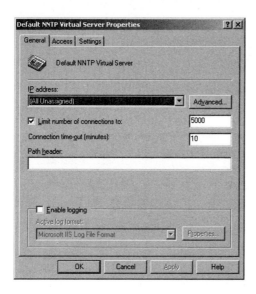

■ **Access tab:** authentication, certificate requirements, and connection control

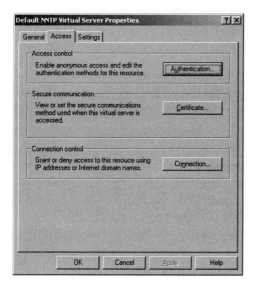

❏ **Authentication** ranges from anonymous (no username or password required for access) to SSL client authorization (certificate required)

❏ **Certificate requirements** set communications security when the server is accessed (The IIS Certificate Wizard handles assignment of certificates.)

❏ **Connection control** allows administrators to use IP addresses or domain names to grant or deny access to the server

■ **Settings tab:** control of messages and newsfeeds, including

❏ Setting posting permission and establishing posting limits, allowing clients and servers to send control messages (for creating and removing newsgroups and deleting articles), and specifying the SMTP mail server responsible for sending articles to moderated newsgroups

❏ Permitting other servers to pull information from this server

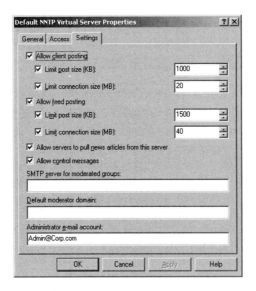

Moderated newsgroups NNTP newsgroups themselves can be either moderated or unmoderated. Although users are free to post articles to either type, a moderated newsgroup offers control over content by ensuring that all submitted articles are reviewed and approved before they are posted. For a moderated newsgroup, the NNTP Service sends articles to the newsgroup moderator.

The moderator then determines whether to post the article or not. If the decision goes against posting, the moderator can explain the decision to the author of the article.

In an NNTP Service moderated newsgroup

- Any NNTP client can submit messages, but the moderator must use an NNTP client that provides moderating capability.

- There must be either an SMTP mail server (for messages sent to the moderator) or a directory (where the messages can be stored for access by the moderator).

- By default, articles are sent to a default moderator domain that takes the format *newsgroup-name@default.domain,* where the periods in the newsgroup name (e.g., rec.weaving.baskets) are replaced by hyphens (*rec-weaving-baskets@default.domain*). The default domain can, however, be changed to the moderator's e-mail domain.

Directories and newsgroups Just as the Windows operating system stores users' personal files in directory hierarchies beginning with a root directory, the NNTP Service stores NNTP articles in one or more directory hierarchies. For each newsgroup created, the NNTP Service automatically creates a corresponding directory, which is assigned the same name as the newsgroup itself. Within these directories, the NNTP Service stores both newsgroup articles (assigned the extension .nws) and a subject file (with the extension .xix) that lists the subjects of the stored articles. Each subject file created lists the subjects for 128 articles in a particular newsgroup.

To reference actual message locations, the NNTP Service makes use of virtual directories. Virtual directories provide newsgroups with both scalability and fault tolerance. That's nice, but what exactly is a virtual directory? It's a public folder store that

- Is used to store part of the newsgroup hierarchy

- Allows newsgroup files to be stored on multiple disk drives

- Allows similarly named newsgroups to be collected under an "umbrella" designation—for example, sports.baseball, sports.skating, and sports.skiing could all be collected in a single virtual directory called sports

- Allows a newsgroup to be physically moved without requiring its name to be changed

In effect, virtual directories enable NNTP administrators to break up and manage the public folder newsgroup hierarchy as subsets stored in different locations, all without affecting the primary tree.

During setup, Exchange creates the following two virtual directories, both of which can be seen by clicking the Virtual Directories node under the Protocols/NNTP folder:

- **The default directory,** located in *Public Folders/Internet Newsgroups,* which is where new newsgroups are created by default

- **The control directory,** stored in the local file system in *[drive:]\Inetpub\nntpfile\root\control*

Newsfeed distribution   For distributing articles among servers, the NNTP Service supports streaming. Messages pass through an intermediate node, which begins streaming to the destination server without waiting for the entire message to be received, as shown in the following illustration.

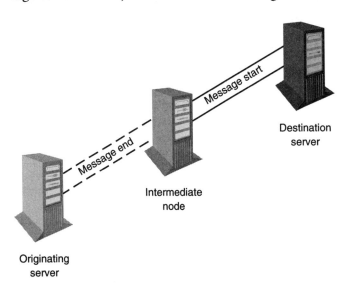

In terms of how newsfeeds travel between servers, NNTP Service supports three types of feeds, at the heart of which is one server that is designated within the organization as a master server. This master server is responsible for managing article numbers—the article or message IDs that enable servers to identify and request articles—and for ensuring that all newsgroups remain synchronized. The role of this server is strictly supervisory and administrative; clients never connect directly to it.

In terms of newsfeeds themselves, the master server and "subservient" (actually, peer and slave) servers take part in these three types of feed:

- **Master feed,** in which local posts are sent for article IDs and all requests are sent to the master server

- **Slave feed,** in which messages (plus article IDs) are sent to slave servers for posting

- **Peer feed,** in which a server exchanges articles with other servers, generally a USENET server

These three different types of feed are typically used in the following ways. (The terminology is a bit confusing here because the terms *master*, *peer*, and *slave*, although they still refer to the servers, are seen in a somewhat different light.)

- **USENET newsfeeds** are those in which the NNTP Service interacts, via the master server, with a USENET news provider to offer internal users access to articles posted to any USENET sites to which the organization subscribes. In this form of distribution, incoming newsfeeds are pushed by one or more of the USENET provider's servers to the NNTP Service in the subscriber's organization, and the NNTP Service pushes outgoing posts to the USENET provider, as shown in the following illustration.

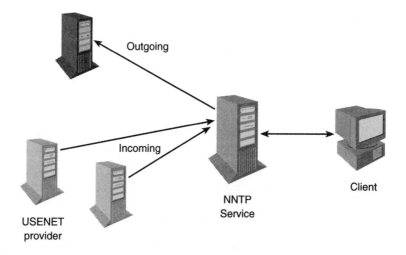

- **Peer newsfeeds** are those in which an organization maintains more than one news server and the master server distributes articles between and among them. Each peer server manages its own newsgroup articles.

■ **A master/slave newsfeed,** as mentioned in the earlier section "The NNTP Service," enables multiple servers to share articles. In this arrangement, there is one server, the master, that is responsible for feeding information to all of its slave servers. The master controls distribution of all articles and ensures that the slave servers are kept synchronized. Each slave has a newsfeed to the master, and clients connect only to the slave servers, never directly to the master. When an article is posted by a client, the recipient slave doesn't post the article. Instead, it sends the article to the master. The master returns the article to all slave sites, and at that time the article appears on the original and all other slave sites. The following illustration shows the relationship between USENET, master, and slave servers.

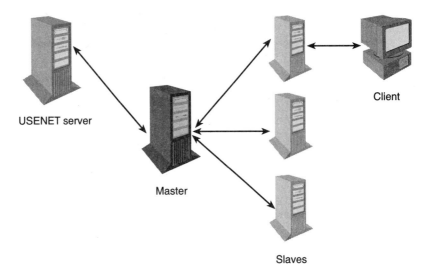

USENET server

Client

Master

Slaves

WebDAV

Chapter 6 introduced WebDAV in relation to the new concept of the Web Store, the Exchange 2000 multimedia-rich approach to unified messaging and collaboration. As described in that chapter, WebDAV is

■ An extension of HTTP version 1.1

■ A means of enabling Web-based file-system-like operations, such as copy and move, and of supporting collaborative operations, including document locking, tracking, and management

WebDAV is also integrated into IIS and is inherently integrated with XML, so a closer look at its features and its potential use as a Web-based tool for document manipulation is certainly in order.

HTTP and WebDAV

HTTP, of course, is the protocol that underlies the Internet, or at least the Web-based portion of the Internet. HTTP is also the protocol that underlies WebDAV, so a look at WebDAV should naturally begin with a look at HTTP—its strengths and, well, its not-quite strengths. (Referring to "limitations" in reference to something as venerable as HTTP seems a little like pointing out warts on the Mona Lisa. True, perhaps, but not quite right somehow.)

At any rate, HTTP is a universal Web standard. It's object-oriented, and its importance to the Web lies in that it defines

- How information is formatted and communicated over the Web

- How Web servers and clients respond to different commands (methods), such as GET, PUT, and POST

Invaluable as HTTP is, it has one significant "wart." It's designed for static (look but don't touch) document viewing and so doesn't lend itself to authoring, collaboration, or other forms of document manipulation, such as file locking. WebDAV, the abbreviation for Web-based Distributed Authoring and Versioning, addresses this shortcoming in HTTP.

Described in detail in RFC 2518, WebDAV extends the HTTP 1.1 protocol with a set of commands that provides clients with the ability to access and manipulate documents and to collaborate over an HTTP connection. WebDAV is designed for situations in which information is stored on a server but used on the client. Because it provides active rather than static access to documents, WebDAV is (or can be) a valuable means of extending use of the Internet or of enhancing the usefulness of an already valuable intranet.

HTTP/WebDAV resources are published to directories on an HTTP virtual server and can be accessed by any of the following:

- Any client that supports the HTTP and WebDAV protocols

- Windows 2000, which connects to a virtual server through the Add Network Place Wizard and then displays the contents of the HTTP/ WebDAV directory as if it were part of the file system on the local computer

- Microsoft Internet Explorer 5.0, which connects to an HTTP/ WebDAV directory and allows the same types of file manipulation (retrieve, modify, drag and drop, and so on) that are allowed by Windows 2000

- Microsoft Office 2000, which supports document creation, publication, editing, and saving directly into an HTTP/WebDAV directory

- Outlook Express, which allows e-mail access from an Internet connection

WebDAV Features

Although the WebDAV specification is a lengthy and detailed document, the benefits of WebDAV in terms of supporting document manipulation, collaboration, and interoperability (between applications) boil down to three major areas:

- **File locking** is the foundation of WebDAV's support for collaboration. Also called concurrency control, file locking ensures that one individual's changes don't overwrite another's during group writing or editing projects.

- **Property access** Resource properties, such as author, title, subject, and so on, are stored as XML metadata. Once these properties are stored, they can be used in searches for specific documents.

- **Namespace manipulation** This feature sounds rather exotic, but it essentially refers to WebDAV support for file management, including copying, moving, and renaming. In this same area, WebDAV also includes the ability to create and list collections, which are comparable to directories in a "normal" file system.

WebDAV Extensions

Although WebDAV is itself an extension to HTTP, and Exchange supports all of the capabilities described above, Microsoft has also extended WebDAV in Exchange in the following ways:

- **Distributed Authoring Search and Location (DASL)** for extending search capabilities

- **Notifications** for messages sent to the client by the server when content changes in public or private folders, when new e-mail arrives, or when there are changes in individual messages

- **Calendar access** for tasks such as creating new calendar items and listing calendar events

XML

XML, the eXtensible Markup Language, is to some degree HTML on steroids. Though still not in wide use, XML is garnering increasing attention from Web developers and professionals as a remarkable tool with the potential to take Web-related operations to a new and higher level of customization and flexibility.

At the heart of all this attention lies the fact that XML, unlike HTML, isn't limited to describing how data should be displayed (bold, italic, red, green, and so on). Although XML can indeed be used for describing how data should be formatted, its greater importance lies in the fact that XML can be used for describing the data itself—for producing usable data about data (metadata).

Furthermore, XML is extensible because it isn't limited to a predefined set of markup symbols, or tags. Its very nature ensures that new tags can be created at any time, and that any new tags created are self-defining. In effect, an XML tag can sit in a document and say "this is what I am," and programs will neither argue with it nor choke on it. At worst, they will ignore it. So, given this extensibility, XML allows for the creation of tags that describe data as, say, phone numbers, credit card numbers, processor speeds, vegetables, vaccines, bank account types...literally any conceivable form of information.

WebDAV and XML

Unlike HTTP, which uses only headers to hold information that needs to be communicated in relation to method requests and responses, WebDAV allows use of either headers or XML. The choice of XML is based on two factors: its extensibility, which leaves open the ability to add new XML elements to existing structures, and its ability to use character sets that support internationalization.

All told, XML not only provides a vehicle for the data itself, but it also contributes the following to WebDAV functionality:

- The ability to support creation of properties that can then be used in searching, indexing, and processing server resources

- A means of formatting instructions that describe how to treat the data rather than simply display it

- A vehicle for formatting complex responses from the server (needed in the kind of give-and-take, interactive environment supported by WebDAV)

- The means of encoding customized information about collections and resources

Outlook Web Access

Outlook Web Access, often abbreviated to OWA, first appeared as a client option in Exchange 5.0 as a means of providing access to e-mail and public folders features through a Web browser. In version 5.5, Outlook Web Access was enhanced to include access to the calendar and to support IIS and Internet Explorer 4.0. With the release of Exchange Server 5.5 Service Pack 1, Outlook Web Access gained additional support for contact creation and management, password changes, name checking, and the ability to convert Outlook forms to HTML.

In Exchange 2000, Outlook Web Access has been redesigned for ease of use and reliability. Architectural changes, such as the ability to rely on a front-end/back-end configuration, address scalability and performance. In terms of the client, Outlook Web Access now adds support for:

- **Internet Explorer 5.0** in addition to providing a more Outlook 2000-like interface, enhances efficiency by offloading processing to the client
- **Public folders** containing contact and calendar information
- **Multimedia** (audio and video) messages and messages containing embedded items, including appointments and ActiveX objects
- **Use of named URLs** (such as *http://server/exchange/mailbox/ inbox*) rather than the GUIDs used in earlier versions

Outlook Web Access provides secure, cross-platform (as in Windows, UNIX, and Macintosh) access to roaming users and to those using computers other than their own or computers with limited capability. Even in Exchange 2000, however, it doesn't provide the functionality of the full-featured Outlook client. In terms of limitations, Outlook Web Access in Exchange 2000 version does *not* support the following:

- Offline use, so users must connect to Exchange Server in order to use Outlook Web Access
- Tasks and journaling
- Printing templates
- Outlook rules
- Copying to or from public and private folders
- Telephony options and user-defined fields for contacts

- Certain mail features, including spell checking, delayed delivery, and expiration options

- Reminders

- The ability to enter and edit information in Calendar view

Outlook Web Access Clients

Although Outlook Web Access supports browsers compliant with HTML 3.2 and the ECMA (European Computer Manufacturers Association) script standards, Internet Explorer 4.0 and later and Netscape Navigator 4.0 and later are recommended for use because they have been tested with Outlook Web Access in Exchange 2000.

The recommended best option, however, is Internet Explorer 5.0, with its support for the rich collaborative functionality provided by Dynamic HTML (DHTML). So, in effect, Outlook Web Access client support boils down to two categories, Internet Explorer 5.0 and other browsers.

Internet Explorer 5.0 not only supports DHTML, but it also provides a working environment close to that of the full-featured Outlook client. Included in its functionality are

- An expandable, tree-style hierarchy for public and private folders

- Drag and drop capability

- Right-click menu options

- HTML composition

- The ability (as mentioned earlier) to process many Outlook Web Access commands on the client rather than having to send the request to the server

The one major drawback to using Internet Explorer 5.0 with Outlook Web Access has to do with speed on older computers or those with limited processing capability. On those machines, Internet Explorer 4.0 can prove to be a better option.

On other browsers, the user interface is closer to the Outlook environment than it was in earlier versions of Outlook Web Access, but the functionality available is less than that provided by Internet Explorer 5.0. These other browsers

- Display Outlook Web Access in two frames. An unchanging left pane is used for navigation, and a right pane is used for rendering pages

(Limiting changes to the right pane reduces the amount of network traffic required.)

■ Display both public and private folders

■ Allow users to move or copy contents of private folders to other private folders

The Logon Process

When a user connects to the Exchange store through Outlook Web Access, he or she is unknowingly taken through a set logon procedure before the individual's mailbox appears on the screen.

1. The address typed into the browser (in the form *http://servername/ exchange/,* as described under "Accessing Mailboxes" below) takes the user to the Outlook Web Access server.

2. IIS authenticates the user.

3. The Outlook Web Access server queries Active Directory services for the location of the user's mailbox and, if the mailbox is on another server, redirects the browser to the other server, where authentication is again performed.

4. Outlook Web Access returns to the browser a page containing a navigation bar in the left pane and a view of the mailbox in the right pane.

5. Mail is then served.

Accessing the Store

In a typical (non-Web-access) Exchange installation, clients interact directly with their Exchange server. When using Outlook Web Access and a browser, however, clients access Exchange and its information store by way of IIS and an ISAPI (Internet Services Application Programming Interface) component of Exchange.

Essentially, the client's browser communicates with Outlook Web Access through HTTP and WebDAV by way of a virtual HTTP server and IIS. When IIS receives the request, the process of retrieving and returning the requested information takes place as follows:

1. IIS passes the request to the ISAPI component, DAVEX.DLL, which parses the request and sends it on to the Exchange store. During parsing, DAVEX.DLL determines the following:

   ❑ Client browser type and version, operating system, and how content should be rendered

❑ The language used for display

❑ Whether the content should be displayed in a browser or returned to a WebDAV application

❑ What action to perform

2. Once this information has been determined, the request passes along to the Exchange store.

3. The store verifies that the user has permission to access the requested item and, assuming there are no problems with access, determines the type of object that has been requested and then returns the item itself and its state, such as read or unread, to the ISAPI component.

4. The ISAPI component then matches this information about the item to a form (stored in the Forms Registry) that can be used for rendering the actual data.

5. The ISAPI component parses the form and asks the information store to retrieve the data.

6. When the store returns the data, the ISAPI component renders the form and its content into browser-usable HTML and XML and sends the result on its way back to the client.

Outlook Web Access Installations

Outlook Web Access is installed automatically when Exchange 2000 is installed, so other than requiring Windows 2000 server and IIS 5.0, there is no real setup involved in enabling this feature. However, depending on the organization and the number of servers handling Exchange, Outlook Web Access can be made available to users in either of two ways: on a single server or through a front-end/back-end configuration.

> NOTE: Organizations that don't want to allow Web access should take care to stop the HTTP virtual server to disable HTTP services on which the physical server is hosting Outlook Web Access.

Single-Server Installation

In a single-server installation, even though Outlook Web Access requests still pass through IIS, clients connect directly to the same server that stores their mailboxes. To enable access to the Exchange store, two virtual directories, an Exchange virtual root and a public virtual root, are added to IIS. These directories point to the corresponding directories in Exchange.

Accessing mailboxes   Users can connect to their mailboxes from either an intranet or the Internet. From an intranet, they use their browser and an address in the form

```
http://servername/exchange/,
```

where *servername* is the name of the Exchange server. Users accessing their mailboxes from the Internet use the same address format but replace *servername* with the organization's domain name or IP address.

If individuals connect to the server from Windows computers running Internet Explorer 4.0 or later, Outlook Web Access reads their logon credentials and automatically connects them to their mailboxes. Users running other browsers are prompted for logon information before being granted access.

It's also possible for one individual to access another's mailbox, providing such access is authorized. In this case, the address in the browser's address bar simply becomes a little longer:

```
http://servername/exchange/userid,
```

where *userid* is the individual's mail alias.

Once again, assuming access is authorized and the request is coming from Internet Explorer 4.0 or later, Outlook Web Access verifies the logon and connects the person to the requested mailbox. Users with other browsers are again prompted for logon credentials.

Accessing public folders   Connecting to public folders by way of Outlook Web Access is similar to connecting to mailboxes, except that the address takes the form

```
http://servername/public/foldername/,
```

where *servername* is the name of the Exchange server hosting public folders and *foldername* is the name of the public folder. Access is granted, however, only if permission to use the requested folder has been granted to the individual.

Multiple-Server Installation

A multiple-server installation is, of course, a front-end/back-end configuration in which users connect to a front-end server that, in turn, acts as a proxy and relays HTTP requests directly to a back-end server running Outlook Web Access and Exchange.

Although a front-end/back-end configuration involves a considerable amount of up-front planning, once the planning is done, this type of setup offers a number of advantages as well. These include the ability to

- Use a single namespace that encompasses all servers, an advantage that not only allows users access through a single name, but also allows a considerable amount of flexibility in terms of adding and removing servers and moving mailboxes when necessary.

- Use front-end servers for SSL encryption and decryption (CPU-intensive processes that can slow performance by about 15 percent). Keeping responsibility for encryption and decryption on the front-end server means that the back-end servers can concentrate on managing the Exchange store itself.

- Enhance security by locating a firewall between the front-end and back-end servers and configuring the firewall to allow only traffic from the front-end server to reach the back-end server.

User authentication   When Outlook Web Access is deployed in a front-end/back-end server configuration, the work performed by the software becomes more involved than in a single-server setup. In particular, authentication takes place on both the front-end and the back-end servers, and users aren't allowed access to Exchange resources until they've been thoroughly validated.

There are different levels of authentication possible, however, and they require some consideration. To begin with, these are the different levels:

- **Anonymous**   doesn't offer security, but does provide easy access to non-secure content in public folders. It has the additional advantage of being supported by all browsers. The user is logged on with an anonymous or guest account.

- **Basic**   requires a valid Windows username and password, and the password is transmitted as clear text unless SSL encryption is used. Basic authentication works with firewalls and proxies and is supported by most browsers.

- **Digest**   offers the same features as basic authentication, but transmits authentication credentials differently. In digest authentication, the password goes through a hashing process that eliminates the possibility that an unauthorized individual can capture and use the password. Digest authentication works with HTTP 1.1 browsers, but doesn't work through the front-end server.

- **Integrated Windows authentication**   transmits the password in encrypted form. Although the most secure of these methods, Integrated Windows authentication works through both front-end and back-end servers only if users are running Windows 2000 and using Internet Explorer 5.0.

Of these, Basic and Integrated Windows authentication are the defaults in Outlook Web Access.

In terms of front-end and back-end servers, Microsoft recommends that Basic authentication be used on front-end servers to enable requests from any browser to be passed successfully to a back-end server. Integrated Windows authentication, for example, would stop all but requests from Windows 2000/Internet Explorer 5.0 clients at the front-end server. For added security, a higher level of authentication can then be implemented on the back-end server.

CHAPTER TEN

Real-Time Communication

E-mail, by its very nature, is an asynchronous process, in every respect comparable to sending, receiving, and responding (or not responding) to snail mail. Exchange is mightily quick at notifying recipients when new messages arrive, but even so, sending a message and receiving a reply are independent events. They are related only by content and by the willingness or ability of the recipient to respond to the message within a reasonable amount of time.

Real-time electronic communication, on the other hand, is much more like a spoken conversation. Comment A evokes comment B in, well, real time. The person who speaks first might have to wait for a minute or so while the person being spoken to thinks matters over, but the speaker doesn't normally hang around for hours, days, or weeks waiting for a response. Time and spontaneous interaction make real-time communication much different from e-mail.

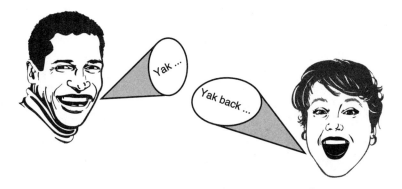

Although real-time communication was, for many years, something best left to telephones, formal business meetings, and water-cooler gossip, it's now in the process of becoming a desirable (or, as some Internet aficionados say, crucial) aspect of electronic communication, too. And so it's no surprise that Exchange 2000, the software whose business is communication, now supports real-time information swapping.

Exchange provides three different ways for people to interact in real time. These different venues—instant messaging, chat, and conferencing—address three types of communication needs:

- **Instant messaging** provides the foundation for private, one-to-one or one-to-many off-the-cuff exchanges
- **Chat** opens the door to many-to-many real-time discussions in an open forum
- **Conferencing** supports both one-to-one and many-to-many communication and collaboration in an organized, invitation-only type of forum

All three types of real-time communication blend the dynamism of face-to-face and telephone exchanges with the convenience (no travel, no sticky notes, no telephone tag) and functionality of e-mail.

Instant Messaging

Instant messaging is now known, even—or especially—to non-business people, as the Internet's "hi and hello there" mechanism for enabling individuals, no matter how widely separated, to interact in real time. (And yes, this chapter plans to steer clear of interoperability issues between and among providers.)

In terms of communicating, instant messaging adds a valuable third benefit—presence information—to the twin advantages of immediacy and familiarity that are provided, respectively, by the telephone and by e-mail. But what, exactly, is presence information? What's it the presence of? The answer is as simple as its value is obvious: Presence information tells an individual whether or not the person he or she wants to send a message to is online and available. Unlike the telephone, which can't yet tell a caller whether the other party is available or will answer the telephone, instant messaging, through presence information, can tell the person wanting to communicate whether there is a responsive human being on the other end of the "line."

Instant Messaging from the Client Side

The instant messaging client in Exchange is a version of the instant messenger software available through Microsoft's MSN service, as can be seen in the installation wizard.

The first time the service is used after installation, the instant messaging logon process prompts for logon name and password, makes the Internet or intranet connection, authenticates the user, and automatically logs the user on. From that point on, instant messaging starts by default when the computer is turned on, logs the user on when the computer is connected to the Internet or intranet, and opens an instant messaging window. This window is where the user can

- See who else is online
- Select contacts and send messages
- Specify how his or her own presence should be displayed to others

Once installed and running, the service can be minimized to an icon in the taskbar and will alert the user to new messages with either a flashing message in the status bar or a user-selected sound.

Instant Messaging Contacts

Even though the Exchange instant messaging service can track the presence of numerous clients, it doesn't automatically show all, or even any, of those clients when a user logs on. Because this service is intended to provide individual users with real-time access to limited groups of people, clients must specify each person they wish to include on their list of contacts. To do this, the client sends a subscription to a host server (more about this in the section "Instant Messaging from the Server Side"), adding the individual to the contact list.

Once a contact list is established, the instant messaging client separates them into two groups that it labels Contacts Currently Online and Contacts Not Online. Those not online are individuals who haven't logged on and those who have chosen not to be available by making use of options that block other users or that make themselves "invisible" (see the status list in the next section, "Client Status"). Those online are available for messaging; users can address them either individually or as part of a group if a "conversation" requires collaboration among several people.

Client Status

For the person running instant messaging, the client software automatically registers two presence settings.

- **Idle**   is associated with the screen saver and comes into effect when there has been no keyboard activity for a period of time defined by the user. The idle state lets others know that the computer hasn't been used for awhile and that it can be switched off simply by pressing a key.

- **Offline**   means that the user hasn't logged on.

When logged on and active, the user is able to select from seven different presence states that are then displayed on others' contact lists.

- Online (and thus available for messaging)
- Invisible
- Busy
- Be Right Back
- Away from Computer
- On the Phone
- Out to Lunch (grin)

Instant Messaging from the Server Side

From the server side, instant messaging is a little more complex than it is (or appears to be) from the client side. To begin with, Exchange instant messaging is described as a federated architecture. This means that its structure allows an organization to choose to enable instant messaging either within company boundaries only, or over the Internet as well—to provide users with the ability to communicate with, say, employees in other businesses.

Whether it's intranet-only or Internet-capable, however, an instant messaging deployment consists of

- One or more instant messaging domains
- One or more instant messaging home servers or routers

Instant messaging domains, home servers, and routers are related as shown in the following illustration.

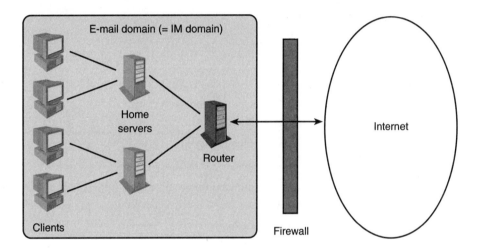

Now for the details about each.

Instant Messaging Domains

An instant messaging domain is a DNS name that identifies a logical collection of instant messaging accounts and home servers represented by an instant messaging router. The domain itself is identified by the letters *im* preceding the organization's DNS name.

Domain organization and naming   To simplify matters for both administrators and users, Microsoft recommends that instant messaging domains correspond, one to one, with an organization's e-mail domain or domains. So, for example, if instant messaging is enabled in an organization with a single e-mail domain—say, *one_domain.tld*—the organization's instant messaging domain would be *im.one_domain.tld*. (Recall that *tld* is used in this book instead of *com* or some other top-level domain indicator as a means of creating completely fake domain names.)

Conversely, an organization with multiple e-mail domains based on country (us, fr, jp, and so on) or business divisions would name its instant messaging domains after each separate e-mail domain—for example, *im.us.multidomain.tld, im.fr.multidomain.tld, im.jp.multidomain.tld,* and so on.

Whether an organization involves one or many instant messaging domains, each domain must include at least one home server and one router. Ideally, though this wouldn't be possible in a small, one-server business, the home servers and routers should be installed on separate servers.

User addresses   Even though instant messaging domains represent groups of users, the messages themselves must be addressed to specific individuals within the domain. Although the messaging service itself refers to users by World Wide Web-like URLs, the users themselves don't have to learn or remember such addresses. Instead, instant messaging allows users to build on familiarity and convenience by using addresses very similar to standard SMTP mail addresses. So, for example, the messaging service might refer to a user by a lengthy and relatively difficult (for people) address such as this one:

```
http://im.one_domain.tld/instmsg/aliases/bogus_user
```

But people wanting to send messages to this user—here, the haplessly named Mr. or Ms. bogus_user—would simply use the familiar:

```
bogus_user@one_domain.tld
```

Given this convenience for users, however, there remains the question of how *bogus_user@one_domain.tld* becomes its corresponding URL. The answer is in the client software, which has the job of converting addresses to URLs—effectively, by taking the two parts of the user's address and plugging them into the URL format, as shown by the part in italics in this URL:

```
http://im.domain_name/instmsg/aliases/username
```

Home Servers

Home servers are virtual servers that host user accounts and interact directly with clients by delivering messages and status (presence) information. Created and viewed in the Instant Messaging (RVP) node under Protocols in the Exchange Management console, a home server is capable of handling up to 10,000 concurrent online users—users who are currently logged in, even if they aren't actively sending messages back and forth.

Home servers are created with the New Instant Messaging Virtual Server Wizard shown in the following illustration.

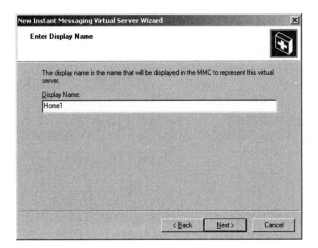

During home server creation, the wizard requests the server's display name, an IIS virtual server, and a default DNS-resolvable domain name. Bear in mind that Exchange requires one IIS virtual server for each new instant messaging home server created, even if the same physical server will be used to host multiple home servers. New IIS virtual servers are created in the Internet Information Services MMC (Start | Programs | Administrative Tools | Internet Services Manager).

The names of home servers, like those of the routers described in the next section, match the DNS name (*server_name.domain_name*) of the server, preceded by the letters *im*—for example, *im.home_server.one_domain.tld*.

> NOTE: Unlike the routers described next, instant messaging home servers have private DNS names. Their names aren't visible over the Internet.

Routers

Although they, too, are virtual servers, routers are one step removed from the client. Rather than hosting users, routers forward the messages they receive to the users' home servers. In fact, routers are prevented from hosting user accounts by the instant messaging service itself. In addition to referring messages to home servers, instant messaging routers, whose names are visible to external users, bolster security by acting as go-betweens that enable the organization to avoid exposing home servers by name on the Internet.

As in the creation of a home server, the wizard requests the router's display name—the name under which it appears in the Exchange Management console—as well as the name of the IIS virtual server that will host the router and a DNS name, in the form *server_name.domain_name*, that will identify the router on the network. Coming full circle (so to speak) back to domains and their names, Microsoft recommends that the router's DNS name correspond to the e-mail domain name.

To maximize performance, Microsoft recommends deploying one router for every two home servers.

Servers and DNS Records

Both home servers and routers must be associated with IP addresses, because DNS names require such mapping. This mapping doesn't happen by magic, of course, and in cases where servers or routers are given fully qualified domain names (for example, *new_name.multi-domain.tld*) created specifically for instant messaging, administrators must create a DNS host address resource record, or A record, for each separate server. This is the record that maps the host name to its IP address and thus enables other computers to resolve the host's domain name to the needed IP address.

For routers only, administrators can also create a service location resource record, or SRV. Instant messaging uses this record, which is normally used to locate network services such as FTP, to map an e-mail domain to an instant messaging domain. But, you might think, if e-mail domains and instant messaging domains correspond on a one-to-one basis, what's the point of creating such a record? The point is convenience, for instant messaging users. Without such an SRV record, a user's instant messaging address would have to include the fully qualified domain name of the messaging router, like this:

```
bogus_user@imrtr.router.multi-domain.tld
```

Once an SRV record exists for the router, however, users can use the same address for both e-mail and instant messages:

```
bogus_user@multi-domain.tld
```

Internet Connectivity

When instant messaging is deployed only within the organization, the entire messaging apparatus is naturally secured because everything can be implemented behind a firewall, thus ensuring minimal contact between the internal network and the outside world.

When the Internet enters the instant messaging picture, however, it brings with it a new layer of complexity or, perhaps more accurately, a bundle of security considerations related to protecting the internal network from the free-for-all of the Web. Security considerations involve both incoming and outgoing messages.

Incoming traffic   Because routers are the only servers visible to Internet users, instant messaging security issues apply to the routers, rather than to the home servers.

In terms of inbound messaging traffic, the connection to the Internet might involve any of the three security-related methods of protecting the network described in the list below. In all three methods, note that HTTP traffic must be able to reach the instant messaging routers through TCP port 80.

- **Packet filters,**   as shown in the following illustration, inspect inbound TCP/IP traffic, checking for criteria such as IP address or port number and allowing only those packets that pass the test to enter to the network.

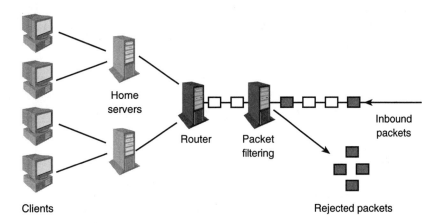

- **Reverse proxies**   Normal proxies stand between the internal network and the outside world with respect to outgoing traffic. Reverse proxies, as their name suggests, do the same, but in reverse. They, too, stand between internal and external networks, but act as relays for external traffic entering the network. As shown in the illustration at the top of the next page, reverse proxies forward external traffic to the instant messaging routers, which, in turn, send it on to the organization's home servers.

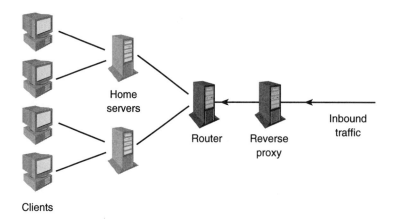

- **A perimeter network, or DMZ (demilitarized zone)** A DMZ, like its military namesake, sets up something of a neutral space between the internal and external networks. Essentially, a DMZ is a portion of the internal network that provides limited connectivity to the outside. If used with instant messaging, a DMZ should house the instant messaging routers, as shown in the following illustration.

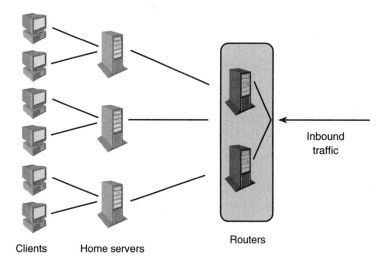

Outbound traffic Instant messaging traffic destined for the outside world can also be secured through the use of Winsock proxy servers or the HTTP proxy servers already used by the organization for Internet access.

Because Winsock proxies are transparent to client software, they need no special configuration. Likewise, because Microsoft Internet Explorer 5 clients use proxy settings entered in the browser, they need no special configuration settings if HTTP proxy servers are in use. However, to conserve network resources, it's advisable to have these clients bypass the HTTP proxies when they are communicating within the organization. Instant messaging relies on the browser to determine whether connections should involve a proxy server, and Internet Explorer 5 supports three ways to determine when to bypass a proxy.

- **Through Web Proxy Auto-Detect,** which is supported by Internet Explorer 5 and enables users to bypass proxies for specific addresses

- **Through a routing script** that resides on the intranet and is accessed by the browser through a URL

- **Through users** manually entering the names of specific instant messaging servers in the proxy exclusion list in Internet Explorer

Authentication Methods

Security, of course, includes more than packet filtering, proxies, and other methods of protecting the internal network from harm. There's also the matter of authenticating the users themselves, ensuring that they are who they claim to be and that they are entitled to use the network.

The instant messaging service supports two methods of authenticating users: Microsoft Windows NT LAN Manager (NTLM) and HTTP Digest information.

NTLM

NTLM, the recommended method of authenticating users, represents a secure, functionally unbreakable means of validation. Like the HTTP Digest method described next, NTLM relies on existing Windows 2000 passwords. The security provided by NTLM authentication is two-pronged.

- The username and password aren't passed over the network

- Authentication is based on an encrypted challenge and response handshake mechanism

NTLM authentication is based on the user account on the client computer, and all domain-authenticated users with logon rights to the server are logged on automatically. There is no prompting for username and password information, unless the authentication attempt fails.

HTTP Digest

As briefly mentioned in the "User Authentication" section of Chapter 9, digest information is a means of authentication in which the user's password and other data are transmitted in encrypted form. Newly supported in Exchange 2000, digest information, like NTLM authentication, relies on the user's existing Windows 2000 password.

Digest information is based on an Internet standard in which authentication is based on a series of challenges and responses over HTTP. Unlike NTLM, the HTTP digest method requires users to supply their passwords when logging on as instant messaging clients.

Although NTLM is the preferred method of authenticating users, digest information is recommended in two situations.

- Installations in which instant messaging clients run on operating system software other than Windows

- Environments in which clients must be able to authenticate themselves to home servers through an HTTP proxy

Messaging Architecture and the RVP Protocol

Instant messaging is easy to use from the user's point of view and, at least superficially, easy to understand from an administrator's point of view. As with any type of software, however, ease of use and ease of understanding are based on some sophisticated internal plumbing. In the case of instant messaging, for example, the process is based on components that run on both the client and the server, and the server itself runs as an IIS process.

The Server Architecture

As shown in the following illustration, on the server side, instant messaging relies on a Server Application Layer, which does the bulk of the work through interaction with three unique instant messaging components, plus Microsoft Windows Active Directory services. Through IIS, the server communicates with the client by means of the Rendezvous Protocol.

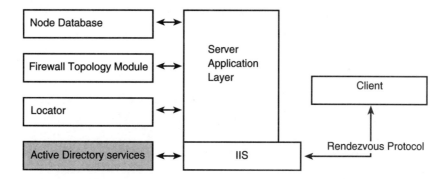

■ **The Node Database,** an instance of the Extensible Storage Engine, is responsible for maintaining subscription information for the local server. Although clients both subscribe and are subscribed to, the Node Database handles the information related to clients who have subscribed *to* users homed (based) on the server.

■ **The Firewall Topology Module, or FTM,** keeps track of which messaging servers are inside the organization's firewall and which are outside the firewall. It also contains information about whether a given source IP can connect to a particular destination IP, as well as whether a proxy is needed. When handling requests, the Firewall Topology Module can do one of three things:

❑ Allow the server to act as a gateway, connecting directly to the destination and returning the request result to the sender

❑ Refer the request by giving the sender a different destination, to which it can connect directly

❑ Reject the request if it can't be handled because of network topology and the IP addresses of the source and destination

■ **The Locator,** as its name indicates, notifies the appropriate home servers when messages pass through bridgehead servers.

The Rendezvous Protocol

The Rendezvous Protocol, generally shortened to RVP, is a protocol developed by Microsoft, in conformance with evolving IETF instant messaging standards, for the development of applications that can make use of instant messaging itself or of the presence information kept on instant messaging servers. The goal of the Rendezvous Protocol is to support compatible instant messaging capabilities for different products, platforms, and vendors.

Based on an extension of HTTP-DAV, the Rendezvous Protocol supports the following methods used in instant messaging:

- **Subscribe**   Adds users to a list of contacts; once a subscription is sent to the user's home server, the server responds by returning information about the user's online status and availability

- **Unsubscribe**   Removes a user from a list of contacts and, in reversing a subscription, ensures that the user's home server no longer sends status and availability information about that individual

- **Proppatch**   Changes (patches) a user's presence (his or her status property) by updating information on the home server

- **Propfind**   Retrieves information about all of a user's subscriptions when the individual goes online—in other words, finds the status property of all subscriptions

- **Notify**   Performs two jobs: it sends an instant message, and it informs home servers other than the user's of any status changes

And that, in a nutshell, is instant messaging, Exchange 2000 style. Next up: real-time chats, another favorite among Internet users.

Chat

Introduced in Exchange 5.5, chat continues as a real-time communication service in Exchange 2000.

Unlike instant messaging, a chat service in general provides an outlet for many-to-many discussions held in an open forum. In essence, a chat service is the real-time equivalent of a bulletin board or a newsgroup. The chat service in Exchange 2000 is based on the widely used, client/server-based Internet Relay Chat (IRC) protocol for real-time communication over TCP/IP, as well as on a set of extensions called IRCX that were developed by Microsoft to provide additional capability for managing chats on a chat server. IRC and IRCX are distinguished as follows:

- **IRC** is an Internet standard developed in 1988, forms the basis for worldwide chat networks, and is defined in RFC 1459. In a sense, IRC *is* Internet chat.

- **IRCX** was developed by Microsoft in 1997 and extends IRC with support for user authentication, security, and the two-byte Unicode characters that enable extended character sets and, by extension, support for languages worldwide.

Just as televisions show different programs on different stations, chat servers host different groups of users in discussion "areas" formally known as channels, but more commonly referred to as chat rooms. These rooms can be either public or private, and the discussions in them can be ongoing or spontaneous. In addition, the administrator can choose to apply filters to restrict use of profanity and can, when necessary, enforce bans based on usernames, nicknames, domain names, or IP addresses, that close chat services to certain users or groups of users. Together, the users and channels configured for a single instance of the chat service are known as a chat community.

Chat Servers

A chat server is essentially the heart of a chat service because it provides the meeting place to which users connect through client software. In Exchange 2000, each chat server operates as an independent entity with its own lists of users and channels. In terms of chat as a whole, however, Exchange 2000 chat servers are characterized by the following features:

- The ability to host as many as 20,000 concurrent users.

- A unique combination of port number and IP address assigned to each chat community. By default, Exchange uses the chat standard, port 6667, but it can also use port 7000 or, if both are in use, port numbers ranging from 1 through 65535. Two chat communities can share the same port or the same IP address, but not both.

- One physical server can host more than one chat community, but one chat community can't run on multiple servers. To support large numbers of users, separate instances of a chat community can be created on multiple servers. Each of these instances would have its own characteristic lists of users and channels.

Chat Channels

Although a chat session can't exist without a chat server, it's the channels that define chat for its users. These channels, or chat rooms, are the actual meeting places where people get together to discuss...whatever. If the chat sessions are limited to business, for example, there might be separate channels devoted to finance, human resources, sales by product group, and so on. If the chat sessions are as wide-ranging as those on the Internet, discussions can obviously range from fishing to baseball, from fashion to photography, and from favorite pets to favorite actors.

The Exchange chat service requires little in the way of setup (simply requiring the installation program) and the creation of one or more channels. Each channel has a name composed of a prefix and either ASCII or Unicode (16-bit) characters.

- The prefixes identify the channel type:
  - ❏ # or & for an IRC channel
  - ❏ %# or %& for an IRCX channel—that is, an extended channel whose name contains Unicode characters and is visible only to clients that support the IRCX protocol
- ASCII names can be 1 to 200 characters long, but can't include any of the following: null, bell, carriage return, line feed, space, comma, or backslash
- Names containing Unicode characters can be up to 100 characters long

The channels, however, can be of two different types and can operate in any of a number of modes. The two basic types of channel are

- **Registered channels,** which are permanent and can either start when someone joins the channel or be created automatically when the chat service is started
- **Dynamic channels,** which are temporary and are created by the chat client

In terms of modes, four are related to whether channels can be seen by users.

■ **Public** All information about the channel other than actual messages can be seen by non-members using their client's IRC List command

■ **Private** Non-members can see only the name, number of members, and content-rating information (PICS property) of the channel

■ **Hidden** The channel can't be found through the List command, but its properties can be displayed by individuals specifying the exact name of the channel

■ **Secret** A members-only chat room, the channel can't be found by any non-members

In addition to these "visibility" modes, a channel can be made

■ **Cloneable,** meaning that it's configured to duplicate itself when it reaches the maximum number of members it can accommodate

■ **Moderated,** which imposes human control over a chat by requiring that messages be granted permission before they can be posted

■ **Auditorium,** which is designed for large gatherings and a speaker-audience type of event in which the speaker can post messages to any member of the audience, but the audience members can't post messages to one another.

Chat Security

Chat doesn't, by default, impose any restrictions on who can use the service, so any user with a chat client can connect anonymously. However, because chat communities, especially those exposed to the Internet, can become vulnerable to undesirable…let's say, influences…Exchange offers administrators ways to ensure channel and network security, to authenticate users, and to protect the system from attack.

Roles for Users and Administrators

By assigning permissions, administrators can control the amount of authority granted to individuals making use of the chat service. Exchange supports three levels of authority.

■ **User,** which grants permission to individuals wanting to log on and use the service.

241

■ **Sysop,** which grants the ability to monitor and control chat community channels from a chat client. Although sysops can't use nicknames containing *system* or *service*, they can make themselves immediately identifiable with nicknames beginning with *sysop, orwell*, and variations on *Serv—ChanServ, CodeServ, HelpServ, MemoServ*, and *NickServ*.

■ **Administrator,** which grants the highest level of authority. An administrator owns any channel he or she joins, can access any channel, can't be removed from any channel, and has the ability to override any sysop. Although even these masterful creatures can't use *system* or *service* in their nicknames, only they have the right to begin their nicknames with *admin*.

Securing Channels

Individual channels can be secured in a number of different ways in addition to the visibility options (Private and Secret, for example) described earlier in the "Chat Channels" section. Administrators can also choose to secure channels by

■ Requiring users to provide a password.

■ Allowing access to only a small or selected number of users.

■ Creating user classes—restrictions applied to whole groups of users—or bans to determine who can access a particular channel. Membership in a user class can be based on any of the following:

❑ The individual's logon as either an authenticated or anonymous user

❑ The individual's identity (domain, IP address, username, and so on)

❑ The time of day

Because any user logging on who matches the criteria in any user class is governed by the restrictions imposed on that class, user classes help secure both channels and the network by protecting them from outside attack and limiting the activities of the users themselves.

Securing the Network

In addition to restricting channel access, administrators can provide for a chat community's security on the network by creating user classes, enacting bans, controlling the number of connections to a chat community, and requiring some level of user authentication.

In terms of controlling connections, administrators can set both the maximum number of connections to a community and the maximum number of anonymous connections allowed. In addition, while a community is active, administrators can disallow new connections to limit the number of users to those currently involved in the community.

For authentication, administrators can choose from three increasingly demanding levels.

- **Anonymous access,** which allows individuals to log on without providing a password

- **Basic authentication,** which requires a password (that is transmitted in clear text)

- **Windows security package,** which supports Windows NTLM security

And now, on to the third, and last, member of the real-time communication triad: conferencing.

Data Conferencing

Although a chat channel in auditorium mode can be thought of as representing a form of conferencing support, it's more suited to a lecture format (one to many), and for the most part it's open to anyone who cares to attend. Exchange data conferencing, in contrast, provides a true forum for give and take sessions—sessions that can range from a small meeting between two individuals to an online, many-to-many discussion among a number of participants. Also, unlike chat, data conferencing provides a structured, invitation-only environment.

The Conferencing Platform

The most sophisticated and the most capable of the three types of real-time communication supported by Exchange 2000, data conferencing provides users with a means of scheduling and conducting online meetings, managed by an Exchange 2000 server (rather than the host's computer). During a conference, participants can make use of

- Video
- Audio
- Shared whiteboards
- Direct file transfer
- Chat

Conferencing Components

To provide these services, the Exchange 2000 Conferencing Server includes a number of different components. By way of introduction and to provide an overview of the conferencing platform as a whole, the following list outlines these components. As you can see from the list, the components essentially fall into two major categories, conferencing management and technology providers.

- **Conference Management Service, or CMS,** handles conference reservations and scheduling by negotiating between requesting clients, such as Microsoft Outlook 2000, and the server on which conferences are actually hosted. To perform these tasks, the Conference Management Service relies on:

  - **Conference resources,** which are mailbox-enabled accounts created in Outlook 2000 and are used for scheduling the Conference Technology Providers described below.

  - **Conference calendar mailboxes,** which are Outlook storage locations and are used for conference-related format, structure, and other information related to online meetings.

- **Conference Technology Provider, or CTP,** extends Conference Management Service capabilities by providing online conferencing technologies. Exchange 2000 includes two Conference Technology Providers that are installed with the Exchange Conferencing Server:

  - **Data Conferencing Service** enables conference hosting and supports application sharing, whiteboards, file transfer, and chat. The Data Conferencing Service includes a component called the T.120 Multipoint Control Unit, or MCU, for hosting client connections.

  - **Video Conferencing Service** enables video conferencing online by multicasting audio and video as a stream over a TCP/IP connection.

Differences from Microsoft NetMeeting

As can be seen from the conferencing capabilities (chat, whiteboard, application sharing) listed above, Exchange data conferencing is at least superficially similar to Microsoft NetMeeting software. Why, then, implement the conferencing in Exchange 2000? There are three main reasons, all of which address limitations in NetMeeting.

- Exchange conferencing supports scheduling through Outlook, an application that may already be familiar to users. In contrast, most clients don't support scheduling with NetMeeting.

■ Exchange conferences are managed by Exchange Server rather than by the client station, as happens with NetMeeting. Thus, whereas NetMeeting works best for small meetings, Exchange conferencing works well for meetings both small and large. Likewise, whereas the host client determines when NetMeeting conferences end, Exchange conferencing isn't reliant on a single workstation.

■ Exchange conferences can include both internal and external participants without compromising security if the data conferencing server is located in a DMZ that minimizes risk to the internal network. In contrast, NetMeeting conferences can be held internally or externally, but not both at the same time. Also, the need to host a NetMeeting conference on a client computer located behind a firewall both increases overhead and risks network security as a whole.

The Conference Management Service

The Conference Management Service is effectively the "boss" component in Exchange online conferencing for three reasons. Not only does it take responsibility for scheduling, starting, and ending meetings, it also directs the Data Conferencing Service to host the meeting itself and, like a greeter at the door, it directs arriving clients to the server that is hosting the meeting.

In terms of the hardware and software environment required to enable Exchange data conferencing, the Conference Management Service should be installed on a server with the following:

■ **Windows 2000 Server**   (Enterprise Server if clustering is required), IIS 5.0, and Exchange 2000 Server

■ **Exchange mailboxes**   for all users allowed to schedule online conferences

■ **HTTP connectivity** with all expected client computers

■ **Membership in the same Windows 2000 Active Directory tree**   as the client computers

■ **A central location**   on the network

The Conference Technology Providers

As mentioned earlier, the Exchange Conferencing Service installs two conferencing providers: the Data Conferencing Service, which enables such features as whiteboards, chat, and file transfer, and the Video Conferencing Service, which adds video to the online experience.

Data Conferencing Service

The Data Conferencing Service provides the technological support needed by the Conference Management Service for hosting online meetings based on the T.120 standard. In effect, the Data Conferencing Service acts as the conduit through which meeting participants communicate and collaborate.

The Exchange Data Conferencing Service consists of two parts:

■ **A controller,** which must be installed on the same server as the Conference Management Service.

■ **One or more T.120 Multipoint Control Units, or MCU servers,** which serve as nodes to which clients connect for conferences. The more T.120 MCU servers available for clients to connect to, the more conferencing capability the site has. However, although the Data Conferencing Service can support more than one T.120 MCU, no more than one MCU can be installed on any Exchange 2000 server.

T.120 T.120 is an International Telecommunications Union (ITU) standard defining communication and application protocols and services designed to support delivery of information to multiple recipients (that's where multipoint comes from) in real time. Usable not only for real-time conferencing and collaboration, but also for fun activities such as multi-player games, T.120 represents an entire family of specifications (T.120 through T.128) that address different aspects of creating and managing multipoint connections and real-time information delivery.

Overall, the T.120 standard brings order to potential chaos in several areas, including

■ Interoperability

■ Support for communications networks ranging from POTS (plain old telephone service) to ISDN- and TCP/IP-based LANs

■ Scalability

MCUs As already mentioned, the Data Conferencing Service connects each participating member of a conference to a T.120 MCU (Multipoint Control Unit). On networks with a number of MCUs, the Data Conferencing Service uses several criteria in finding and connecting a client to the nearest available MCU. These criteria include

- The total number of MCUs that are available to be used
- Whether the conference is already using an MCU
- The current load on the MCU
- The location of the user in relation to the conferencing site
- Any administrative restrictions on the server that can be used

Because the Data Conferencing Service is able to support multiple MCUs, the Conference Management Service has the ability to dynamically host concurrent conferences across more than one server to improve performance and availability.

The Video Conferencing Service

Exchange video conferencing allows audio and video to be streamed to meeting participants. This capability is supported by the Telephony Application Programming Interface (TAPI) 3.0 and requires the network to be able to handle both IP multicasting and the MADCAP technology.

On the client side, the user's workstation must be equipped with the appropriate multimedia hardware—video camera, full duplex sound card, and either a headset or an echo-canceling microphone. In addition, the client must have multicast connectivity to other meeting participants (a capability that can be checked with the Windows 2000 MCAST utility, which essentially "pings" the client with a multicast packet). Finally, because audio and video are processed on the client, the computer must be adequately powered and have enough memory to handle the conferencing demands placed on it.

IP Multicasting

IP multicasting is a means of efficiently distributing the same information to multiple recipients. Instead of broadcasting over the entire network and using excessive bandwidth, multicasting sends a single copy of each data packet to a group IP address. This group address, in turn, ensures that the information is delivered to all recipients participating in the conference. To minimize the number of times the information must be copied as it travels from the source to multiple destinations, IP multicast delivers over a single path between routers and copies the data stream only when the paths go in different directions, as shown in the following illustration.

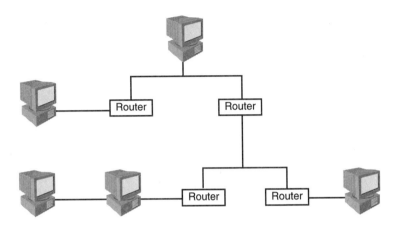

Because of IP multicasting, Exchange conferencing supports the ability to schedule a video conference from Outlook, have an HTTP address sent to each participant as part of the meeting invitation, and allow members to participate through their browsers. To join in the conference, participants either elect to join the meeting when Outlook sends them a reminder, or they can use their browser and the HTTP URL to sit in. In both cases, the person invited is automatically included in the multicast conference.

MADCAP

MADCAP, formerly known by the acronym MDHCP, is short for Multicast Address Dynamic Client Allocation Protocol. A means of enabling individual Exchange conferences to have their own IP group address, MADCAP is part of the Windows 2000 DHCP (Dynamic Host Configuration Protocol) service.

Windows 2000 DHCP servers can assign both multicast and unicast addresses but, because MADCAP and DHCP run independently, it's also possible to set up a MADCAP server to multicast addresses and keep it separate from DHCP servers on the network.

Essentially, MADCAP provides a way for hosts to request and receive a group address. Thus, when a conference is started, the conferencing host looks for a MADCAP server and then requests a conference address from it. For flexibility and control, MADCAP servers can also be used to divide the multicast IP address space into subregions called scopes. These scopes can be associated with specific routers to divide the network into multiple "zones" of multicast regions, and these regions can be presented to users by TAPI applications to control where traffic can and can't be allowed to travel.

TAPI 3.0

TAPI (Telephony API) support, though essential to Exchange conferencing, is incorporated in the Windows 2000 operating system to provide uniform support for computer-based telephony in general—telephone calls and faxes, as well as conferencing. Through TAPI service providers, which are DLLs designed to work with specific devices, applications designed for telephone communications can work with and control communications hardware. Because the TAPI service providers perform the low-level, device-specific tasks associated with communicating over the telephone or over an IP network, applications can concentrate on what they need to do, providing similar interfaces and functionality across a range of hardware devices, network protocols, and network architectures. TAPI is, in this sense, the unifying "principal" underlying network telephony.

In relation to Exchange conferencing, two TAPI service providers are of special interest: the H.323 service provider that enables IP telephony multimedia communication and the Multicast Conference service provider that enables multiparty conferencing.

The H.323 service provider   H.323, like T.120, represents a family of standards. In this case, those standards define the way H.323-compliant terminals (PCs) communicate over IP networks—that is, over networks, including the Internet, that don't provide a guaranteed quality of service. Through H.323, products from different hardware and software providers can interoperate to carry voice, video, and data in real time.

Covering both high-bandwidth and low-bandwidth network connections, H.323 defines

- **How multimedia streams are formatted for transmission**   It uses the Real Time Protocol and the Real Time Control Protocols specified by the IETF for framing, sequencing, and error detection, and thus enables the recipient device to ensure that packets being delivered are put together in the correct order

- **How calls are established**

- **Audio and video codecs**   for converting audio and video streams between analog and digital formats

The H.323 service provider in Windows 2000 is designed to work with TAPI applications to provide multimedia telephony over LANs or through standard telephones and telephone gateways.

The Multicast Conference Service Provider   The Multicast Conference Service Provider, also installed with Windows 2000, enables IP multicasting and, thus, multiple-participant videoconferencing for TAPI clients. As mentioned above under "IP Multicasting," multicasting forwards packets of videoconferencing information only to certain routers, rather than to the entire network, and makes efficient use of network bandwidth.

TAPI supports multicasting through the MADCAP "half" of the DHCP service. Whereas DHCP provides unicast (single address) information, MADCAP provides the multicast IP addresses required by conference participants.

When conferences are created, they can use the Site Server ILS (Internet Locator Service) service to publish information on the network. As part of its duties, the Site Server ILS service maintains a directory of conference descriptors which, in turn, contain the names and multicast IP addresses of individual conferences. This is where the Multicast Conference TAPI service provider enters the picture. In a manner reminiscent of the way "friendly" DNS names are resolved to IP addresses, the TAPI service provider uses the conference descriptors to resolve conference names to multicast IP addresses.

Conferencing security   TAPI works with Windows 2000 Active Directory services to ensure secure conferencing over the Internet and other such nonsecure networks. To address security issues, the TAPI conference security system enables security descriptors—information that defines access rights based on groups or individuals—to determine who can create, view, and join a meeting. These security descriptors can then be associated with SDP (Standard Description Protocol) conference descriptors and stored in Active Directory services. Once this is done, conference creators can then specify individuals with access to conference announcements, and Windows 2000 security takes care of authenticating users.

A Final Word

And there you have it. In Chapter 10, you saw three different, but highly complementary ways in which Exchange supports real-time messaging and collaboration. In previous chapters, you saw the many other ways in which Exchange supports scalable, reliable, and efficient communication and collaboration, especially now that it (as Exchange 2000) is so closely integrated with—and dependent on—Windows 2000 and its Active Directory and security services.

Although there is much more to be learned about Exchange 2000, this book has provided you with an overview of the ways in which Exchange has grown and improved over earlier versions.

If your organization is planning on, or considering, deploying Exchange 2000, there's a significant amount of planning, thought, and just plain learning "how-to" yet ahead of you, but this book has shown you ways in which Exchange can help with these processes. With Exchange, your organization can provide the messaging and collaboration support required by knowledge workers, at the same time that it provides administrators with a uniform, centralized administrative model for management and control. Although the rest is in your hands, there's help to be had when you need it, starting with this address: *http://www.microsoft.com/exchange/*.

PART III

APPENDIXES

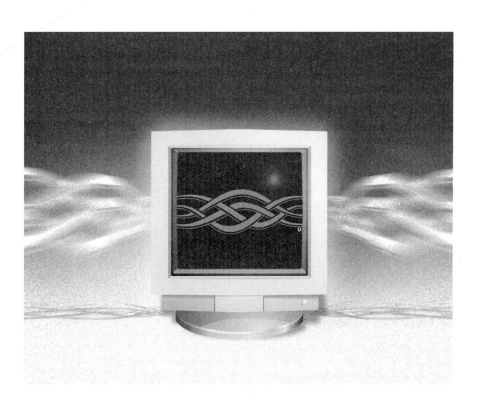

GLOSSARY

access control list (ACL)   In Windows 2000, a list of entries associated with an object that controls individual and group access to the object. An access control list is a security feature. Administrators can assign entries on a per-property basis.

ACL   *See* **access control list**

Active Directory Connector (ADC)   In Exchange 2000, the connector that enables replication between Exchange 5.5 installations and Active Directory services. The Active Directory Connector is the means by which administrators ensure that directory information is synchronized between Exchange 5.5 and Exchange 2000 systems.

Active Directory services   The directory service implemented in Windows 2000 in which classes of network objects (users, groups, resources) are organized and managed in the context of a forest and one or more trees, domains, and organizational units. Active Directory services stores information about network objects—both users and resources—and makes this information available to authorized individuals throughout the network. *See also* **directory, directory service, domain, forest, organizational unit.**

Active Directory Services Interface (ADSI)   An object-oriented interface to Active Directory services that enables developers to use high-level tools such as Visual Basic and Visual C++ to create directory programs. ADSI is designed to provide a means of creating programs that use a common set of commands to access directory services provided by different vendors. It is supported by Novell Directory Services, LDAP, and Windows NT.

Active Messaging   *See* **Collaboration Data Objects**

Active Server Pages (ASP)   A server-based scripting environment that supports creation of dynamic Web pages. Active Server Pages can call on ActiveX components to add functionality or interactivity to otherwise static HTML pages. Recently, the acronym ASP has also, somewhat confusingly, become associated with application service providers—businesses that provide software to clients over a network such as the Internet.

active/active clustering   The form of clustering supported by Windows 2000 that enables Exchange 2000 to run simultaneously on more than one server. *Compare* **active/passive clustering.** *See also* **cluster.**

active/passive clustering   The form of clustering used with versions of Exchange earlier than Exchange 2000, in which Exchange ran on a single server within a cluster, but could be restarted on another in event of failure. *Compare* **active/active clustering.**

ActiveX Data Objects (ADO)   A Microsoft programming model designed to provide easy-to-use, high-performance access to all types of data sources. ADO can be used for developing data-driven client/server and Web-based products. *Compare* **OLE DB.**

ADC   *See* **Active Directory Connector**

address (A) record   A DNS record that matches a fully qualified domain name to its associated IP address. An address record is required for every SMTP server included in the mail exchange (MX) records used to send e-mail over the Internet to SMTP servers.

address list   A list of Active Directory services objects, including users, contacts, groups, public folders, and other resources. Exchange 2000 supports creation of two types of address lists: default address lists and custom address lists. Default address lists include objects throughout the organization, are generated during setup, and are automatically available to users. Custom address lists are subsets of the default address list and are created to show addresses that match certain rules or criteria, such as region or department. *See also* **Global Address List.**

address space scoping   A form of traffic management introduced in Exchange 5.5 that allows restrictions to be applied to different connectors on a per-site, per-server, or per-organization basis.

administration model   In Exchange 2000, an approach to visualizing the configuration of an organization's network and Exchange installation. An administration model can be centralized, decentralized, or a combination of the two.

A centralized administration model revolves around a core IT group that is responsible for the entire installation. A decentralized model, although it also relies on a core IT group, also delegates day-to-day administrative responsibility to subgroups within the organization.

administrative group   In Exchange 2000, a logical grouping of servers that matches the administrative structure of an organization. Administrative groups are a means of grouping objects in a way that makes permissions easier to assign and manage. *Compare* **routing group.**

ADO   *See* **ActiveX Data Objects**

ADSI   *See* **Active Directory Services Interface**

anonymous access   In Windows 2000 and Exchange 2000, allows access to the network and publishes resources in which the user isn't authenticated at logon. Anonymous access in Windows 2000 must be enabled; it isn't turned on by default.

API   *See* **application programming interface**

application programming interface (API)   A set of routines designed to enable programmers to access operating system or application services. An API essentially provides a consistent intermediary (interface) between the programmer and an operating system or other application.

ASP   *See* **Active Server Pages**

asynchronous   Not dependent on timing—for example, communications that can start and stop at any time and aren't controlled by a clock. Modem communications and e-mail are both examples of asynchronous communication, one hardware-based and the other people-based.

attribute   In terms of objects, a feature associated with a particular object—for example, a name associated with a User object, or a network location associated with a Printer object. *See also* **mandatory attribute, optional attribute.**

backup   A copy of important data created to ensure that the original can be restored or duplicated if it's lost or damaged. Backups typically vary in the amount of data copied at a given time. In Exchange, a normal, or full, backup copies all databases and log files in the information store and deletes the log files to free space on the hard disk; a copy backup is the same as a normal backup but doesn't delete log files; a differential backup copies log-file data that has changed since the last normal backup; an incremental backup copies log-file changes since the last normal or incremental backup.

BBS *See* **bulletin board system**

bridgehead server In Exchange, a server that transfers information (messages) between one server and another. In Exchange 2000, a bridgehead server is the connecting point between two routing groups or between a routing group and a remote or other external system.

bulletin board system (BBS) A network-based "meeting place" where interested individuals can post and respond to messages on particular areas of interest, such as technology, games, or politics. Like a corkboard at the supermarket, a bulletin board system is a "come when you want, post when you want" type of forum. In this respect, it's unlike a chat room, which is based on real-time messaging.

CA *See* **certification authority**

canonical name (CN) In Windows 2000, an object name generated by Active Directory services in which the object's distinguished name (its name plus the containers and domains it belongs in) is represented without LDAP attribute tags (such as cn for common name). A canonical name starts with the root and separates elements with forward slashes, e.g., *microsoft.com/WallSitter/ Hdumpty. Compare* **distinguished name, relative distinguished name.**

CDO *See* **Collaboration Data Objects**

centralized administration *See* **administration model**

certification authority (CA) A security-related third-party organization or business that is responsible for issuing digital certificates and public key pairs for data encryption and decryption. A certification authority, also called a certificate authority, verifies the identifications of individuals granted certificates and thus guarantees the identities of communicating parties.

channel A virtual forum, commonly known as a chat room, that is set aside by the system administrator for use in online chats. Exchange 2000 allows the creation of registered (permanent) channels and dynamic (temporary) channels. *See also* **chat.**

channel name   The name assigned to a chat channel. In Exchange 2000, channel names can consist of 1 through 200 ASCII characters or 1 through 100 dual-byte Unicode characters. All names are prefixed by either one or two characters: a single # or & to indicate an IRC channel, or %# or %& to indicate an extended channel whose name contains Unicode characters and which can only be viewed by clients that support IRCX. *See also* **Internet Relay Chat, Internet Relay Chat Extensions.**

chat   A form of real-time messaging in which channels are designated as "chat rooms" in which interested individuals can meet and participate in reading and posting messages on particular topics of interest. Unlike instant messaging and conferencing, chat represents an open, ad-hoc, many-to-many environment. *Compare* **bulletin board system, conferencing, instant messaging.**

circular logging   In Exchange, a form of transaction logging in which log files are overwritten after their changes have been committed to disk. Circular logging saves disk space, but allows restoration of information only from the last full backup, rather than from the last transaction, and doesn't allow incremental or differential backups. Circular logging isn't recommended and is turned off by default in Exchange 2000.

class   In object-oriented programming and applications, the definition of a category of objects—in effect, a blueprint for actual instances of the type of object defined by the class. For example, if *car* is considered a class of objects; a *Porsche911* would be an instance of the *car* class.

cluster   A group of servers with shared storage that work together to provide data or services to users. A means of attaining scalability and fault tolerance, a cluster is viewed by users as a single entity, even though it consists of two or more individual servers. In event of failure, the load on the failed server can be redistributed to the other server(s) in the cluster. During normal operations, clusters can also be used for load balancing, in which processing is evenly distributed across servers to avoid overwhelming any single server.

CMS   *See* **Conference Management Service**

CN   *See* **canonical name**

Collaboration Data Objects (CDO)   A Microsoft scripting-object library designed to provide developers with a high-performance environment for creating client-side and server-side collaboration applications. CDO replaces Active Messaging objects and is language independent, working with VBScript, Java, C++, Visual Basic, and other languages.

committed   The state in which a database transaction has been safely written from memory to disk.

Conference Management Service (CMS)   The Exchange conferencing component that handles conference reservations and scheduling by negotiating between a requesting client, such as Outlook 2000, and the server on which conferences are hosted. The CMS is responsible not only for scheduling, but for starting and ending meetings, directing the Data Conferencing Service to host meetings, and directing clients to the servers hosting their meetings.

Conference Technology Provider (CTP)   The Exchange conferencing component that provides online conferencing technologies. Exchange conferencing installs two conference technology providers: Data Conferencing Service, which enables conference hosting, application sharing, and so on, and Video Conferencing Service, which enables video conferencing. *See also* **Data Conferencing Service, Video Conferencing Service.**

conferencing   A form of real-time messaging in which individuals gather online in a one-to-one or many-to-many meeting. Exchange conferencing supports several forms of interaction, including whiteboards, shared applications, file transfer, and videoconferencing. Like real-world conferences, Exchange conferences are organized and closed to all but invited participants. *Compare* **chat, instant messaging.**

connection agreement   In Exchange 2000, the mechanism used to enable directory replication between Exchange 5.5 sites and Active Directory services. A connection agreement can be either one-way or two-way and specifies not only the servers to be connected, but such information as the Exchange and Windows objects to be replicated and the replication schedule. *See also* **Active Directory Connector, connector.**

connector   In Exchange, a component that enables information to pass between two systems—for example, between Exchange and a "foreign" messaging system such as Lotus Notes. Connectors are invisible to users and ensure that users of each system see the information as they're accustomed to viewing it.

console An administrative tool displayed and manipulated in the Microsoft Management Console window. A console consists of various snap-ins and other tools (controls, wizards, and so on) that are used to perform specific management tasks. Windows 2000 consoles deal with such tasks as administering domains, sites and trusts, and users and computers. The primary Exchange 2000 console is the Exchange System Manager, which is used for managing servers, administrative groups, routing groups, and so on. *See also* **Microsoft Management Console.**

contact In Exchange 2000, an individual who can't log on to the system but who is associated with an e-mail address and to whom Exchange e-mail can be routed. The Exchange 2000 contact is the equivalent of a custom recipient in earlier versions.

CTP *See* **Conference Technology Provider**

custom recipient The equivalent, in earlier versions of Exchange, of an Exchange 2000 contact. *See also* **contact.**

data conferencing *See* **conferencing**

Data Conferencing Service One of two Conference Technology Providers (CTP) installed with Exchange 2000 Conferencing Server. The Data Conferencing Service is the component that enables conference hosting, including application sharing, whiteboards, file transfer, and chat. *See also* **Conference Technology Provider, T.120 Multipoint Control Unit, Video Conferencing Service.**

DAV *See* **Distributed Authoring and Versioning**

DC *See* **domain controller**

decentralized administration *See* **administration model**

DHCP *See* **Dynamic Host Configuration Protocol**

DHTML *See* **Dynamic HTML**

differential backup   *See* **backup**

directory   Generally, a collection of information. In terms of a file system, a directory (folder in Windows) represents a collection of documents. In terms of Active Directory services in Windows 2000, the directory is the collection of information about objects—network users and resources—required for such activities as logon, security, authentication, resource permissions, and, in Exchange, sending and receiving e-mail. *See also* **Active Directory services.**

directory partition   A self-contained, or contiguous, section of the Active Directory services hierarchy that forms the unit of replication. Active Directory services recognizes three types of directory partition: domain (directory object data), schema (object classes and attributes), and configuration (information including the identity of the domain controller identity and replication topology). Every domain controller holds schema and configuration partitions, as well as a domain partition for its own domain.

directory service   A network service that makes information about all objects on a network available to users. The directory service in Windows 2000 is Active Directory services. Other directory services include LDAP and the Netware Directory Service (NDS) implemented on Novell networks.

distinguished name (DN)   An object name, based on X.500 naming conventions, that includes the same elements as a DNS name but with additional two-letter abbreviations that identify the components of the name. In Windows 2000 and Exchange 2000, the abbreviations used are cn (common name), ou (organizational unit), and dc (domain component)—for example, *cn=Hdumpty,ou=WallSitter,dc=microsoft,dc=com*. A distinguished name includes the full path from the object to the domain root. It's the basis for routing messages throughout the organization and serves both to identify the object itself and its position in the domain hierarchy. *See also* **canonical name, relative distinguished name.**

distributed administration   *See* **administration model**

Distributed Authoring and Versioning (DAV)   Extended functionality added to HTTP that allows for development of tools designed to enable remote users to edit, save, and otherwise manipulate information over the World Wide Web. *See also* **WebDAV.**

distribution group   An Active Directory services group created to allow delivery of e-mail to a group of recipients. *See also* **group.** *Compare* **security group.**

distribution list   A means of enabling mass mailing to a group of recipients.

DMZ (demilitarized zone)   *See* **perimeter network**

DN   *See* **distinguished name**

DNA   *See* **Windows Distributed interNet Applications**

DNS   *See* **Domain Name Service**

domain   (1) In the Domain Name Service, the portion of a domain name that identifies the organization that owns the address; essentially equivalent to the organization's site name plus the .com, .org, and top-level domain identifiers. (2) In Windows, a uniquely named collection of servers that share a common directory database and security policy. (3) In Exchange 2000 instant messaging, a collection of instant messaging accounts represented by an instant messaging router. *See also* **second-level domain, top-level domain.**

domain controller (DC)   A server running a version of Windows 2000 Server that is responsible for managing user logon, authentication, and access to resources. A domain controller contains a complete replica of its own domain naming context as well as a replica of the configuration and schema for the entire forest. In Windows 2000, each domain must include at least one domain controller. In a mixed-vintage domain, a Windows 2000 domain controller acts as the primary domain controller required by Windows NT domains. *See also* **primary domain controller.**

domain local scope   A feature associated with a Windows 2000 security or distribution group that restricts membership in Windows 2000 and Windows NT domains. A group with domain local scope can be assigned permissions only in the same domain. *See also* **scope.**

Domain Name Service (DNS)   The hierarchical system used in naming sites on the Internet. DNS names consist of a top-level domain (such as .com, .org, or .net), a second-level domain (the site name of a business, organization, or individual), and possibly one or more subdomains (servers within a second-level domain). The DNS is used to match human-friendly site names to the IP addresses used by computers in communicating. DNS naming conventions also form the foundation of Active Directory services.

Dynamic Host Configuration Protocol (DHCP)   The protocol that enables assignment of IP addresses dynamically—that is, temporarily and on an as-needed basis when computers connect to the Internet—instead of requiring those addresses to be statically mapped ("hard-wired") to specific machines. DHCP automates the process of assigning IP addresses and eases this aspect of network administration considerably.

Dynamic HTML (DHTML)   An object-oriented form of HTML that can be used to add interactivity to Web pages. Dynamic HTML is supported by Internet Explorer 4.0 and later.

.edb   In Exchange 2000 and earlier versions, the rich-text file database. *See also* **information store.** *Compare* **.stm.**

Epoxy   *See* **EXIPC**

ESE   *See* **Extensible Storage Engine**

EXIPC   Short for Exchange Interprocess Communication layer, an intermediate queuing layer between IIS and the Exchange information store that facilitates rapid communication, even though protocols in Exchange 2000 are now part of IIS rather than, as before, part of the information store. To support such communication, EXIPC relies on shared memory and queues to enable information transfer on a protocol-by-protocol basis. EXIPC is also referred to as "Epoxy," perhaps because of the pronunciation and, perhaps, because it forms the "glue" binding IIS and the information store.

Extensible Markup Language (XML)   A markup language (roughly, a document-description coding scheme) that enables developers to create their own, customized tags and schemas for describing document contents—that is, to design tags for working with metadata (data about data). In this respect, XML is more flexible than HTML, which limits description to the structure and format of the document.

Extensible Storage Engine (ESE)   The database engine on which Windows 2000 Active Directory services is based. ESE works on the basis of discrete, individual transactions that are recorded in log files to ensure the integrity of the directory database. ESE is an improved version of the JET (Joint Engine Technology) database implemented in earlier versions of Exchange.

failback   To move a resource from an alternate node in a cluster back to the original node on which it was running, after the original node has been brought back online following a failure.

failover   To move a resource from a failed or overloaded server in a cluster to another node (server) in the cluster.

File Transfer Protocol (FTP)   A fast application-level TCP/IP protocol widely used for transferring both text-based and binary files to and from remote systems, especially over the Internet.

Firewall Topology Module (FTM)   In Exchange instant messaging, a security-related component that keeps track of which servers are inside and outside an organization's firewall. The FTM also holds information about whether proxies are needed and whether connections are allowed between specific source and destination IPs.

forest   In Windows 2000, a group of domains and domain trees that don't form a contiguous namespace. *See also* **tree.**

FQDN   *See* **fully qualified domain name**

front-end/back-end   In Exchange 2000, a server configuration in which separate sets of servers handle protocols and the data store. In a front-end/back-end configuration, clients access front-end protocol servers, and these servers in turn connect to back-end (database) servers to retrieve data.

FTM   *See* **Firewall Topology Module**

FTP   *See* **File Transfer Protocol**

fully qualified domain name (FQDN)   A DNS domain name that completely and unequivocally identifies the position of the domain in relation to the domain namespace. A fully qualified domain name like this—*server-a.subdomain-a.microsoft.com.*—typically ends with a trailing period (.) indicating the root of the DNS tree.

GAL   *See* **Global Address List**

Global Address List (GAL)   The list of all Exchange recipients in the organization. The GAL includes all of the organization's users, groups, public folders, contacts, and conferencing resources. The GAL is stored on a Global Catalog server.

Global Catalog A Windows 2000 domain controller that holds information about every object in an Active Directory services forest. Each Global Catalog server holds a complete replica of the configuration and schema naming contexts for the forest. In addition, it holds a complete replica of the naming context for the domain in which it's installed (in other words, it has complete information about the objects in its domain), and it holds a partial replica of all other domains in the forest (that is, it has enough information about objects in other domains to be able to locate complete information about those objects).

global scope A feature associated with a Windows 2000 security or distribution group that restricts membership in the group to the domain in which the group is defined, but also allows the group to be granted permissions in any domain. *See also* **scope.**

globally unique identifier (GUID) A unique 128-bit value that can be associated with a COM object for purposes of identification across computers and networks.

group (1) In Active Directory services, a collection of objects—users, computers, contacts, or other groups—pulled together for either of two purposes: distribution (e-mail only) or security (e-mail and access to resources). *Compare* **organizational unit.** (2) In clustering, a collection of resources, typically those needed to run an application or service, administered as a single object. When applications or services are moved from one server to another in the cluster, they're moved in groups. *See also* **administrative group, distribution group, resource group, routing group, security group, storage group.**

group management domain A means of enabling interoperability between Exchange 2000 and earlier versions. A group management domain is a Windows 2000 domain running in native mode that supports distribution-list functionality with Exchange 5.5 through an Active Directory Connector connection agreement that extracts the distribution list information from the Exchange 5.5 site.

GUID *See* **globally unique identifier**

H.323 An umbrella designation for an ITU-T family of standards that address the way H.323-compliant terminals (PCs) communicate over TCP/IP to transmit voice, video, and data in real time. H.323 is designed for networks, such as the Internet, that don't provide guaranteed quality of service. It's one of the two standards that support Exchange 2000 videoconferencing. *See also* **T.120.**

home server (1) The Exchange server on which an individual's mailbox resides. (2) In Exchange instant messaging, a virtual server dedicated to hosting user accounts and interacting with clients by delivering messages and presence information. An instant messaging home server can handle up to 10,000 concurrent users. *See also* **instant messaging.**

hop One segment, or leg, of a journey in which the route taken by a message from sender to destination involves multiple separate segments—the equivalent of a two-"hop" flight from Los Angeles to Denver to New York, as opposed to a nonstop journey.

host (1) A network computer (assume Windows 2000) running server software or a service for access by clients on the network. (2) In Exchange conferencing, the server running the conferencing service.

hostname The name of a device on a network; often, but not always, the name of a computer.

HTML *See* **Hypertext Markup Language**

HTTP *See* **Hypertext Transfer Protocol**

HTTP digest One of two methods of user authentication used in Exchange instant messaging. HTTP digest relies on existing Windows passwords and a series of challenges and responses over HTTP. Unlike the recommended NTLM method, HTTP digest requires instant messaging clients to supply their passwords when they log on. *Compare* **Windows NT LAN Manager.**

Hypertext Markup Language (HTML) The coding scheme used to tag the elements of Web documents (text layout, font, color, image identifier, and so on) so that browser software can display the documents correctly on screen.

Hypertext Transfer Protocol (HTTP) The protocol used on the World Wide Web to enable browsers to request Web pages and servers to respond to those requests. The *hypertext* portion of the name refers to the ability of the protocol to transfer multimedia (hypertext) content—that is, images, sound, video, and animation in addition to text.

IETF *See* **Internet Engineering Task Force**

IFS   *See* **Installable File System**

IIS   *See* **Internet Information Service**

ILS   *See* **Internet Locator Server**

IMAP4   *See* **Internet Message Access Protocol 4**

incremental backup   *See* **backup**

information store   The Exchange storage used to hold messages in users' mailboxes and in public folders. In Exchange 2000, with its support for the concept of a Web Store, the information store supports two types of content files: multimedia in an .stm file and rich text in an .edb file.

infrastructure master   The server in a domain that is responsible for finding outdated object information, requesting the updated information from the Global Catalog, and replicating the new information to other domain controllers in the domain.

Installable File System (IFS)   In Exchange 2000, the storage technology that exposes objects in folders and mailboxes as file shares. Through the IFS, Internet Explorer and other clients can access and query the Exchange information store.

instant messaging   A form of real-time messaging that enables individuals to communicate, typically on a one-to-one basis. With instant messaging, users build up lists of contacts by sending subscriptions indicating the individuals they wish to add to their list. These individuals' home servers then notify the subscriber of the online status of those contacts. In Exchange 2000 instant messaging, users can choose whether or not they wish to be "visible" and can choose to display several types of presence information, including busy, be right back, and so on. *Compare* **chat, conferencing.**

Integrated Services Digital Network (ISDN)   A high-speed communications network developed to provide all-digital service over the existing telephone network. ISDN was designed to carry not only voice but also data, images, and video. It's available in two forms, known as BRI (Basic Rate Interface) and PRI (Primary Rate Interface), which are distinguished by the number of B (bearer) channels they use to carry data.

International Telecommunications Union-Telecommunication Standardization Sector (ITU-T)   One of three branches of the International Telecommunications Union, which is based in Geneva, Switzerland, and now includes the standards body formerly called the CCITT (Comité Consultatif International Télégraphique et Téléphonique). The ITU-T branch focuses on analog and digital telecommunications. The other branches cover radio communications and telecommunications development.

Internet   The open, worldwide communications network characterized—technically—by its use of the TCP/IP protocol suite and its reliance on the hierarchical Domain Name System for matching domain names to IP addresses. The World Wide Web is the graphical, multimedia-oriented segment of the Internet.

Internet Engineering Task Force (IETF)   A worldwide organization of individuals interested in networking and the Internet. The work of the IETF is carried out by various working groups that concentrate on specific topics, such as routing and security. The IETF is the publisher of the specifications that led to the TCP/IP protocol standard.

Internet Information Service (IIS)   In Windows 2000, the software services that support Internet-related functions ranging from Web site creation to development of server-based Web applications. The IIS services include support for the widely used Internet protocols NNTP, FTP, and SMTP. Exchange 2000 extends the Windows-installed IIS capabilities and relies on IIS for message routing.

Internet Locator Server (ILS)   The Windows 2000 services that support telephony applications, including the videoconferencing capabilities in Exchange 2000.

Internet Message Access Protocol 4 (IMAP4)   An Internet messaging protocol used to access e-mail messages stored on a remote server. IMAP4 is used to enable clients to connect to the Exchange information store and download their messages. Like POP3, it's intended for temporary connections. IMAP4 is more capable than POP3, however, and supports public folder access, searches by keyword while messages are on the server, and selective downloading, such as attachments only. *Compare* **Post Office Protocol 3.**

Internet Protocol (IP)   The TCP/IP protocol responsible for routing packets. The Internet Protocol runs below TCP, at the internetwork layer in the TCP/IP networking model—equivalent to the network layer of the ISO/OSI reference model.

Internet Relay Chat (IRC)   A chat system widely used on the Internet for real-time online conversation. Developed in 1988, IRC is an Internet standard defined in RFC 1459.

Internet Relay Chat Extensions (IRCX)   A set of extensions to IRC developed by Microsoft to provide support for user authentication, security, and Unicode characters.

Internet service provider (ISP)   A business that provides Internet access to businesses and to individuals.

IP   *See* **Internet Protocol**

IP address   The 32-bit numeric address that corresponds to a computer's DNS name and that identifies the computer to other hosts on the Internet (or in an intranet).

IP multicasting   A means of distributing information to multiple recipients in which single packets of data are sent to a group IP address rather than being broadcast over the entire network.

IRC   *See* **Internet Relay Chat**

IRCX   *See* **Internet Relay Chat Extensions**

ISDN   *See* **Integrated Services Digital Network**

ISO/OSI reference model   A well-known standard that defines networks in terms of seven protocol layers, each concerned with a different level of service that contributes to preparing data for transmission over a network. The ISO/OSI model covers all aspects of a network, from the physical medium to the ways in which applications access the network. It's a fundamental blueprint designed to help guide the creation of networking hardware and software. *Compare* **TCP/IP reference model.**

ISP   *See* **Internet service provider**

ITU-T *See* **International Telecommunications Union-Telecommunication Standardization Sector**

JET *See* **Joint Engine Technology**

Joint Engine Technology (JET) *See* **Extensible Storage Engine**

knowledge worker An individual whose job or profession is based on access to and work with information, rather than with materials as in manufacturing.

LAN *See* **local area network**

LDAP *See* **Lightweight Directory Access Protocol**

Lightweight Directory Access Protocol (LDAP) A network access protocol based on X.500 standards that is designed to work on TCP/IP stacks and that provides for extracting information, such as user names or e-mail addresses, from a hierarchical directory.

link state In Exchange 2000, status information regarding the availability of the links used to transfer messages between routing groups. Links can have either of two states, UP or DOWN. This information is maintained in link state tables and is propagated in near real time to all servers in the system.

local area network (LAN) A network that is relatively limited in scope, as in a single department or building. Unlike larger networks, such as wide area networks, LANs typically offer permanent, high-speed connections between the computers and other devices connected to them. *Compare* **wide area network.**

Locator In Exchange instant messaging, the component that notifies the appropriate home servers when messages arrive through bridgehead servers.

MADCAP *See* **Multicast Address Dynamic Client Allocation Protocol**

MADMAN MIB *See* **Mail and Directory Management, Management Information Base**

Mail and Directory Management, Management Information Base (MADMAN MIB) An Internet-standard means of managing network objects through SNMP.

mail exchange (MX) record   In the transmission of e-mail over the Internet, a DNS record that associates an e-mail domain with the fully qualified domain name of one or more SMTP servers. *See also* **address (A) record.**

mailbox   The storage location on a network where an individual's e-mail is delivered.

mailbox-enabled   An Active Directory services object associated with a mailbox. In other words, one that can both send and receive e-mail. *Compare* **mail-enabled.** *See also* **contact.**

mail-enabled   An Active Directory services object associated with an e-mail address but not with an e-mail mailbox. In other words, one that can't use Exchange for sending and receiving mail. *Compare* **mailbox-enabled.** *See also* **contact.**

mandatory attribute   An object attribute (Must Contain) that must be present in every object in a class of objects. A user name, for example, would be a mandatory attribute. *Compare* **optional attribute.**

MAPI   *See* **Messaging API**

MCU   *See* **T.120 Multipoint Control Unit**

MDHCP   *See* **Multicast Address Dynamic Client Allocation Protocol**

message transfer agent (MTA)   The Exchange component responsible for routing messages. Depending on the destination, the message transfer agent routes messages to other MTAs, to the information store, to Exchange connectors, and to third-party gateways.

Messaging API (MAPI)   An application programming interface developed by Microsoft to enable messaging applications to work with different messaging systems and on different platforms through a single client.

Microsoft Management Console (MMC)   The tool in Windows 2000 and Exchange 2000 designed to unify and simplify administrative tasks. Not truly functional in and of itself, the MMC serves as the frame for various special-duty consoles made up of units called snap-ins. These consoles are displayed in the MMC frame and are the actual tools used in managing Windows 2000 and Exchange 2000 installations. *See also* **console, snap-in.**

migration file importer   A component of the Exchange Migration Wizard that takes information prepared by the source extractor component, makes the information usable to Exchange, and places the information where Exchange users can access it. *See also* **source extractor.**

MIME   *See* **Multipurpose Internet Mail Extensions**

mirroring   A means of protecting data on a network by duplicating it in its entirety on a second disk. Mirroring is one strategy implemented in RAID security. *See also* **Redundant Array of Independent Disks, striping.**

mixed mode   In Exchange 2000, the mode of operation in which Exchange 2000 and earlier versions of Exchange are running at the same time in the same organization. Mixed mode is the default in an Exchange 2000 installation. *Compare* **native mode.**

MTA   *See* **message transfer agent**

Multicast Address Dynamic Client Allocation Protocol (MADCAP, or **MDHCP)**   A part of the Windows 2000 DHCP service that enables Exchange conferences to have their own individual IP group addresses.

Multipoint Control Unit (MCU)   *See* **T.120 Multipoint Control Unit**

Multipurpose Internet Mail Extensions (MIME)   A protocol widely used on the Internet for enabling e-mail to include multiple types of information, including text, graphics, sound, and video. MIME is based on the use of MIME types to describe document content. Sending applications assign these MIME types to documents; receiving applications consult a list of standard MIME types to determine how the document should be interpreted.

MX   *See* **mail exchange (MX) record**

name   *See* **canonical name, distinguished name, fully qualified domain name, relative distinguished name, security ID, user principal name**

name resolution   The process of resolving (matching) a computer's DNS name to its corresponding IP address.

namespace   In Active Directory services, a bounded area within which names can be resolved to the objects they represent. In other words, a namespace represents a collection of objects that can be managed or referred to as a single unit.

naming context (1) In Active Directory services, a section of the directory hierarchy with its own properties, such as replication configuration. Active Directory services includes three naming contexts: the schema and configuration naming contexts, which are the same on all domain controllers, and the user naming context, which is unique to each server. (2) The X.500 and LDAP term for a branch or subtree within a tree. The preferred term in Active Directory services is directory partition. *See also* **directory partition.**

native mode In Exchange 2000, the mode of operation in which all servers are running Exchange 2000—that is, the organization doesn't support both Exchange 2000 and an earlier version of Exchange. Servers must be explicitly switched to native mode. Once done, the switch is irreversible. *Compare* **mixed mode.**

NDR *See* **non-delivery report**

NetBIOS *See* **network basic input/output system**

network basic input/output system (NetBIOS) An API designed for use on a local area network that provides programs with a uniform set of commands for accessing low-level services of the type required to manage names, conduct sessions, and send datagrams.

Network Load Balancing service A feature of Windows 2000 Advanced Server and Datacenter Server designed to distribute workload across up to 32 servers to provide high performance and scalability in demanding environments such as Web service and e-commerce.

Network News Transfer Protocol (NNTP) A protocol designed to support the posting and distribution of USENET news and group discussions on the Internet. NNTP works between NNTP clients and news servers and is described in RFC 977. It's based on the two concepts of newsgroups, which consist of messages posted by individuals interested in particular topics, and newsfeeds, which are collections of newsgroup articles fed from server to server.

newsfeed A collection of newsgroup articles delivered with the NNTP protocol from one news server to another on the Internet. A newsfeed can either be pushed to a destination server or pulled by a requesting server. A push newsfeed is comparable to a newspaper delivery; a pull newsfeed is comparable to buying the newspaper at a newsstand.

newsgroup   A collection of messages through which interested individuals "converse" by posting, reading, and responding to messages related to a particular topic of interest.

NNTP   *See* **Network News Transfer Protocol**

NNTP Service   The service in Windows 2000 that sends and receives all NNTP-based news. As built into Windows 2000, the NNTP service supports the creation of news and discussion groups on standalone servers. Exchange installation enhances this service with the ability to support newsfeeds through interaction with other NNTP servers, to store newsgroups either in the local file system or in public folders, and to support a master/slave arrangement that allows client access to a farm of servers.

node   (1) In general, a network device, such as a computer or a printer, that is capable of communicating with other devices on the network. (2) One of the servers in a cluster.

Node Database   In Exchange instant messaging, an instance of the Extensible Storage Engine (ESE) that's responsible for managing subscription information for the local server—that is, information related to clients that have subscribed to users homed on the server.

non-delivery report (NDR)   An Exchange report generated when a message can't be delivered.

nontransitive trust   A Windows 2000 trust relationship in which one domain trusts another, but the reverse isn't true. A nontransitive trust is always a one-way trust; that is, the trust relationship exists only between the trusting and trusted domains, so even if domain A trusts domain B and domain B trusts domain C, domain A doesn't trust domain C. *Compare* **transitive trust.**

NTFS   A file system used within the Windows NT and Windows 2000 operating systems that offers support for long filenames, full security access control, file system recovery, extremely large storage media, and various features for the POSIX subsystem. NTFS supports object-oriented applications by treating files as objects with user-defined and system-defined attributes.

NTLM   *See* **Windows NT LAN Manager**

object   An instance of an object class. In Active Directory services, an object is an entity associated with a named set of attributes that represents a real-life "object" such as a user, printer, file, or other network resource.

OLE DB   A COM-based API that provides applications with low-level access to data records. OLE DB is designed for system-level development requiring high performance or access to SQL Server features not provided by ActiveX Data Objects. *Compare* **ActiveX Data Objects.**

optional attribute   An object attribute (May Contain) that needn't be present in every object in a class of objects. A fax number, for example, might be an optional attribute. *Compare* **mandatory attribute.**

organizational unit (OU)   In Active Directory services, a container in which objects can be grouped to make administration easier. The smallest Active Directory services unit that can be given administrative authority, an organizational unit can contain different types of objects, including users, groups, computers, and resources, and it can be used to assign specific permissions to groups of objects.

OU   *See* **organizational unit**

Outlook Web Access (OWA)   In Exchange, a browser-based means of accessing e-mail, public folders, and calendars.

OWA   *See* **Outlook Web Access**

packet filtering   A means of monitoring inbound TCP/IP traffic that inspects packets for criteria such as IP address or port number and allows only approved packets to enter the network. *Compare* **perimeter network, reverse proxy.**

PDC   *See* **primary domain controller**

perimeter network (DMZ)   A portion of an internal network that provides something of a neutral zone between the internal network and the Internet. A perimeter network provides limited connectivity in both directions through the use of internal and external screening routers.

policy   A concept new in Exchange 2000 that represents a set of configuration settings that can be applied to one or more than one configuration object. Exchange supports server-side system policies, which are applied to servers, public stores, and mailbox stores, and client-side recipient policies, which are applied to mail-enabled objects.

POP3 *See* **Post Office Protocol 3**

Post Office Protocol 3 (POP3) An Internet messaging protocol used to access e-mail from a remote location or on a computer with limited hardware capability. Like the similar IMAP4, POP3 provides for downloading e-mail, typically over a temporary TCP/IP connection. POP3 is defined in RFC 1081. Like IMAP4, it supports downloading, but not sending messages.

primary domain controller (PDC) A Windows NT domain controller that authenticates logons and maintains the directory database for its domain. In Windows 2000, one domain controller in each domain is identified as a primary domain controller for backward compatibility with Windows NT. *See also* **domain controller.**

protocol A set of rules governing the way in which computers communicate, either with one another or with attached devices. The numerous existing protocols operate at different levels in widely used networking models, including ISO/OSI and TCP/IP. A set of protocols designed to work together through all levels of a networking model is known as a protocol stack.

public folder An Exchange folder used for sharing information of interest to multiple users. Depending on the permissions assigned to it, a public folder can be made accessible to only a specific group of users, such as project team members, or to all users who can access the Exchange organization.

RAID *See* **Redundant Array of Independent Disks**

RAS *See* **Remote Access Service**

RDN *See* **relative distinguished name**

Real Time Control Protocol (RTCP) A transport control protocol used in conjunction with the Real Time Protocol to monitor real-time transmissions, such as videoconferencing. RTCP uses packets of control information, transmitted at regular intervals, to determine how well transmissions are being delivered to recipients on the network. *See also* **Real Time Protocol.**

Real Time Protocol (RTP) An Internet-standard transport protocol used in real-time transmissions, including audio and video. RTP is often used with the Real Time Control Protocol and can be used in both unicast and multicast transmissions.

recipient policy   *See* **policy**

Redundant Array of Independent Disks (RAID)   A means of improving network performance and ensuring data integrity and security by storing information on multiple disk drives. Different levels of RAID security can be implemented, depending on the levels of reliability and performance desired.

relative distinguished name (RDN)   The part of a distinguished name that represents an attribute of the object itself—for example, in the distinguished name *cn=Hdumpty,ou=WallSitter,dc=microsoft,dc=com*, *cn=Hdumpty* would be the relative distinguished name of the object Hdumpty.

Remote Access Service (RAS)   A feature of Windows operating systems that enables users to gain access to network servers by modem.

remote procedure call (RPC)   A call made by a program on one system to a program on another (remote) system. The program on the remote system carries out whatever task is required and returns the results to the calling program.

Rendezvous Protocol (RVP)   A protocol based on HTTP-DAV and developed by Microsoft in conformance with evolving IETF instant messaging standards. RVP is designed for the development of applications that use either instant messaging or presence information. It's intended to support instant messaging across different platforms, products, and vendors.

replication   In Active Directory services, the process of updating directory contents between sites and servers.

resource   (1) In general, any item that can be accessed and used. In this sense, a resource can be hardware (such as a printer), software (such as a font), or information (such as a file or shared folder). (2) In Exchange conferencing, an object that can be used for scheduling.

resource group   In Windows 2000 clustering, a set of resources that are managed by the cluster, brought online (or taken offline) as a unit, and hosted by one node at a time. Any resource group is associated with two policies related to the cluster: the server the resource group should run on and the server to which it should be moved in the event of failure.

reverse proxy   A proxy server that, like a normal proxy, stands between the internal and external network but, as the name indicates, acts as a relay for inbound, rather than outbound, traffic.

Rich Text Format (RTF)   A standard means of transferring formatted documents between applications.

root   In general, the highest level in a hierarchical structure, as the root directory in a subdirectory tree or the root (first) domain in an Active Directory services tree or forest.

router   (1) In networking, a network device that transmits message packets, routing them over the best route available at the time. Routers are used to connect multiple network segments, including those based on differing architectures and protocols. (2) In Exchange instant messaging, a virtual server that forwards messages to a user's home server.

routing group   In Exchange 2000, a grouping of servers that matches the topology and capabilities of the underlying physical network. Unlike administrative groups, which are designed to group related objects for ease of management, routing groups are used to define groups of servers joined by permanent, high-bandwidth connections. In this respect, routing groups are similar to sites in Exchange 5.5 and earlier. *Compare* **administrative group.**

routing group master   In an Exchange routing group, the server responsible for tracking link state information and propagating it to the other servers in the group.

RPC   *See* **remote procedure call**

RTCP   *See* **Real Time Control Protocol**

RTF   *See* **Rich Text Format**

RTP   *See* **Real Time Protocol**

RVP   *See* **Rendezvous Protocol**

SAM   *See* **Windows NT Security Accounts Manager**

SASL   *See* **Simple Authentication and Security Layer**

scalability   The ability of hardware, software, or a network to expand to meet growing needs.

schema   (1) A set of definitions that define a database to a database management system. (2) In relation to Exchange 2000, the definitions stored in the directory that define both class objects and the attribute objects that specify the properties of the objects in each class.

scope (1) In Windows 2000, in relation to the DHCP service, a range of IP addresses that are available for assignment to clients. (2) In Windows 2000, in relation to security and distribution groups, a feature that defines, or delimits, the membership in a group and determines its relationship to the rest of the domain tree or forest. Windows 2000 recognizes three scopes: universal, global, and domain local. *See* **domain local scope, global scope, universal scope.**

second-level domain The level immediately beneath the top-level domain in the DNS hierarchy.

Secure Sockets Layer (SSL) A protocol developed by Netscape Communications Corporation (now part of America Online) for ensuring security and privacy in Internet communications. SSL supports authentication of client, server, or both, as well as encryption during a communications session.

Security Accounts Manager *See* **Windows NT Security Accounts Manager**

security group An Active Directory services group that is used both for assigning permissions for use of shared resources and for sending group e-mail. *See also* **group.** *Compare* **distribution group.**

security ID (SID) A unique number generated by Windows 2000 and assigned to each user, group, or computer account created. The security ID, rather than the account name, is used to manage permissions and access to resources.

security principal A Windows 2000 user, group, or computer that has been assigned a security identifier; essentially, a Windows account with logon capability. *See also* **security ID.**

server A network computer that provides shared services, applications, or resources to network users.

service Specialized, software-based functionality provided by network servers—for example, directory services (such as that provided by Active Directory services) that provide the network equivalent of a telephone book for locating network users, groups, and resources.

SID *See* **security ID**

Simple Authentication and Security Layer (SASL) A standard method of adding support for user authentication to connection-based protocols.

Simple Mail Transfer Protocol (SMTP) (1) A protocol in the TCP/IP suite used to transfer e-mail over the Internet. (2) The native mail transport in Exchange 2000.

Simple Network Management Protocol (SNMP) A protocol in the TCP/IP suite used for network monitoring and management.

single-instance storage In Exchange, the process of keeping a single copy of a message in the information store, even if the message is destined for multiple recipients.

site (1) In Windows 2000, one or more IP subnets; essentially, a group of computers linked by permanent, high-speed connections, but not necessarily belonging to the same namespace. (2) In Exchange 5.5 and earlier, a group of computers linked by high-speed connections. Unlike the site concept in Windows 2000, a site in Exchange 5.5 also defined an administrative unit and namespace.

site link A low bandwidth or unreliable connection joining two Windows 2000 sites—for example, two sites that communicate over WAN connections.

SMTP *See* **Simple Mail Transfer Protocol**

snap-in A COM object used to create Microsoft Management Consoles for Windows 2000 and Exchange 2000 administration. Technically defined as representing one unit of management behavior—that is, a tool that can be used to perform one management task—snap-ins come in two varieties: stand-alone snap-ins that are functional as-is and don't rely on other snap-ins, and extension snap-ins that must be invoked by a parent snap-in.

SNMP *See* **Simple Network Management Protocol**

source extractor A component of the Exchange Migration Wizard that copies and saves directory and calendar information and messages in migration-ready format for moving from a non-Exchange message system to Exchange. *See also* **migration file importer.**

SRV (service) resource record   A resource record used to locate TCP/IP services. In Windows 2000, an SRV record is used in locating domain controllers. In Exchange instant messaging, an SRV record can also be used to map an e-mail domain to an instant messaging domain.

SSL   *See* **Secure Sockets Layer**

.stm   In Exchange 2000, a new database used to store streaming media. *Compare* **.edb.** *See also* **information store.**

storage group   In Exchange 2000 multiple-database support, a set of one to six databases and an associated set of transaction log files. Exchange 2000 can work with up to 90 databases in 15 storage groups per server. Such use, however, isn't recommended.

striping   A means of protecting data on a network by spreading it across multiple disks. In the most commonly used approach, striping is combined with parity (error-correcting information) to ensure that if some portion of the data is lost, it can be reconstructed. Striping is implemented in RAID security. *See also* **mirroring, Redundant Array of Independent Disks.**

subdomain   A domain, often representing an administrative or other organizational subgroup, within a second-level domain.

subscription   In Exchange instant messaging, the means by which a user adds another individual to a personal list of contacts.

system attendant   The Exchange component responsible for maintenance and ensuring that operations run smoothly.

system policy   *See* **policy**

T.120   An umbrella designation for an ITU standard that defines communication and application protocols and services needed to support multipoint connections (delivery of information to multiple recipients) in real time.

T.120 Multipoint Control Unit (MCU)   A server that supports the T.120 standard, to which clients connect for Exchange conferencing.

TAPI   *See* **Telephony API**

TCP/IP   *See* **Transmission Control Protocol/Internet Protocol**

TCP/IP reference model A networking model designed around the concept of internetworking—the exchange of information among different networks, often built on different architectures. The TCP/IP model, often called the Internet reference model, consists of three or four layers (depending on interpretation), the most distinctive of which is the internetwork layer that deals with routing messages and that has no equivalent in the ISO/OSI reference model. *Compare* **ISO/OSI reference model.**

Telephony API (TAPI) An API designed to provide Windows client applications with access to telephone services, including phone calls, faxes, and conferencing.

top-level domain The highest-level domain in the DNS hierarchy.

transaction A discrete unit of activity in a system, usually an operation associated with a database.

transaction log In Exchange, the file in which all messages are recorded as a safeguard so that lost or damaged information can be reconstructed and recovered if necessary.

transitive trust The type of trust relationship that is standard between Windows 2000 domains and between domain trees in a forest. In a transitive trust, which is always two-way, the trust flows in both directions and is automatically extended to child domains created in either of the domains in the trust relationship. In addition, two-way trust relationships are also automatically created between the root domain of a forest and the root domains of the trees in the forest. *Compare* **nontransitive trust.**

Transmission Control Protocol (TCP) The TCP/IP protocol responsible for creating and reassembling packets and ensuring that information is delivered correctly. TCP runs at the transport layer and relies on IP (Internet Protocol) for delivery.

Transmission Control Protocol/Internet Protocol (TCP/IP) A protocol suite (set of protocols) designed for enabling communications over interconnected, sometimes dissimilar, networks. TCP/IP is supported by almost all networks. It lies at the heart of Internet communications.

tree (1) In general, a hierarchy of nodes beginning with a root node and descending through child nodes, each of which arises from one and only one parent node. (2) In Windows 2000, a hierarchy of domains that form a tree structure and share a contiguous namespace. *See also* **forest.**

trust relationship In Windows 2000, a relationship between two domains in which one honors the authentications performed by the other and thus enables users to access resources in different domains. A trust relationship can be one-way (between a trusting and a trusted domain) or two-way (between two equally trusting domains), transitive or nontransitive. *See also* **transitive trust, nontransitive trust.**

UDP *See* **User Datagram Protocol**

unified messaging Microsoft's goal, embodied in the Exchange 2000 concept of the Web Store, for providing users with access to multiple types of information (messages, voice, fax) in a single location, at any time, and from any device.

universal scope A feature associated with a Windows 2000 security or distribution group that allows the group to include members from any Windows 2000 domain. A group with universal scope can also be assigned permissions in any domain. *See also* **scope.**

UPN *See* **user principal name**

USENET The worldwide network of UNIX servers that support the thousands of special-interest newsgroups in which individuals post, read, and respond to messages on topics of particular interest.

User Datagram Protocol (UDP) A transport-level TCP/IP protocol that breaks messages into packets for delivery by the IP protocol. Unlike TCP, UDP is a connectionless, unreliable protocol, meaning that it doesn't establish a path between sender and receiver before transmitting and doesn't verify that packets arrive correctly.

user principal name (UPN) A user name that consists of the user's account, or logon, name and the domain in which the account is located—for example, *user@microsoft.com.*

user principal name suffix (UPN suffix) The part of a user principal name that identifies the domain in which the account resides—the part following the @ symbol in an e-mail address. By default, the UPN suffix is the same as the account's domain name. However, because the UPN suffix is used only within Windows 2000 and its domains, the suffix doesn't necessarily have to be a valid DNS name.

Video Conferencing Service   One of two Conference Technology Providers installed with Exchange 2000 Conferencing Server. The Video Conferencing Service is the component that supports multicast video conferencing through streaming audio and video. *See also* **Conference Technology Provider, Data Conferencing Service.**

virtual directory   In the Exchange NNTP Service, a directory on a physical disk drive or a folder in a public folder tree that is used to store part of the newsgroup hierarchy and that allows newsgroup files to be stored on multiple disk drives.

virtual server   An instance of a service that appears (to clients) to be a physical server. A virtual server typically has its own name and IP address, and can also be assigned a particular port number and authentication type.

WAN   *See* **wide area network**

Web Store   In Exchange 2000, the concept of a one-stop, Web-based information store that provides access to all types of information, ranging from e-mail to multimedia. The Web Store concept essentially combines messaging, file access, and collaborative capability with Exchange database features such as multiple databases and transaction logging. The Web Store is the technology embodied in the Exchange 2000 information store. *See also* **information store.**

WebDAV   In Exchange 2000, the extension to the HTTP 1.1 protocol that provides clients with the ability to manage documents (move, copy, delete, and so on) and document properties over an HTTP connection on the Internet or an intranet. WebDAV is an IETF draft standard described in RFC 2518 and is used by clients to create and manipulate content on an Exchange server. WebDAV is valuable not only for allowing file manipulation, but also in supporting collaborative applications.

wide area network (WAN)   A geographically disperse network that relies on communications capabilities to link the various network segments. *Compare* **local area network.**

Win32 The Windows API that enables applications to take advantage of 32-bit instructions.

Windows Distributed interNet Applications (DNA) A Windows framework, based on the Microsoft Component Object Model (COM), for creating multitier applications that incorporate client/server networking and Web technologies. Windows DNA is intended to provide an environment that supports development of corporate, Internet, intranet, and e-commerce solutions.

Windows Internet Name Service (WINS) A Windows software service that associates IP addresses with NetBIOS computer names.

Windows NT LAN Manager (NTLM) One of two methods of user authentication used in Exchange instant messaging. NTLM relies on existing Windows passwords and provides security in two ways: by not passing usernames and passwords over the network, and by basing authentication on an encrypted challenge and response handshake mechanism. *See also* **HTTP digest.**

Windows NT Security Accounts Manager (SAM) The Windows NT database containing user account and password information.

WINS *See* **Windows Internet Name Service**

Winsock Short for Windows Sockets. An API designed to provide a TCP/IP interface under the Windows operating system.

X series A set of recommendations adopted by the ITU and ISO for standardizing network communications. The X series includes a number of recommendations that address specific aspects of networking and communications. Those most relevant in terms of this book are X.400 and X.500. X.400 covers the format at the ISO/OSI application level for e-mail transmitted over various transports including Ethernet and TCP/IP. X.500 deals with client/server protocols that maintain and access directories and network resources in X.400 form.

XML *See* **Extensible Markup Language**

INDEX

A

access, role of domain controllers in, 108

access control lists (ACL), 21, 38, 255

ACL. *See* access control list

Active Directory Cleanup Wizard, 76, 102

Active Directory Connector (ADC), 72–74, 255

Active Directory Domains and Trusts, 60, 62–63

Active Directory group types, 86

  relationship to scope and operating mode, 87–88

Active Directory services, 255

  comparison with DNS, 114–15

  Exchange 2000 integration with, 20–21, 34–38, 49–51

  features of, 105–06

Active Directory Services Interface (ASDI), 255

Active Directory Sites and Services, 60–62

Active Directory Users and Computers, 60, 63–66

Active Server Pages (ASP), 255–56

  Exchange 2000 integration with, 24

Active Server platform, in Exchange 5.0, 13

active/active clustering, 22, 143, 148, 256

  scalability/reliability and, 130, 156, 159, 163–67

active/passive clustering, 156, 163–67, 256

ActiveX Data Objects (ADO), 140, 256

ADC. *See* Active Directory Connector

address (A) record, 256

address book views, 128–29

address books, 125–27

address lists, 125–27, 256

  custom vs. global, 128

  views, 128–29

address space scoping, 256

administration models, 256–57

  centralized/decentralized, 49, 78–83

  mixed, 81

administrative authority, 42

  delegating through Active Directory services, 110–12

administrative groups, 50, 79–80, 257

  coexistence and, 94

  managing, 68–71

Administrative Groups container, 71

Administrative Tools menu, 60

administrators, Web Store and, 142–44

ADO, 140. *See also* ActiveX Data Objects

animation, in messages, 134

anonymous access, 257

application development, Exchange 2000, 24–25

Application layer

  ISO/OSI model, 201

  TCP/IP model, 202–3

Archive importers, 76

ASDI. *See* Active Directory Services Interface

ASP. *See* Active Server Pages

asynchronous processing, 141, 257

attribute objects, 41

attributes, 257

  mandatory vs. optional

audio, in data conferencing, 243

auditorium channels, 241

authentication

  in instant messaging, 230–36

  for NNTP Server, 210

  in Outlook Web Access, 223

  role of domain controllers in, 108

authentication options, SMTP configuration, 181

authoring, WebDAV and, 215. *See also* application development; WebDAV

authority, chat levels of, 241–42

B

back-end servers, routing requests to, 170–71. *See also* front-end/back-end servers
  SMTP configuration and, 181
backups, 257–58
  in Exchange 5.5, 15
  incremental or differential, 162
Badmail directory, 180
BBS. *See* bulletin board system
bridgehead servers, 258
  in Exchange 4.0, 9
  link state information and, 198
  multiple, for load balancing and stability, 181
  replication with, 125
bulletin board system (BBS), 258
  Exchange 4.0 support for, 7

C

calendar querying, 94
canonical name (CN), 119, 258
CDO 3.0 programming model, 24, 141. *See also* Collaboration Data Objects
CDO Workflow Objects, 24
centralized administration, 78–83
certificate requirements, for NNTP Server, 210
certification authority (CA), 258
channel name, 259
channels, 258–59
  chat, 240–41
  cloneable, 241
  securing, 242
chat, 78, 259
  in data conferencing, 243
  dedicated servers for, 33
  security, 241–43
chat channels, 240–41
Chat Server, 25–26, 239–40
chat services, 238–243
circular logging, 150, 259
  disadvantages of, 163

class objects, 41
classes, 40–41, 259
client system requirements, 30
cloneable channels, 241
Cluster Server, 15, 164
cluster, 259
clustering, 78, 155–57
  in Exchange 2000, 22
  functions of, 164
CMS. *See* Conference Management Service
CN. *See* canonical name
coexistence, 55, 88, 90–95
Collaboration Data Objects (CDO), 17, 141, 260
  in Exchange 5.0/5.5, 13
collaboration, 142
  Exchange 2000 support for, 25–26
  tools, in Exchange 5.5, 16–17
Collabra Share, migrating from, 75, 101
color, in messages, 134
command verbs, added, 184
committed data, 162, 260
computers, managing with Active Directory Users and Computers, 63
concurrent connections setting, 180
concurrent users, in chat services, 239
Conference Management Service (CMS), 244–45, 260
Conference Technology Providers (CTP) , 244–47, 260
conferencing, 260, 243–50. *See also* data conferencing
  components, 244
  dedicated servers for, 32–33
configuration, naming contexts and , 46
configuration information, stored by domain controllers, 121
connection agreement, 260
connection control, for NNTP server, 210
connection schedules, controlling, 192
connectivity, 4
  in Exchange 5.5, 15–16

connectors, 32, 260–61
  coexistence installations and, 94–95
  ensuring availability of, 102
  functions of, 94
  linking routing groups, 191–95
  message delivery and, 189–90
Console Root, 59
consoles, 261
  creating new, 59
  Exchange System Manager, 66–76
  representative, 60–76
contact management, in Outlook 97
contacts, 50, 261
content indexing, 137, 149
content searches, 137
contiguous namespaces, 107
cost of ownership, 21, 77
CPU requirements, 29
CTP. *See* Conference Technology Provider
custom address lists, 128
custom recipient, 50, 261
customer concerns, installation related, 77–78

D

Data Conferencing Service, 244, 246, 261
data conferencing, 243–50
  Exchange 2000 support for, 25
data conversion, 152–53
data drives, protecting, 162
data, stored by domain controllers, 121
database recovery, 162
database services, 142
databases
  multiple, 149–51
  recommended practices for, 162–63
  single-instance, 8
data-link layer, 201
DAV. *See* Distributed Authoring and Versioning;
  WebDAV

decentralized administration, 78–83
dedicated servers, 31–33
default containers, 90
default group accounts, 71
Default SMTP Virtual Server, 178
Default SMTP Virtual Server Properties sheet
  Access tab, 181
  Delivery tab, 183–84
  General tab, 180–81
  Messsages tab, 182–83
delegating administrative authority, 85
delivery. *See* message delivery
delivery retries, specifying, 183
DHCP. *See* Dynamic Host Configuration
  Protocol
DHTML. *See* Dynamic HTML
digital certificates, SMTP configuration options
  and, 181
directories, 262
  as centralized topological hierarchy, 6
  in Exchange 4.0, 8
  functions of, 105–06
  newsgroups and, 211–12
directory, 262
directory access, 36
directory management, simplified in Exchange
  2000, 21
directory objects, naming contexts and, 46
directory partition, 262
directory replication, 50–51
  in Exchange 4.0, 10
  optimizing, 61
directory services, 262
  functions of, 35–36, 105–06
directory synchronization, 94
disk mirroring, 162
display requirements, 30
distinguished names (DN), 118, 262
  compared with X.500, 119
  vs. canonical names, 119

distributed administration, 82

Distributed Authoring and Versioning (DAV), 262

distributed configuration architecture
  scalability/reliability and, 159, 169–72

distributed services, scalability and, 131

distribution groups, 86, 262
  scope and, 88

distribution list, 50, 263

DMZ (demilitarized zone), in instant messaging,
  235

DNA. *See* Windows Distributed InterNet
  Applications

DNS. *See also* Domain Name Service
  as name resolution service, 113
  as locator service, 113
  comparison with Active Directory services, 114
  round-robin, 170–71

DNS integration, 112–15

DNS mail exchanger record, 193

DNS name, 116
  forest names and, 110

DNS records, in instant messaging, 232

document content, searches for, 137

document properties
  searches for, 137
  Web Store and, 23

document tracking, with WebDAV, 138–39

domain component names, 118

domain controllers (DC), 42, 47, 263
  connecting to, 61
  functions of, 108
  managing with Active Directory Users and
    Computers, 63–66

domain local scope, 86–88, 263

domain mode. *See* mode

Domain Name Service (DNS), 36–37, 263

domain organization, 108–10

domain-naming operations master, 63

domains, 263
  functions of, 107–08
  hierarchy of, 84–85

in instant messaging, 229
  logical organization of objects through, 84
  relationship to sites, 39, 42

DOWN link state, 195–98

duplicate accounts, 102

dynamic channels, 240

Dynamic Host Configuration Protocol (DHCP),
  263–64

Dynamic HTML (DHTML), 264

Dynamic RAS Connector, in Exchange 4.0, 9–10

Dynamic RAS X.400 transport stack, 195

E

ease of use, with front-end/back-end servers, 206

.edb files, 152, 264

enterprise benefits, Web Store, 141–42

enterprise, defined, 19

Epoxy, 169, 175

Exchange 2000
  accessibility features in , 25–26
  active/active clustering in, 156
  Active Directory services integration with, 49–
    51
  chat services in, 238–43
  coexistence with earlier versions of, 90–94
  infrastructure, 20–21
  installation considerations, 55–57
  Internet integration in , 23–24
  new features in, 12–26
  server requirements for, 29–30
  Web Store support in, 148
  Windows integration with, 126–31

Exchange 4.0, 5–7

Exchange 5.0, 12–14

Exchange 5.5, 14–16
  clustering in, 156
  SMTP connector and, 194
  Web Store support in, 148

Exchange 5.5 sites, as administrative groups, 80

Exchange Admins account, 71

Exchange Application Services, 76

Exchange Chat Service, 17

Exchange Connectors, 32

Exchange extensions to SMTP, 184

Exchange features, versions 4.0 through 5.5, 17–18

Exchange Installation Wizard, 55–57

Exchange Scripting Agent, 16–17

Exchange Server Site Connector, 9

Exchange Servers account, 71

Exchange System Manager, 66–76

Exchange technology, Web Store and, 147–57

EXIPC, 169, 175, 263. *See also* Epoxy

expiration periods, 183

extended permissions, 70

Extensible Markup Language (XML), 264

Extensible Storage Engine (ESE), 149, 264

F

failback server, 22, 264

failover, 265

file attachments, 134

file conversions, minimized by Web Store, 136

file system services support, 141–42

File Transfer Protocol (FTP), 265

Firewall Topology Module (FTM) , 237, 265

flexibility, 77

folder replication, 143

folders, similarity to organizational units, 43

forests, 265

  connecting to, 61

  functions of, 109–10

  noncontiguous domain trees and, 44

four-node clusters, 167

front-end servers

  creating, 169–70

front-end/back-end servers, 21, 78, 148, 154–55, 265

  Outlook Web Access and, 171–72

  POP3 and IMAP4 benefits, 206–7

  scalability and, 131

FrontPage 2000, 30

  Exchange 2000 integration with, 24

FTM. *See* Firewall Topology Module

FTP. *See* File Transfer Protocol

full-text search capabilities, 23

fully qualified domain name, 116, 265

G

gateways, ensuring availability of, 102

Global Address List, 128, 265

  in Exchange 4.0, 8–9

Global Catalog, 46–47, 106, 266

  functions of, 121–22

global scope, 86-88, 266

globally unique identifier (GUID), 120, 266

group management domain, 266

groups, 266

  domains as, 84

  logical vs. physical organization of, 83–88

  organizational units as, 84

  sites as, 84

GUID, 120. *See also* globally unique identifier

H

H.323 service provider, 249

H.323 standard, 266–67

Help, in Microsoft Management Console, 57

Hierarchies, logical and physical, 49–59

home server, 267

  in instant messaging, 230

hops, 267

  maximum number of, 183

host, 267

host computers, 116

hostname, 267

HTML. *See also* Hypertext Markup Language

  Exchange 5.0 support for, 12

  Web Store support for, 139–40

HTTP. *See also* Hypertext Transfer Protocol

  Exchange 5.0 support for, 12

HTTP *(continued)*
  WebDAV and, 215–16
  Web Store support for, 138
HTTP 1.1, 214
HTTP digest information, 267
  instant messaging using, 236
Hypertext Markup Language (HTML), 267
Hypertext Transfer Protocol (HTTP), 267

I

IBM OfficeVision, 16
IBM PROFS Connector, 16
IETF. *See* Internet Engineering Task Force
IIS. *See* Internet Information Service
ILS. *See* Internet Locator Service
IMAP4, 205–6. *See also* Internet Message Access
    Protocol 4
  comparison with POP3, 205
  folder tree views, 153
  migration from, 75, 101
inbound message flow, 185–86
incoming traffic, instant messaging and, 233
indexing capabilities, 23
indexing mechanism,, 106
information storage, domains and, 42
information store, 268
  administering through permissions, 70
  in Exchange 4.0, 7–8, 11
infrastructure master, 268
in-place upgrade, 95–96, 99
Installable File System (IFS), 155, 268
installation, Exchange 2000 options, 55–57
instant messaging, 25, 268
  client-side considerations, 226–28
  client status, 228
  dedicated servers for, 33
  domains, 229
  server-side considerations, 228–35
Integrated Services Digital Network, 268
integration, with Windows 2000, 4. *See also*
    Windows 2000; Active Directory services

International Telecommunications Union-
    Telecommunication Standardization Sector
    (ITU-T), 269
Internet, 269
  Exchange 5.5 support for, 16
Internet connectivity, instant messaging and,
    232–35
Internet directory, migrating from, 75, 101
Internet Engineering Task Force (IETF), 269
Internet Explorer 5.0, 216, 218–19
Internet Information Server, Exchange 2000
    integration with, 24
Internet Information Service (IIS), 269
Internet Information Services 5.0, 175
Internet integration, 77
  Internet protocols and, 200–14
  networking models and, 200–4
  newsgroups and, 207–14
  Outlook Web Access and, 218–24
  WebDAV and, 214–17
Internet Locator Server (ILS), 17, 269
Internet mail servers, 32
Internet Mail, migration from, 75
Internet Message Access Protocol 4, 269. *See also*
    IMAP4
Internet protocol (IP), 270
Internet protocols
  ISO/OSI, 200–2
  IMAP4, 205–6
  messaging functions of, 175–76
  NNTP, 207–14
  POP3, 204–5
  in replication, 124
  TCP/IP, 202–4
Internet Relay Chat (IRC), 270.
Internet Relay Chat Extensions (IRCX), 270
Internet Service Provider (ISP), 270
Internetwork layer, 202–3
interoperability, Exchange 5.0 and, 14
inter-routing group communication messages, 80
intra-routing group communication messages, 80
IP. *See* Internet Protocol

IP address, 270
IP multicasting, 247–48, 270
IRC. *See* Internet Relay Chat
IRC protocol, 238–39
IRCX, 238–39 *See also* Internet Relay Chat
Extensions
ISDN. *See* Integrated Services Digital Network
ISO/OSI networking model, 200–2, 270
ISP. *See* Internet Service Provider

J
JET database. *See* Extensible Storage Engine
Joint Engine Technology (JET), 149. *See also*
Extensible Storage Engine

K
Kerberos security, 62
key message fields, searches for, 137
knowledge workers, 271
Web Store benefits for, 135, 144–47

L
LAN. *See* local area network
LAN connections, 27
LDAP, 113–14
Exchange 5.0 support for, 13
naming conventions, 118
LDAP. *See* Lightweight Directory Access Protocol
Lightweight Directory Access Protocol (LDAP),
271
link state, 271
algorithm, 196
information, 195–98
load balancing, scalability/reliability and, 159,
167–68
local area network (LAN), 271
locator service, 112–13
Locator, 271
logon
in Active Directory services, 106
domain controller sand, 108

Lotus cc:Mail, 195
connector for, 95
migration from, 75
Lotus cc:Mail Connector, 14
Lotus Notes, 195
connector for, 95
migration from, 75
Lotus Notes Connector, 16

M
MADCAP, 248–49. *See also* Multicast Address
Dynamic Client Allocation Protocol
MADMAN MIB. *See also* Mail and Directory
Management, Management Information Base
in Exchange 5.5, 15
Mail and Directory Management, Management
Information Base (MADMAN MIB), 271
mail exchange (MX) record, 272
mail systems, coexistence with other, 90–95
mailbox, 50, 272
mailbox management, 207
mailbox server, 31
mailbox-enabled, 272
mail-enabled, 272
contacts, 127
groups, 127
users, 127
Mailmig, 76
mandatory attribute, 272
MAPI. *See also* Messaging API
folder tree views, 153
MAPI content, 152–53
masquerade domain, 183–84
master newsfeed, 213–14
master/slave arrangement, NNTP Service and,
208
MayContain attributes, 40
media types, supported in conferencing, 243
message categorizer, 184
message databases, scalability and, 130
message delivery
connector links, 191–95

message delivery *(continued)*
  different routing group, 188–89
  dynamics of, in Exchange 4.0, 11–12
  link state information and, 195–98
  other mail systems, to, 195
  outside the organization, 189–90
  single vs. multiple routing groups, 190–91
  same server, 187
  same routing group, 187–88
message flow, 174–75
message looping, 196
message priority, controlling, 192
message recovery, 162
message routing, 186–98
message size limits, controlling, 192
message size, specifying, 182
message transfer agent (MTA), 272
  in Exchange 4.0, 9–10
messages per connection, 182
messaging, enterprise-level, 14–16
Messaging API (MAPI), 272
messaging architecture, Rendezvous Protocol and, 236–38
Microsoft Application Converter for Lotus Notes, 101
Microsoft Importer for Lotus cc:Mail Archives, 101
Microsoft Mail Connector, 10
Microsoft Mail, 195
  migrating from, 101
Microsoft Management Console (MMC), 22, 56–76, 272
Microsoft Office, Web Store integration with, 145
migration, 55, 74–76, 100–02
  phased, 102
migration considerations, 101–02
migration file importer, 273
migration tools, 100–01
Migration Wizard, 74–76, 100–1
MIME. *See* Multipurpose Internet Mail Extensions
MIME content, 152–53, 136
  Exchange 4.0 support for, 5
mirroring, 273

mixed administration model, 81–83
mixed mode, 88, 125, 172, 273
  switching to native mode, 63
MMC. *See* Microsoft Management Console
mode
  mixed, 125
  native, 126
moderated channels, 241
moderated newsgroups, 210–11
move mailboxes upgrade, 95–96, 99
MS Mail, migration from, 75
MS-DOS prompt, 30
MTA. *See* message transfer agent
Multicast Address Dynamic Client Allocation Protocol (MADCAP), 273
Multicast Conference Service Provider, 250
multi-phase migrations, 102
multiple databases, 78, 149–51
  in Exchange 2000, 22
  scalability/reliability and, 159–63
multiple domains, 39
multiple public folder trees, 153–54
multiple sites, Exchange 4.0 support for, 5–6
Multipoint Control Unit. *See* T.120 Multipoint Control Unit (MCU)
Multipurpose Internet Mail Extensions (MIME), 273. *See also* MIME content
multi-server organizations, 29
multi-site organizations, 29
multithreaded virtual servers, 177
MustContain attributes, 40

N

name resolution, 112–13, 273
  in Windows 2000 and Exchange, 129–30
namespaces, 37–38, 107, 273
  contiguous, 43
  in Active Directory services and DNS, 115
naming context, 46, 274
naming conventions
  canonical names, 119

common names, 118
distinguished names, 118
domains, 116, 118
organizational units, 118
relative distinguished names, 118
security principals and identifiers, 117–18
user principal names and suffixes, 117
native mode, 87–88, 126, 274
conversion to, during coexistence installations, 93
switching to, from mixed mode, 63
NDR, 183. *See also* non-delivery report
NetBIOS. *See* network basic input/output services
NetMeeting, comparison with Exchange 2000 data conferencing, 244–45
Netscape Navigator 4.0, 219
network, logical view of, 40–47
Network access layer, 202–3
Network basic input/output system (NetBIOS), 274
Network layer, 201
Network Load Balancing Service, 167–68, 274
network load, adjusting messages per connection to optimize, 182
Network News Transfer Protocol (NNTP), 274
network topology, 27–33
distributed, in Exchange 2000, 20–21
installation considerations and, 56
network views, 38–47
Networking models
ISO/OSI, 200–2
TCP/IP, 202–4
new installations, Exchange, 88–90
newsfeed distribution, 212–14
newsfeed timing, 207
newsfeeds, 207, 274
newsgroup clients, recommended, 30
newsgroups, 207, 275
Exchange support for, 153
moderated, 210–11
NNTP, 207–14. *See also* Network News Transfer Protocol
Exchange 5.0 support for, 12

NNTP server configuration, 208–10
NNTP Service, 208–14, 275
node, 275
Node Database, 237, 275
nodes
storage groups and, 166–67
virtual servers and, 156–57
non-delivery report (NDR), 275
non-Exchange systems, MAP and mail routed to, 194
nontransitive trust, 275
Novell GroupWise, 195
connector for, 95
migration from, 75, 101
NTFS, 275
NTLM. *See* Windows NT LAN Manager

O
object, 276
object administration, Active Directory services and, 35
object name changes, 127
object property sheet, 65
objects, 40–41
specifying replication for, 73
Office 2000, 216
Office 2000 documents 3
OLE DB, 141, 276
Exchange 2000 integration with, 24
Open Shortest Path First algorithm, 196
operating costs, reducing, 142
optional attribute, 276
organization size, centralized/decentralized administration and, 79
organizational unit (OU), 276
organizational units, 43, 112
as containers, 85
managing with Active Directory Users and Computers, 63
OU. *See* organizational unit
outbound message flow, 186

outbound traffic, in instant messaging, 234
Outlook 97, 13–14, 30
Outlook 98, 30
Outlook Express, 30, 216
Outlook Web Access (OWA), 31–32, 146, 276
   clients, 219–20
   front-end/back-end servers and, 171–72
   logon process, 220
   multiple-server installations, 222–24
   single-server installations, 221–22
   Web Store access with, 220–21

P

packet filtering, 276
packet filters, instant messaging and, 233
paging file, 30
parent/child relationships, 11
   tree and domain relationships and, 43
PC Networks, connector for, 95
peer newsfeeds, 213
perimeter network (DMZ), 276. *See also* demilitarized zone
   instant messaging use, 234
permissions, 88
   extended, 70
phased migrations, 102
physical connections, routing groups and, 71
Physical layer, 201
Pickup directory, 180
policies
   access/configuration/use, 85
   client-side, 68
   cluster-related, 166
   as configuration settings, 68
   server-side, 68
policy, 276
POP3, 204–5. *See also* Post Office Protocol 3
   comparison with IMAP4, 205
   Exchange 5.0 support for, 12
   folder tree views, 153

Post Office Protocol 3 (POP3), 277
Presentation layer, 201
primary domain controller, 277
printers, managing with Active Directory Users and Computers, 63
private information store, 7
programming support, Web Store and, 140–41
property sheet, new user, 65–66
protocol, 277
Proxy Server, 4
proxy servers, in instant messaging, 235
public database, 7
public folder trees, 148
   multiple, 153–54
public folders, 127, 277
   dedicated server for, 31
   permissions and, 70
pull newsfeeds, 207
push newsfeeds, 207
Queue directory, 180
queuing, 176

R

RAID drives, 162. *See also* Redundant Array of Independent Disks
RAM requirements, 29
RAS. *See* Remote Access Service
Real Time Control Protocol (RTCP), 277
Real Time Protocol (RTP), 277
real-time communication, 225. *See also* instant messaging; chat; data conferencing
recipient policies, 68
recipients per message, 182
recommended practices, 162–62
Redundant Array of Independent Disks (RAID), 278
registered channels, 240
relative distinguished names, 118, 278
reliability, 4, 77, 142–43
Remote Access Service (RAS), 278

remote procedure call, 278
  in Exchange 4.0, 9
Rendezvous Protocol (RVP) , 236–38, 278
replication schedule, 73
replication service, 106
replication, 50–51, 122–25, 278
  direction of, 73
  folders, 143
  Global Catalog and, 46
  managing, 73
resource groups, 157, 278
  virtual servers and, 165–66
Resource Monitor, 165
resources, 278
  role of domain controllers in accessing, 108
restricted bandwidth, adjusting messages per
    connection to optimize, 182
reverse DNS lookup, 184
reverse proxies, 233, 278
rich formatting, in messages, 134
Rich Text Format (RTF), 279
risk factors, in move mailboxes upgrade, 96
root, 279
root domain, 36–37, 109, 116
round-robin DNS, 170–72
routers, 279
  instant messaging, 231–32
routing engine, 184
routing group connectors, 191–92
Routing Group container, 71
routing group master, 197, 279
routing groups, 50, 80, 279
  coexistence and, 94
  delivery to same/different, 187–89
  link state information, with multiple, 197
  managing, 71–72
  single vs. multiple, 190–91
  virtual server requirements, 178
routing scripts, 235
RTF. *See* Rich Text Format
RVP. *See* Rendezvous Protocol

S

SAM. *See* Windows NT Security Accounts
    Manager
SASL *See also* Simple Authentication and Security
    Layer
  Exchange 5.5 support for, 16
scalability, 4, 77, 142–43, 279
  active/active clustering and, 130
  message databases and, 130
  distributed services and, 131
  front-end/back-end servers and, 131
  multiple databases and, 22
  native mode advantages for, 126
  security boundaries and, 110–12
Schedule +, connector for, 95
scheduling, group, in Outlook 97, 14
schema, 40–41, 279
  forest organization and, 44
  naming contexts and, 46
  stored by domain controllers, 120
scope, 86–88, 280
search mechanism, 106
second-level domain, 36–37, 116, 280
Secure Sockets Layer (SSL), 280
  reduced server load and, 206
security
  chat channels and, 242–43
  data conferencing and, 250
  scalability/reliability and, 160
  SMTP configuration options and, 181
  Windows 2000, 35, 38, 143–44
security boundaries, domains as, 110–12
security groups, 86, 280
security IDs (SID) , 117–18, 280
  in Active Directory Services, 116
security policies, 42
security principals, 117–18, 280
server event model, 25
server load, reduced, 206
server requirements, 29–30
servers, 280

servers *(continued)*
    configuring, in Windows 2000, 53–54
    dedicated, 28, 31–33
    delivery to same, 187
    instant messaging, 232
service, 280
Session layer, 201
shared folders, managing with Active Directory
        Users and Computers, 63
SID. *See* security IDs
Simple Authentication and Security Layer (SASL),
        281
Simple Mail Transfer Protocol (SMTP), 281
Simple Network Management Protocol (SNMP),
        281
single-instance database, 8
single-instance storage, 134–35, 148, 281
    scalability/reliability and, 160–61
single-phase migrations, 102
site link, 281
Site Server, 4
sites, 281
    in Active Directory services, 39
    creating, renaming, deleting, 61
    directory replication of, 84
    relationship to domains, 42
slave newsfeed, 213–14
small businesses, 27
smart host, 193
smart host, identifying, 184
SMTP *See also* Simple Mail Transfer Protocol
    advantages, 177
    administrative considerations, 177–84
    Exchange extensions to, 184
    Exchange 2000 support for, 4, 22–23
    features of, 184
    inbound message flow in, 185–86
    outbound message flow in, 186
    in replication, 124
SMTP configuration options, 180–84
SMTP Connector, 71

SMTP connectors, 192–94
SMTP session size, specifying, 182
SMTP virtual servers, 177–78
SNADS Connector, 16
snap-ins, 22, 58, 281
SNMP. *See* Simple Network Management
        Protocol
sound attachments, 134
source extractor, 281
SQL Server, 4
SRV (service) resource record, 282
SSL. *See also* Secure Sockets Layer
    Exchange 5.0 support for, 13
.stm files, 136, 152, 282
storage groups, 149–51, 282
    nodes and, 166–67
storage space requirements, 30
streaming media, 136, 151–52, 249
streaming video, 3
striping, 282
subdomains, 116, 36–37, 282
subnets, creating/deleting, 62
subscription, 282
swing server upgrade, 97–98, 100
synchronous processing, 141
System Attendan, 282
    in Exchange 4.0, 10–11
system policies, 68
system requirements, servers, 29–30
Systems Management Server, 4

T

T.120 Multipoint Control Unit (MCU), 246–47,
        282
T.120 standard, 246, 282
TAPI, 249. *See also* Telephony API
task management,
    in Outlook 97
TCP/IP. *See* Transmission Control Protocol/
        Internet Protocol
TCIP/IP X.400 transport stack, 195

TCP/IP networking model, 202–4, 283
TCP/IP stack protocols
    application layer, 203
    internetwork layer, 204
    transport layer, 204
Telephony API (TAPI), 283
terminology, Active Directory services changes to, 50
timeout period setting, 180
top-level domain, 36–37, 116, 283
training costs, reducing, 142
transacted store, 148
transaction, 283
transaction logs, 134, 283
    recommended practices for, 162–63
    scalability/reliability and, 160–62
transitive trust relationships, 110–11, 283
Transmission Control Protocol (TCP), 283
transport, 129
Transport layer
    ISO/OSI model, 201
    TCP/IP model, 202–3
transport processing, 141
trees, 43, 283–84
trust relationships, 284
    between domains, 62
    transitive, 110
    two-way, 44
two-node clusters, 167
two-way trust relationships, 44, 111

U
Unicode characters, in chat channels, 240
unified messaging, 25–26, 284
units of replication, domains as, 107–08
universal scope, 86–88, 284
unlimited storage, 78
UP link state, 195–98
upgrade installations, 95–100
upgrade options, advantages and concerns, 99–100
UPN. *See* user printipal name

URL, for Exchange 2000, 251
USENET, 284
USENET newsfeeds, 207–8, 213–14
user accounts, managing with Active Directory
    Users and Computers, 63
user addresses, instant messaging, 230
User Datagram Protocol (UDP), 284
user principal name (UPN), 117, 284
user principal name suffixes, 62–63, 117, 284–85
user, adding a new, 64–65
user-based names, 116

V
video, in data conferencing, 243
video attachments, 134
Video Conferencing Service, 247–50
virtual directory, 285
Virtual Server Properties sheet
    for NNTP servers, 208–10
virtual servers, 285
    Current Sessions node, 179
    instant messaging, 230–31
    nodes and , 156–57
    parameters set for, 178–79
    queues, 179
    resource groups and, 165–66
    SMTP, 177–78
voice mail, 3

W
WAN. *See* Wide Area Network
WAN connections, 28
Web browsers, 30
Web content, delivery of, 3
Web integration, 4, 199–224
Web Proxy Auto-Detect, 235
Web Store, 23–24, 285
    administrators and, 142–44
    client software for, 144
    concepts behind, 133–34

Web Store *(continued)*
    content, 135
    Exchange technology supporting, 147–57
    HTTP and, 138
    HTML and, 139
    indexing and searching, 137
    knowledge workers and, 144–47
    Microsoft Office integration with, 145
    Office document properties and, 145
    programming support in, 140
    scalability/reliability and, 159
    WebDAV and, 138
    XML and, 140
Web Store folder, accessing, 146
WebDAV, 285
    document management through, 23
    extensions, 216–17
    features, 216
    folder tree views, 153
    HTTP and , 215–16
    Internet integration and, 214–17
    Web Store support for, 138–39
whiteboards, in data conferencing, 243
wide area network (WAN), 286
Win32 APIs, 140
Win32, 286
Windows 2000
    Exchange 2000 integration with, 4, 20–21, 34–38, 126–31
    features and functions, 54
Windows 2000 Advanced Server, as prerequisite for clustering, 163

Windows 2000 Datacenter Server, as prerequisite for clustering, 163
Windows 2000 security, scalability/reliability and, 160
Windows 2000 Server, 47, 53–54
Windows Application Server, 54
Windows Distributed InterNet Applications (DNA), 286
Windows File Server, 54
Windows folders, organizational units similar to, 43
Windows Internet Name Service (WINS)
Windows NT LAN Manager (NTLM), 286
    instant messaging authentication using, 235–36
Windows NT Security Accounts Manager (SAM), 286
Windows NT Server 4.0 Enterprise Edition, 15
Windows Print Server, 54
Winsock, 286
World Wide Web. *See* Web
write-ahead transaction logging, 143

X

X series, 286
X.25 X.400 transport stack, 195
X.400 Connector, 72, 194–95
X.400 standard, 23
X.500, compared with distinguished names, 119
X.500 Directory Access Protocol (DAP), 114
XML. *See also* Extensible Markup Language
    Web Store support for, 140
    WebDAV and, 217

About the Author

JoAnne Woodcock is the author of several popular computer books, including *Understanding Groupware in the Enterprise*, *The Ultimate Microsoft Windows 95 Book*, *The Ultimate MS-DOS Book*, *PCs for Beginners*, and *Step Up to Networking*, all published by Microsoft Press. She is also a contributor to the *Microsoft Press Computer Dictionary*.

The manuscript for this book was prepared and submitted to Microsoft Press in electronic form. Text files were prepared using Microsoft Word 97. Pages were composed by Microsoft Press using Adobe PageMaker 6.52 for Windows, with text in Galliard and display type in Helvetica bold. Composed pages were delivered to the printer as electronic prepress files.

Cover Graphic Designer
Girvin|Branding & Design

Cover Illustrator
Tom Draper

Interior Graphic Artist
Sybil Ihrig, Helios Productions

Principal Compositor
Sybil Ihrig, Helios Productions

Technical Editor
Douglas Giles

Copy Editor
Fran Aitkens, ELS

Principal Proofreader
Deborah O. Stockton

Indexer
Helios Productions

Introducing Microsoft® Exchange 2000 Server

WHERE DID YOU PURCHASE THIS PRODUCT?

CUSTOMER NAME

Microsoft®

mspress.microsoft.com

Microsoft Press, PO Box 97017, Redmond, WA 98073-9830

OWNER REGISTRATION CARD

Register Today!

0-7356-0960-8

Return the bottom portion of this card to register today.

Introducing Microsoft® Exchange 2000 Server

FIRST NAME

MIDDLE INITIAL

LAST NAME

INSTITUTION OR COMPANY NAME

ADDRESS

CITY

STATE

ZIP

(   )

E-MAIL ADDRESS

PHONE NUMBER

U.S. and Canada addresses only. Fill in information above and mail postage-free.
Please mail only the bottom half of this page.

For information about Microsoft Press®
products, visit our Web site at
mspress.microsoft.com